THE UNITED STATES AND
THE MIDDLE EAST

THE
UNITED STATES
AND THE
MIDDLE EAST

Philip L. Groisser

Seymour P. Lachman

CONSULTING EDITOR

Prepared under the auspices of the
National Committee for Middle East Studies

State University of New York Press

ALBANY

Published by
State University of New York Press, Albany

Printed in the United States of America

For information, address State University of New York
Press, State University Plaza, Albany, N.Y., 12246

Library of Congress Cataloging in Publication Data

Groisser, Philip L.
  The United States and the Middle East

  1. Near East—Foreign relations—United States.
2. United States—Foreign relations—Near East.
3. Near East. I. Title
DS63.2.U5G76   327.73056   81-8967
ISBN 0-87395-547-1   AACR2
ISBN 0-87395-548-X (pbk.)

Contents

Preface

In recent years it has become increasingly clear that the Middle East is an area of strategic importance and concern for Americans. Teachers on all levels, however, have not had easy access to textual materials that describe and interpret the rush of ongoing events in relation to their historic, cultural, and other backgrounds. This is particularly true for American history courses. These courses invariably deal with United States foreign affairs and policy as a topic of major importance. *The United States and the Middle East* is a curriculum unit designed primarily to provide essential study and background materials for teachers and students concerned with understanding the role of the United States in the tangled web of Middle East affairs. The unit may be used in part or whole, for brief or more extended study, as a basic or supplementary text within the required American History and American Studies course. It may also be used in World or Global History and other social science courses.

The book is published under the auspices of the National Committee for Middle East Studies, which seeks to meet the curriculum needs of American education by conducting seminars, publishing educational materials, and organizing study missions to the Middle East. The Committee represents a cross section of prominent American educators. It is an affiliate of the American Academic Association for Peace in the Middle East, an educational and research organization that utilizes the special skills and talents of the academic community to elicit new ideas for the solution of the Arab-Israel conflict. AAAPME publishes a quarterly journal, *Middle East Review*, and books on the contemporary Middle East.

Included in *The United States and the Middle East* are sections dealing with the importance of the Middle East today and in the past, tension and instability in the Middle East since World War II, and American policy and involvement in the Middle East from the nation's early beginnings. Socioeconomic and cultural backgrounds as well as political and diplomatic developments are detailed and brief case studies of a number of Middle

vii

East nations, including Israel and its Arab neighbors, are provided. The entire study is placed in a world as well as a regional context.

The book is thoroughly up to date and written in a clear yet scholarly fashion for today's student. Important facts and concepts are repeated in different chapters and contexts for reenforcement of understanding. In addition to the text, the unit contains useful reference and supplementary materials, including self-testing exercises, maps, pictures, and a bibliography.

The United States and the Middle East asks and answers these questions: (1) Why should Americans be interested in the Middle East today? (Chapter 1); (2) What is the Middle East like today? (Chapters 2 and 3); (3) Why has the Middle East been a region of crisis and tension in recent years? (Chapter 4); (4) Why and how has the United States become involved in the Middle East? (Chapters 5 and 6); (5) What are the United States' goals in the Middle East and how has it attempted to achieve these goals? (Chapter 7); (6) What challenges and dilemmas does the United States face in its dealings with the Middle East and in formulating its foreign policies in the region? (Chapter 8).

Instructors who are unable to devote more than a week to the topic can focus on Chapters, 1, 5, 6, 7 and 8. In this context Chapters 2 and 3 could be omitted or made the subject of student reports or independent study. Instructors with two weeks or more who teach mini and elective courses on the Middle East can utilize the entire text for full class study and discussion.

The author would like to express his gratitude to a number of people who read and reread the manuscript as it developed or who assisted in other ways. Dr. Seymour P. Lachman, Chairman of the National Committee for Middle East Studies and University Dean and Professor of Education at the City University of New York, served as consulting editor, giving insightful direction, analysis, and support at every juncture, with particular attention to updating the manuscript in its final stages. Rita Lefkort, National Coordinator of the National Committee for Middle East Studies, was supportive at every stage, giving helpful advice, reading the manuscript and serving as coordinator of the different ongoing processes that breathe life into any text. Dr. Joseph Churba, former chief intelligence analyst of the Middle East, U.S. Air Force, and Professor of Middle East Studies, Air University, Maxwell Air Force Base, Alabama, Dr. Benjamin Rivlin, Professor of Political Science, Graduate School and University Center, CUNY, and Dr. Frank N. Trager, Director of Studies, National Strategy Information Center, Inc., reviewed the manuscript in its early stages and made valuable suggestions. Ricki Rosen did picture research and selection with sympathetic insight and assembled a series of photographs that enhance the text in significant dimension. Christopher Brest prepared a series of carefully drawn maps that strengthen and make more graphic geographic and strategic understandings and relationships. Lois Gottesman assisted in the preparation of meaningful and useful bibliography. Myrna David Hamada served ably as typist for the manuscript throughout all its revisions. The index was compiled by Ralph Freeman Goldman.

Thanks must also be given to my wife Louise Groisser, who graciously and uncomplainingly accepted the silences and sacrifices that writing imposes on an author's family. Without her understanding no task would be worth doing.

P.L.G.

Introduction

FRED G. BURKE
New Jersey State Commissioner of Education

Within the life span of American students, the Middle East has emerged from mysterious obscurity to stark reality. The histories of some of our planet's earliest civilizations were nurtured in this cradle of Western civilization. From this crossroads of three continents there evolved three of the world's most powerful and influential religions. Although philosophers, theologians, and warriors for centuries have contested the relative merits of these religions, they do share, nonetheless, many fundamental values and common histories. Buried beneath the desert sands and river valleys lie the footprints of Moses, Jesus, and Mohammed; footprints that traveled to the far reaches of our planet.

The lives of Americans are vitally affected by what occurs and what does not occur in the Middle East. Within the lifetime of our high school students the United States has become dependent on Middle East oil to generate electricity, fuel aircraft, energize industry, and to propel automobiles. In an energy dependent world, large reserves of oil attract the conflicting interest of major world powers. The Middle East, as it has for thousands of years, again dominates the affairs of nations and therein lies a potential for peace and prosperity or for war and devastation. American youth, if it is to successfully shoulder responsibility for decisions concerning the Middle East that could determine war and peace, cannot rely on myth or rhetoric. Knowledge of the history, ancient as well as modern, of the culture, Islamic and Judaic, and of its strategic geographic importance, is absolutely necessary for responsible decision making.

The United States and the Middle East provides students with the necessary historical and cultural background to aid in comprehending contemporary events. Combining the insights and disciplines of anthropology, history, geography, political science, and economics, this volume objectively, but interestingly, enables students to appreciate the contributions that this ancient region and its culturally diverse peoples have made to contemporary Western life. It provides an insight into the vital issues that keep the nations of the Middle East on the front pages of our newspapers and the forefront of the minds of politicians, industrialists, and generals.

THE UNITED STATES AND
THE MIDDLE EAST

1

Importance of the Middle East

The Middle East has become a focus of growing world attention. Americans are increasingly aware of its significance as an important oil-producing region, as an area of tension and unrest, and as a major field for big-power rivalry and involvement.

Despite the importance of the Middle East in international affairs, few areas are more misunderstood. The purpose of this curriculum unit is to give students a better understanding of this highly complex region and its relationships to the United States.

The Middle East Defined

The Middle East is a large geographic region extending over parts of southeastern Europe, southwestern Asia, and northeastern Africa. As referred to in this book, it includes the following countries: Bahrain, Cyprus, Egypt, Iran, Iraq, Israel, Jordan, Kuwait, Lebanon, Oman, Qatar, Saudi Arabia, Sudan, Syria, Turkey, United Arab Emirates, Arab Republic of Yemen, and People's Democratic Republic of Yemen.[1] Together these countries cover an area of about 3.8 million square miles and have a total population approaching 200 million.

Most geographers and historians agree that any definition of the Middle East should include the eighteen countries just mentioned. This definition encompasses the Arab countries of the eastern Mediterranean, plus Turkey, Israel, Iran, Cyprus, and Sudan. At times, however, authorities have also

[1] The United Arab Emirates were formerly British protectorates known as the Trucial States until they combined to form an independent nation in 1971. The Arab Republic of Yemen, an independent nation since 1918, is usually referred to as Yemen. The People's Democratic Republic of Yemen consists of Aden and other former British-owned or -protected territories in southern Arabia that received independence in 1967. It is frequently referred to as Southern Yemen.

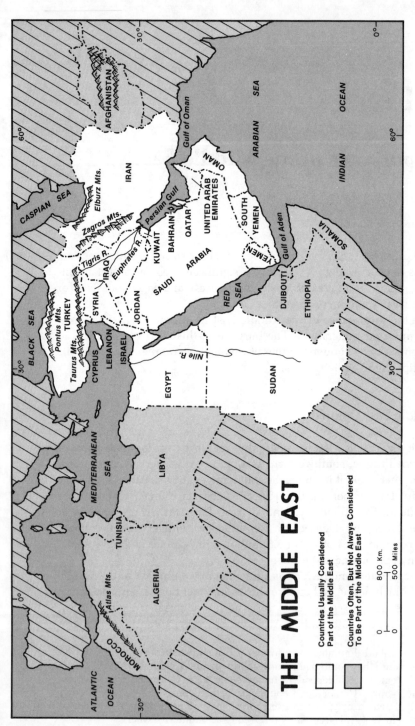

THE MIDDLE EAST

Although it is generally agreed that the Middle East is a large region extending over parts of southeastern Europe, southwestern Asia and northeastern Africa, there is disagreement among scholars and other authorities over exactly where it begins and ends. The map legend (key) attempts to make this clear.

included the following: the North African countries of Libya, Tunisia, Morocco, and Algeria (sometimes referred to as the Maghreb); Afghanistan (in southwestern Asia); and on some occasions, African nations bordering the Red Sea on the eastern "Horn of Africa" — Ethiopia, Somalia, and Djibouti (formerly the French-protected territory of Afars and Issas).

The term *Middle East* has been in popular use since World War II. Before that time, it was more usual to refer to the region as the *Near East* and to include in its coverage the Balkan states, in addition to the area of the eastern Mediterranean ("The Levant").[2]

Importance of the Middle East

The Middle East has long been important. It is strategically located. It has given mankind a rich cultural heritage and has produced three of the world's great religions. It has been a seat of empire and a field of conflict and international rivalry. It is today an area of major concern for the United States and other nations.

Each of these factors will be discussed in the following sections of this chapter in order to make clear why Americans are and should be interested in the Middle East.

Strategic Position

The Middle East occupies a central position at the crossroads of three continents: Asia, Africa, and Europe. The region is deeply penetrated by the Mediterranean Sea, the Red Sea, and the Persian Gulf. Its shores are also washed by the Caspian and Black seas and by the Indian Ocean. The Middle East includes some of the world's most strategic waterways, including the Suez Canal, the Dardanelles, the Straits of Hormuz (through which ninety percent of the region's exported oil passes), the Persian Gulf, and the Red Sea. The area provides a third of the world's annual oil output and over half of its known oil reserves. Although geographically most of its land area lies within Asia, the Middle East's largest city, Cairo, capital of Egypt, is situated in Africa. One of the region's important countries, Turkey, is located in both Europe and Asia.

The strategic location of the Middle East as a "bridge" among three

[2] The term "Balkans" refers to the countries occupying the Balkan Peninsula in southeastern Europe. Today the Balkan states include Albania, Bulgaria, Greece, Rumania, and Yugoslavia. Countries that occupied the area before World War I, such as Serbia, have become part of one or more of the present Balkan states. "The Levant," a term once used to designate the countries of the eastern Mediterranean, is rarely used today.

continents makes more understandable its role as a "middleman" throughout world history. During the Middle Ages important spice routes passed through the Middle East, linking Europe with the Orient. For more than a century the Suez Canal has been a vital part of one of the world's great trade routes, connecting the Atlantic Ocean and the Mediterranean Sea with the Red Sea and the Indian and Pacific oceans. The Middle East's central position also helps explain why foreign invaders — for example, the Mongols from Central Asia and the Crusaders from Europe — have in past times often overrun its territories and conquered its peoples.

The Middle East is also the shortest convenient air and water route between Europe and Asia. In the 20th century it has benefited from Europe's increasing reliance on foodstuffs and raw materials from Africa, the Far East, and the Middle East itself.

Access to the vast oil reserves of the Middle East has become a vital factor for the industrial plants of Western Europe and the United States, the growing industries of Japan, and the rest of Asia and Africa. Oil-supplying states have begun to capitalize on the importance of this precious commodity by using it as a political and economic weapon. They have raised prices and withheld oil from countries with which they have major disagreements. In addition, billions of oil-profit *petrodollars* have been invested largely in foreign industries, securities, and properties in the West. This has caused some countries to be concerned about an actual or possible increase in economic pressure by oil-rich Arab nations. Greatly increased expenditures by these nations for arms, industry, and other purposes have contributed to world trade inflation.

Finally, and perhaps most essential today, the strategic importance of the Middle East makes it a chief concern of the world's major power blocs and especially of the two greatest "superpowers," the United States and the Soviet Union. Each bloc has been trying to gain influence in the region through political, economic, and military support to Middle East nations in order to check or counterbalance the efforts of the other side.

Cradle of Civilization

The Middle East was a cradle of world civilizations. According to archeologists, people lived there as early as 25,000 years ago.

Many scholars believe that civilization began in the Middle East. There is evidence that the peoples of the region practiced agriculture in the prehistoric period. Agriculture made men food producers instead of food gatherers. As a result men settled down, established organized societies, and developed the arts and crafts of civilization. As early as 10,000 years ago, they grew plants and domesticated animals in the Nile Valley in Egypt; along the shores of the eastern Mediterranean in the area of present-day

BIRTHPLACE OF RELIGIONS

Religion has long played an important role in the history and development of the Middle East and continues to do so today. The three inserts in these photographs symbolize this fact. Can you identify each religious symbol? Is it correct to call the Middle East a cradle of religion? Religious News Service

Syria, Lebanon, and Israel; and in the valley of the Tigris and Euphrates rivers in parts of present-day Iraq (ancient Babylonia; later also called Mesopotamia). Two of the best-known of these early civilizations were those of Babylonia and Egypt.[3]

Birthplace of Religions

Three of the world's major religions had their origins in the Middle East: *Judaism, Christianity,* and *Islam.*

JUDAISM. Judaism was the first great religion to stress the idea of a single Supreme Being, God, who created the universe and ruled it with justice and goodness. This belief, called ethical monotheism, became the basis of both the Christian and Muslim religions, as well as of the Hebrew faith. All three faiths accept the ethical teachings of the Hebrew Bible, popularly known as

[3] Other important early civilizations developed in northeastern China and in northwestern India.

MOSES AND THE TEN COMMANDMENTS
As the text indicates Moses was the Hebrew leader who in Ancient Times led the Jews out of captivity and slavery in Egypt. According to the Bible God called Moses to the top of Mount Sinai and gave him the Ten Commandments, which were written on two stone tablets. They are God's laws to guide Jewish conduct. This famous engraving by Gustave Dore shows Moses descending the mountain with the Ten Commandments.

the Old Testament (the five Books of Moses, or *Torah*, plus the Prophets and the Sacred Writings). Judaism stresses good deeds and righteous living. The *Ten Commandments*, given to Moses by God, are still part of the moral code of mankind. Moses was the famous early Jewish leader who led the Jews out of captivity in Egypt.

The Hebrews (Jews), also known as Israelites, originally lived in Palestine, the ancient land of Canaan. The name Palestine comes from the ancient Philistines who lived along the coast. In biblical times the Hebrews made Jerusalem their capital and chief city and built their holy Temple there. Despite the fact that most Jews were dispersed or forced to flee after the Roman Conquest and for most of their history thereafter, many continued to live in Palestine until the establishment of the State of Israel nearly 2,000 years later. In addition, Jews outside of Palestine continued to regard Palestine as their homeland and spiritual center and Jerusalem as their holy city. Since the establishment of the State of Israel in 1948 in what was formerly called Palestine, well over a million and a half Jews from many parts of the world — over one-half from Africa and Asia — have returned to Israel to live.

The Jewish population of the world is now approximately fifteen million. Of this number, about six million live in the United States and over three million in Israel.

CHRISTIANITY. Christianity, another of the world's great religions, is the most widespread. Its major denominations have approximately a billion followers, most of whom live in North America, South America, and Europe. Christianity also continues to be an important religion in the Middle East. Today there are two main traditions within the Christian faith; Eastern and Western. The Eastern tradition includes the Orthodox, the Copts, and others. Within the Western tradition are the Roman Catholic and the Protestant faiths.

Christianity began as a movement among Jews in Palestine who believed that Jesus of Nazareth was the savior for whom they had been waiting. Jesus was born in Bethlehem and died in Jerusalem. The followers of Jesus called him the Messiah ("anointed of the Lord"). The name Christ comes from Christos, the Greek word for "anointed one."

CHRISTIANITY: EASTER PROCESSION
ON VIA DOLOROSA, JERUSALEM

During Easter Christians around the world commemorate the Resurrection of Jesus Christ, whose life and teachings became the basis for Christianity. In Jerusalem part of this commemoration is a retracing of the route (Via Dolorosa) along which Christ was taken by his Roman captors to Calvary, the hill outside the city on which he was crucified. Via Dolorosa means route of pain or sorrow. Israel Government Tourist Office

Christianity spread to peoples in all parts of the world. Saul of Tarsus (Paul), one of the greatest preachers and organizers of the early Christian church, was among the first to spread the new religion to Gentiles as well as Jews. His Epistles or letters written to friends and various churches make up a large part of the *New Testament*.

Christians consider both the *Old Testament* of the Hebrew faith and the *New Testament* as their Bible. Christianity rests on the belief that Jesus Christ is the Son of God. Jesus urged love of God, peace on earth, and the brotherhood of man. Christian doctrines also stress God's love for His people and love and community among individuals.

Christians consider Jerusalem holy because it was the place where many important events in Christ's life occurred, including the Crucifixion.[4]

ISLAM. Islam, one of the world's great religions and the faith of more than 750 million people today, was born in the Arabian Peninsula. Islamic civilization has been dominant in this area for thirteen centuries.

Islam means submission to the will of Allah (the Arabic word for God). Those who accept Islam as their religion are called *Muslims* (or Moslems). In the Arabic language, "Muslim" means one who submits (to God). Contrary to popular belief, the majority of Muslims live outside of the Middle East, in the Indian subcontinent (Pakistan, India, Bangladesh), in sub-Saharan Africa, in the Soviet Union, China, and Europe (mostly in the Balkans). One out of seven persons in the world today is Muslim.

The Muslim religion is the faith first taught by the Prophet Mohammed (570–632) in the early 600s A.D. Mohammed was born in Mecca, in Arabia, in 570 A.D. When enemies forced him to flee from Mecca in 622 he went to Medina. This flight, called the *Hegira*, is the first date in the Muslim calendar.

Mohammed's successors built a great empire. At its height it stretched from Spain to India. As growing numbers of people adopted the Muslim faith, Islam gradually became the predominant religion in North Africa and the Middle East. Arabic gradually replaced other languages as the language of the Islamic world.

In the 11th, 12th, and 13th centuries, the Christian nations of Europe sent military expeditions to the Middle East to recover the Holy Land from the Muslims. These wars, known as the Crusades, had the backing of the popes.

Islamic civilization reached its political height between the 8th and 10th centuries under the leadership of the Abbasid caliphs (rulers). Thereafter its political cohesiveness fell apart until the coming of the Ottomans in the 15th century.

The once great Muslim empire no longer exists. Nevertheless, in many

[4] The Crucifixion refers to the death of Jesus Christ by nailing on a cross.

ISLAM: WOMEN PRAYING
The Islamic religion calls for prayer five times a day. On Fridays such prayers are expected to take place at noon in Muslim houses of worship, called mosques. Here we see women praying in the Selimiye mosque in Edirne, Turkey. Turkish Ministry of Tourism and Information

countries Islam is either the official religion or the faith of the majority of the population. Muslims everywhere pray in Arabic. In Arab countries they speak Arabic in their daily lives. However, Muslims in non-Arab countries use their native language in everyday speech, for example, in Iran and Turkey in the Middle East, Pakistan and India in West Asia, and the Philippines and Indonesia in Southeast Asia.[5]

The basic doctrine of the Islamic faith, as preached by Mohammed and accepted by all Muslims, is that there is one God, Allah, and Mohammed was His apostle and His messenger to all mankind. The Muslim Bible is the *Koran*, which contains Allah's revelations to Mohammed.

Muslims believe that Mohammed was the last and greatest of the prophets. They consider Jesus and many of the prophets of the Old Testament as his predecessors and they refer to Jews and Christians as "people of the book." The Koran teaches that God is just and merciful and calls on man

[5] It will be useful at this point for the student to note that: (1) Not all Arabs are Muslims and not all Muslims are Arabs. (2) Although most people in the Middle East are Arabs, millions are non-Arabs (particularly in Iran and Turkey). (3) Although Islam is the predominant faith in the Middle East, most Muslims live outside the Middle East.

to repent and purify himself while on earth so that he can go to Paradise after death.

The Islamic religion requires the performance of religious duties. Faithful Muslims must profess faith in Islam, pray five times a day, fast (during the month of Ramadan they may eat only after sundown), give alms to the poor, and make a pilgrimage to the holy city of Mecca at least once in their lifetime if it is within their means. Like the Bible, the Koran forbids lying, stealing, adultery, and murder.

As with Christianity and Judaism, there are major sects dividing Muslims. The most important division is between the Sunnis and the Shiites.

The Muslims have always considered Mecca and Medina to be their holiest cities. Jerusalem is considered the third most holy city because it, too, contains shrines and places important in the history of Islam.

PHOENICIAN DAGGER

The advanced level of craftsmanship among peoples of the ancient Middle East is shown in this picture of a Phoenician dagger found in the ruins of the Temple of Byblos. In addition to inventing the alphabet which we now use, the Phoenicians were great traders. Their achievements also included the development of textile, purple-dyeing, glass and metal-working industries. Phoenicia extended along the coastal areas of present-day Syria, Lebanon, and Israel. Lebanon Tourism and Information Office

Cultural Heritage

Peoples of the Middle East have made valuable contributions to the history of mankind. The region's cultural heritage has influenced the development of Western civilization in important ways. Many peoples and civilizations played a role in shaping this heritage.

PEOPLES OF THE FERTILE CRESCENT (4000–300 B.C.).[6] Middle Eastern civilization was probably born in the Fertile Crescent between the Tigris and Euphrates rivers in Mesopotamia (now Iraq). The many peoples of the Fertile Crescent were important cultural innovators. The *Sumerians* (3250–2000 B.C.) probably invented the first known system of writing, called *cuneiform*. The Sumerians and the *Babylonians* (1850–550 B.C.) made many studies in the fields of astronomy, medicine, mathematics, and finance. They produced excellent pottery, textiles, and metal objects. They drew up one of the first known law codes, the *Code of Hammurabi*. They built huge irrigation works and developed a lunar (moon) calendar, based on a 12-month year, seven-day week, and 24-hour day. We have inherited the 60-minute hour and the 360-degree circle from them.

Other early peoples of the Fertile Crescent made noteworthy accomplishments. The *Chaldeans* (approximately 612–539 B.C.) made important astronomical discoveries. *Astrology* developed from their belief that the future could be foretold by studying the stars. The ancient *Persians* (550–330 B.C.) developed an efficient system for governing an empire, the best features of which were later copied by the Greeks and Romans. It was based on a system of military roads to tie the empire together and promote trade, careful checkups on the performance of provincial governors by government inspectors known as "The Eyes of the King," and respect for the language and customs of subject peoples. The *Phoenicians* (1200–750 B.C.) invented an alphabet that became the basis of our present-day alphabet.

The ancient *Hebrews* (Jews) (1200 B.C.–135 A.D.) developed the idea of a *single* Supreme Being, called God, at a time when other peoples were worshipping many gods. The Hebrew Bible or "Old Testament," is considered one of the world's great literary masterpieces as well as a great religious work.

The *Hittites* (1750–1200 B.C.) of Asia Minor (western Asia, including parts of Turkey) were among the first peoples to smelt iron in order to fashion it into agricultural tools and war weapons. The *Lydians* (600–500 B.C.), also of Asia Minor, developed a system of weights and measures.

---

[6] It should be noted that scholars differ on the dating of many ancient historical eras, just as they differ on precise population figures for countries that lack scientific data-collection systems.

The Pathway of Civilization in the Middle East

3250–2000 B.C.	Sumerians
3400–1000 B.C.	Ancient Egyptians
1850–550 B.C.	Babylonians
1750–1200 B.C.	Hittites
1200–750 B.C.	Phoenicians
1200 B.C.–135 A.D.	Ancient Hebrews (Jews)
612–539 B.C.	Chaldeans
600–500 B.C.	Lydians
550–330 B.C.	Ancient Persians
322–90 B.C.	Hellenistic Period
200 B.C.–476 A.D.	Roman Empire
395–1453 A.D.	Byzantine Empire
622–1200 A.D.	Muslim Empire
750–1258 A.D.	Abbasid Caliphate
1096–1300 A.D.	Crusades
1030–1110 A.D.	Seljuk Turks
1200–1260 A.D.	Mongols
1300–1918 A.D.	Ottoman Turks

The dates given in this chart indicate the approximate period when the civilizations of the various peoples had an important influence on the life of their times. One should not make the mistake of believing that the first date given was the year in which each civilization began; nor should one make the mistake of believing that the second date marks the disappearance of the people mentioned. We know, for example, that although most of the Jews of ancient Palestine went to other lands after 135 A.D. when the Romans finally crushed Jewish resistance and destroyed Jerusalem, other Jews continued to live in Palestine until the founding of the State of Israel in the middle of the 20th century.

EGYPTIAN CIVILIZATION (3400–1000 B.C.). The ancient Egyptians made significant contributions in the fields of religion, art, writing, and science. They excelled as artists, astronomers, engineers, and merchants. They developed ideas about life after death, built giant pyramids and great temples, carved lifelike statues and crafted beautiful jewelry. They made paper from the papyrus reed and developed *hieroglyphics*, a form of picture writing. Egyptians preserved their dead by embalming, used geometry for surveying and building, developed a decimal system of arithmetic, and invented a twelve-month solar calendar of 365 days, based on movements of the sun.

BYZANTINE EMPIRE (395–1453 A.D.). Although the Roman Empire fell in 476 A.D., its eastern portion, the Byzantine Empire, continued on for almost a thousand years to 1453, when the Turks captured Constantinople, its capital and most important cultural and commercial center. By warding off

SPHINX AND PYRAMIDS IN EGYPT
The famous Sphinx and pyramids symbolize the greatness of the civilization of ancient Egypt. The treasures recovered from Egypt's pyramids, temples and other "finds" have brought worldwide respect for the abilities of the Egyptians and other peoples of the ancient Middle East. It took approximately 20 years and the efforts of 100,000 workers to build the Great Pyramid of Egypt near Gizeh. American Museum of Natural History

attacks by the Arabs and Turks for hundreds of years, the Byzantine Empire gave Europe time to recover from the fall of the western Roman Empire.

A significant contribution of the Byzantine Empire was the preservation of Greek and Roman culture, though as time went on this was blended with Eastern culture. During the so-called "Dark Ages" in Western Europe, the Byzantine Empire was the chief cultural influence among the Slavic peoples of Eastern Europe. Western European contacts with Byzantine art during the Crusades helped pave the way for the Italian Renaissance.

Byzantine art and architecture were characterized by unusual color and design. The Church of St. Sophia in Constantinople (later Byzantium and Istanbul) is considered the masterpiece of Byzantine architecture and has been called a "symphony of space and light." Byzantine textiles were greatly prized throughout Europe. The empire was also famous for its mosaics and carved luxury items, particularly miniature icons and ivory carvings. The law systems of many countries are based on the law code drawn up by the Emperor Justinian I (the Justinian Code).

BYZANTINE CIVILIZATION: SANTA SOPHIA

Nothing represented the flowering of Byzantine civilization more than the famous Church of Santa Sophia. As originally built, the interior of this famous church is considered to be the finest example of Byzantine architecture. Shown above is one of the brilliantly colored religious mosaics which adorned its walls and ceilings. St. Sophia was built in Constantinople, capital of the Byzantine Empire during the Sixth century. Turkish Ministry of Tourism and Information

MUSLIM EMPIRE (622–1200 A.D.). During the Middle Ages, the Middle East was one of the world's most advanced cultural centers. This important culture, often called *Islamic* or *Muslim culture*, was originated by the Arabs, who established a new religion, Islam, in the 7th century. Arab conquests spread Islam to millions of peoples who were converted to its beliefs. So great was the Arab impact that the entire region is often (though inaccurately) called "the Arab world." Arabic is its chief language and Islam its chief religion.

Arab conquests brought them into contact with more highly developed cultures in Persia (now Iran), Syria, Egypt, and Mesopotamia (now Iraq). The influences of these and other peoples who accepted Islam merged into a distinct and unique "Muslim culture" which still dominates life in the Middle East. During the Middle Ages and until the Renaissance of the 14th century, this culture had developed far more than its European counterpart in most branches of learning and the arts. During this period the Muslims did much to spread knowledge of the arts and sciences.

MUSLIM CRAFTS

The tradition of excellence in intricately designed and crafted metalwork developed during the height of the Arab empire is still much in evidence today in many parts of the Middle East. Here we see a traditional Muslim metalwork craftsman working in the main square of Isfahan, in Iran. Isfahan was the capital and cultural center of the Muslim empire for over 100 years (17th and early 18th centuries). United Nations

Muslim culture was a blend of ancient cultures in the Middle East, India, and China. It also included important elements of Greek culture. It reached its height during the Abbasid Caliphate (750–1258 A.D.).[7] The Muslims built universities and attracted scholars of all faiths to their great centers of learning (Damascus, Cairo, Baghdad, Cordova). At such centers important work was done in mathematics, chemistry, medicine, geography, and astronomy.

Muslim scholars translated the works of Greek scientists and philosophers into Arabic and enriched these studies with contributions by scholars of various nationalities and faiths serving under Islam. Noteworthy in this regard were Avicenna, a pioneer physician of the Middle Ages, Averroes, an able philosopher and authority on Aristotle, and Moses Maimonides, an outstanding Spanish-Jewish scholar, mathematician, and philosopher. An important original Arab contribution to Muslim culture was the invention of the Arabic numerals, which became the basis of our own today.

[7] The Abbasids were of Meccan Arab descent; many of the officials and army were Persian and Turkish.

The Islamic literary and poetic masterpieces of this period that are still admired include the *Arabian Nights* and the *Rubaiyat of Omar Khayyam*. Islamic artists developed a distinctive style of ornamental design, which, because of religious prohibitions, did not include lifelike images of living creatures. In the field of architecture the most unique contribution of the Muslims was the Arab *mosque* or temple.

The Arabs were also skilled merchants and craftsmen. They excelled in the manufacture of many varieties of textiles including damasks (named for the city of Damascus, where such fabrics were first made), linens, brocades, and carpets. In addition they produced steel products, tooled leather, Oriental rugs, and ceramics of high quality.

During the Middle Ages, Arabs performed a middleman's role in trade between Europe and the Orient. Medieval trade routes and Arab exchange centers in the Middle East made possible the introduction into Europe of many new products, for example, citrus fruits, sugar, silk, paper, gunpowder and the compass.

OTTOMAN EMPIRE (1300–1918 A.D.). Following the Mongol assaults in the 13th century, which destroyed much of Islamic-Arabic civilization, the Ottoman Turks built a vast new Islamic empire that extended into the Balkans in Europe as well as the Middle East. It reached its greatest territorial extent in the 16th century and lasted until the early 20th century. Islamic, Arab, and Persian influences were strong. The Ottoman Turks looked down on Europeans as uncultured barbarians but, out of financial necessity, encouraged trade with Europe.

At the same time, gold and silver working as well as wood and stone carving, wood and metal inlaying, and gem setting became highly developed. Impressive mosques were designed and built. Turkish ceramic artists produced beautiful clay tiles, dishes, and bowls, and Turkish weavers produced textiles that became famous for their designs.

The Ottoman Empire began to decline late in the 16th century. Agriculture was neglected and huge areas remained uncultivated. By the middle of the 18th century much of the Fertile Crescent had become a desert. The population decreased as famine, plagues, and poverty stalked the land. Nearly all the good land passed into the hands of absentee landlords, and poor peasants (fellahin) fled to the cities. In addition, in the 19th century the Ottomans lost nearly all their European territories. Turkey, heart of the empire, became known as the "sick man of Europe." In the 20th century the Ottoman Empire disintegrated completely.

A Region of Struggle and Conflict

Throughout the ages the Middle East has been a region of struggle and conflict. It has seen the sweep of empire and has felt the might of invaders

REGION OF STRUGGLE AND CONFLICT
The theme of struggle and conflict as part of the Muslim heritage is reflected by this miniature painting of the Ottoman period, part of the collection of the Islamic Museum in Turkey. For several centuries before the final collapse of their empire after World War I, the Ottoman Turks controlled most of the Middle East.
Turkish Ministry of Tourism and Information

and conquerors. It has also experienced the force of peoples struggling to be free and to throw off foreign domination.

ANCIENT AND MEDIEVAL TIMES. In ancient times many empires sought control of the Middle East. The region became a battleground again and again as such ancient powers as Egypt, Mesopotamia (Babylonia), Assyria, Persia, Greece, and Rome conquered and ruled large portions of it. The Middle Ages witnessed Arab conquest, Crusader attacks from Western Europe, and devastation of the region by the Mongols.

MODERN TIMES. In the last few centuries the Middle East has continued to be a sought-after region. In the 16th century the Ottoman Turks built an extensive empire in the Middle East and the Balkans which lasted for several hundred years, until the end of World War I. European influence became important in the 19th century. By the late 1800s, European nations had begun to look on the Middle East as a field for their imperialistic, empire-building ambitions. In the period before and after World War I, large portions of the region came under the domination of England, France, and other powers. Since World War II, the Middle East has seen the rise of newly independent Arab nations and a newly established Jewish state.

In recent years, unrest and instability have frequently erupted into violent struggles for power. Arab states such as Jordan, Saudi Arabia, Egypt, Iraq, and Syria have fought against other Arab states. Internal divisions have torn apart Iran and the Christian–Muslim republic of Lebanon. Greeks and Turks have fought each other in Cyprus. The Jewish state of Israel and its Arab neighbors have fought four wars. Internal social and religious conflict brought about the overthrow of the monarchy in Iran.

Nearly everywhere in the Middle East there have been struggles and rivalries between conservative and radical leaders, groups, parties, and sects; between those who want to cling to old ways of life and those who desire change and modernization; and between those who favor a united "Pan-Arab Empire" of all Arab peoples and those who prefer separate, independent Arab nations. In addition two of the world's mightiest nations, the United States and the Soviet Union, have become seriously involved in a struggle for power and influence in the Middle East.

Mastery Activities

1. Complete the following chart by referring to data supplied in a reliable atlas, almanac, or encyclopedia.

The Middle East in Facts and Figures

Country	Size (Sq. Miles)	Population[8]	National Capital
Bahrain			
Cyprus			
Egypt			
Iran			
Iraq			
Israel			
Jordan			
Kuwait			
Lebanon			
Oman			
Qatar			
Saudi Arabia			
Sudan			
Syria			
Turkey			
United Arab Emirates			
Yemen			
Southern Yemen			

[8] Population figures for the Middle East are inexact. The figures used in this book are estimates as of 1980.

2. Explain or identify each of the following terms used in this chapter.

Middle East	Old Testament	Crusaders
Fertile Crescent	Monotheism	Mongols
"Cradle of civilization"	New Testament	Abbasid Caliphate
Horn of Africa	Islam	Ottoman Empire
Petrodollars	Koran	

Homework and Discussion Questions

1. Explain why the Middle East has been called a region of continuing tension and crisis.

2. Bring to class and be prepared to discuss one newspaper article that has appeared within the past week that illustrates the truth of the statement in the above question (Question 1).

3. Why does each of the following aspects of the Middle East make it important for Americans to understand this complex region?
A. Its strategic position, B. Its religious heritage, C. Its cultural heritage

2

The Middle East Today

The Middle East stretches over a large area where the continents of Asia, Europe, and Africa come together. It is about the same size as the United States (about 3.8 million square miles), with almost ninety percent as many people (nearly 200 million).

The Land

The physical features that shape the Middle East are mountains, plateaus, rivers, and deserts. Although four-fifths of the area is desert, nearly all the countries have geographic variety. The region has some of the world's greatest deserts, some of the highest and most rugged mountains, and some of the longest rivers.

Mountains

High mountains dominate Turkey and Iran — sometimes referred to as the "Northern Tier" countries of the Middle East, separating the region from Russia and China. High plateau areas are found within the mountainous areas. The central plateau of Turkey (the Anatolian Plateau) and the great plateau that covers much of Iran are hilly highlands, 2,000 to 5,000 feet high. The few lowland areas of Turkey and Iran are narrow plains bordering the Caspian, Black, and Aegean seas; and along the Mediterranean seacoast. Mountainous areas are also found in Lebanon, Saudi Arabia, Iraq, Yemen, and the southern coast of the Arabian Peninsula.

Deserts

Most of the Middle East consists of deserts. These are waterless (arid) wastelands without any vegetation to support man or animals. In addition,

22

A REGION OF DESERTS

Most of the Middle East is made up of deserts. The Rub' al-Khali or "Empty Quarter" of Saudi Arabia is the largest and hottest sand desert on the Arabian plateau. Some parts of this desert do not have rainfall for several years at a time. Only a few Bedouin tribesmen manage to live here. In recent years the discovery of oil in the desert areas of Saudi Arabia and other countries of the Middle East has resulted in the establishment of a growing number of refineries in such regions. The above picture shows a desert vehicle setting out from an oil exploration camp in the Empty Quarter of Saudi Arabia. Aramco Photo

there are semidesert steppe lands with small amounts of scrubby vegetation, barely sufficient for grazing. The deserts are usually lowland or elevated plateaus. They are sandy or rocky, and often hilly.

The region's deserts are among the most arid and desolate in the world. They include parts of the vast Sahara Desert in Africa, the Syrian Desert in the Fertile Crescent, and the Arabian Desert in Saudi Arabia. The southern Arabian Desert, a vast area the size of Texas, is almost completely uninhabited.

Here and there in the vast stretches of the deserts are highly prized oases, with their own natural water supplies. Many of the oases contain cultivated land and living facilities for travelers.

The most noteworthy exception to the arid, desertlike appearance of most of the Middle East is the famous "greenbelt." This is a narrow strip of land suitable for raising crops that stretches from the Persian Gulf up and around the Fertile Crescent through Iraq, Syria, Lebanon, and Israel and continues into the Valley of the Nile in Egypt.

NILE IN EGYPT
One of the world's earliest important civilizations developed is the valley of the Nile River in Egypt, in large measure because of the fertile soil deposited by its annual overflow. Less than five percent of Egypt's land is cultivated and nearly all of the nation's farm land is in the Nile Valley and Delta. Over 95% of Egypt's population of more than 40 million live in this narrow ribbon of green, in the midst of a vast expanse of desert. New York Public Library

Rivers

The two most important river systems of the Middle East are the Nile and Tigris–Euphrates systems. The Nile originates in large mountain lakes in Uganda and Ethiopia. The longest river system in the world, it flows north over 4,000 miles through the Sudan and Egypt to the Mediterranean. The Tigris and Euphrates rivers begin in the mountains of eastern Turkey and flow in a southeasterly direction through Iraq, where they meet to form the Shatt-al-Arab River, which empties into the Persian Gulf. There are also a number of smaller river systems, including the Jordan River, whose waters are shared by Jordan, Israel, Syria, and Lebanon; the Yarmuk River in Jordan and Israel; and the Litani River in Lebanon.

Climate

The climate of the Middle East largely consists of mild to cool winters and hot dry summers. However, extremes of heat and cold prevail in certain areas during some seasons. With the exception of certain mountain sections and the mountain-backed coastal lowlands along the seacoasts of the region, there is little rainfall. Some areas in the south, notably in Arabia and

Egypt, receive no rain for years at a time. Among the few areas that receive enough rain to be fertile and green are the coastal plains of Turkey, Syria, Lebanon, and Israel.

Natural Resources

Aside from oil, the Middle East is not rich in natural resources.

Minerals

Present estimates are that over half the world's known oil deposits are located in the Middle East. Saudi Arabia, Iran, Iraq, Kuwait, Bahrain, Qatar, the United Arab Emirates, and Libya (in North Africa) are leading oil-producing nations. (Before recent discoveries of extensive oil deposits in Mexico, estimates were that *two-thirds* of the world's oil resources were in the Middle East.)

Other Middle East mineral resources include chrome, coal, asphalt, copper, lead, manganese, salts, and silver. However, aside from Turkey (where there are abundant supplies of coal, copper, salt, iron, and chrome), minerals are distributed thinly and unevenly and are as yet too expensive to develop or mine.

Soil

Most of the soil in the Middle East is poor. Ninety percent of the topsoil has been destroyed by centuries of neglect. As a result, few regions in the Middle East are suitable for agriculture, aside from mountain slopes, coastal regions, and a few fertile areas, such as the Fertile Crescent.

Forests

The Middle East has few large forests. Trees cut down over the centuries have not been replaced. Most of the major forests are found on the slopes of the Elburz Mountains in Iran and the Lebanon Mountains in Lebanon.

Peoples of the Middle East

It is a common misconception that the Middle East is a single "Arab world" with a common background, culture, language, and identity. The truth is that more distinct groups of people have lived together in the Middle East over the centuries than almost anywhere else in the world.

While living close to other groups, each group has been able to maintain its identity by living in separate areas of cities and towns, by speaking its own language, by retaining its own customs, and often by engaging in particular occupations.

Peoples

Among the more numerous peoples in the Middle East "mosaic" are Arabs, Jews, Turks, Iranians, Kurds, and Copts. The racial spectrum of the Middle East ranges from fair skins to dark skins.

ARABS. Arabs are the largest population group in the Middle East. They constitute the majority in every country in the Middle East with the exceptions of Turkey, Iran, Cyprus, and Israel. In these countries there are Arab minorities.

Most Arabs are tied together by a language (Arabic), a religion (Islam), and a common desire to be identified as Arabs. They consider Muslim and Arab traditions and history to be part of their common heritage.

The term Arab is not racial. Although most Arabs and other peoples of the Middle East belong to the Mediterranean branch of the Caucasoid (white) race, with darker skins and hair than other European peoples, there are also Arabs of the black (Negroid) and yellow (Mongoloid) races.

Although *most* Arabs are Muslims, not *all* are. There are several million Christian Arabs. In addition, it is important to note — as has been stressed in Chapter 1 — that though many Muslims are Arabs, not *all* Muslims are Arabs. The only true or "original" Arabs today are the Bedouins living in the Arabian Peninsula and the surrounding area in Israel, Jordan, and Sinai. With the expansion of Islam in the 7th century, some Arab tribes moved out of the peninsula and settled in parts of North Africa and elsewhere, bringing with them the Arab language which became the dominant language from Iraq to Morocco. Because they spoke Arabic and became Muslims, people in these areas have identified themselves with the Arab people. At the same time they retain separate and distinct identifications as Egyptians, Tunisians, Algerians, and Moroccans.

Although *most* people who speak Arabic as their daily language are Arabs, not all *consider* themselves to be Arabs. Hundreds of thousands of Jews who came to Israel after its establishment as a separate nation formerly lived in Arabic-speaking countries.

Although reference is made to the "Arab world," there is no one all-encompassing Arab nation. Since the breakup of the Ottoman Empire after World War I, separate Arab states have emerged. Some are more hostile to one another than to non-Arab nations.

BEDOUINS: NOMADS OF THE DESERT

Although there may be oil deposits under his feet likely to change his country's economy, this Bedouin continues his traditional nomadic life, tending his flock of sheep in a harsh environment. Bedouins consider themselves to be the only "true" Arabs, tracing their origins to Biblical times. United Nations

JEWS. Most Jews of the Middle East live in Israel. They make up the majority of its population. Traditionally Jews are a people of the Middle East. Even before Israel was established, large numbers of Jews lived in Turkey, Iraq, Lebanon, Egypt, Syria, Iran, Yemen, Tunisia, Morocco, and other countries in the Middle East — as well as in Palestine. Most have since migrated to Israel. They and their descendants outnumber Jews who have come from Europe (including survivors of the Nazi Holocaust, in which six million European Jews were slaughtered).

Although of varying national backgrounds, the Jews of Israel share a common Jewish heritage. Hebrew is the national language of Israel; Arabic, spoken by the Arab minority and by many Jews, is also recognized as an official language.

TURKS. The Turks were the dominant people in the Middle East for over five centuries. Until the end of World War I, the Ottoman Empire which they created and dominated included all of the Middle East except Iran. Throughout the Ottoman era most Turks continued to live in Asia Minor (Anatolia), which makes up nearly all of present-day Turkey.

Nearly all Turks are Muslims. The Turkish language is a separate and distinct tongue that originated in Central Asia. It is different from Persian or Arabic.

IRANIANS (PERSIANS). Iran is another name for Persia. The population of Iran is predominantly Muslim of the Shii sect. The Persian language (Farsi) is related to European languages but is very different from Turkish and Arabic. Iranians, who have lived in the Middle East for forty centuries, share a common proud heritage. Since the 1940s there has been a great deal of social and political unrest in Iran. The situation was heightened in the late 1970s with the overthrow of the Shah and the establishment of an Islamic Republic.

KURDS. The Kurds are a people of the Islamic faith. Most of them live in Iraq within the mountainous region known as Kurdistan, which stretches from southeastern Turkey and across northeastern Iraq and northwestern

KURDS

Many peoples in the Middle East continue to maintain their separate customs, languages, and identities. The Kurds are one such people. Most Kurds live in Iraq; others in Iran and Turkey. Here we see Kurds in Iraq making bread outside their tents. Kurdish women wear lengthy colored clothes, rings in their ears and noses, and jewelry made of coins and beads. United Nations

Iran. They are essentially a seminomadic people of pasture shepherds living in tribal communities to which they give their first loyalties.

Originally the Kurds, descendants of the ancient Medes, lived in an independent kingdom. Later they became part of the Persian and Ottoman empires and then part of modern Turkey, Iran, and Iraq. Despite many periods of persecution and the loss of land to Arabs, Turks, Iraqis, and Iranians, the Kurds have maintained their own traditions, customs, and sense of identity. They have long complained of oppression and have sought cultural autonomy and self-determination.

COPTS. The Copts are Egypt's largest religious minority. Although Christian, they consider themselves Egyptian since they trace their ancestry to ancient Egyptians who were converted to Christianity in the 2nd and 3rd centuries A.D. The Coptic church has existed as a separate branch of Christianity since the 5th century. Under Arab and Ottoman Muslim rule, the Copts were often victims of discrimination and persecution.

The overall economic level of the Copts in Egypt is higher than that of the Muslim masses. Many are proud of their identity as Egyptians and feel that they are an accepted part of Egyptian society. Others feel that there is discrimination against them in jobs and government positions.

Religions

The major religions of the Middle East are Islam, Christianity, and Judaism.

ISLAM. Islam, the predominant faith in the Middle East, is split into two major divisions plus a number of smaller sects.

The major divisions of Islam are Sunni and Shii. Sunni Islam, the more numerous branch, is predominant in Egypt, Jordan, Syria, the Arabian Peninsula, Turkey, and North Africa. Shii Islam is the majority denomination in Iraq, Iran, and Yemen. Sunnis regard the first four caliphs as the legitimate successors of Mohammed; Shiites regard Ali, the son-in-law of Mohammed, as the legitimate successor of Mohammed. They disregard the three caliphs who actually did succeed him. There are also Alawites and other Muslim sects, each of which maintains its own beliefs.

CHRISTIANITY. Christianity preceded Islam as the major religion of the Middle East. It is still a "living" religion in the Arab world, with millions of adherents. The approximately four million Copts of Egypt make up the largest Christian group. The Orthodox church has large numbers of adherents in Syria and Lebanon. Roman Catholicism is represented by several groups that acknowledge the supremacy of the pope but have their own forms of worship and services. The churches that are in communion with the Roman Catholics include the Maronite, Melkite, and Chaldean churches. Most are found in Lebanon, where the Maronite church is most important.

JUDAISM. Judaism has been an important faith of the Middle East since ancient times. Although Jerusalem was destroyed by the Romans in 70 A.D. and most Jews later dispersed, substantial Jewish communities continued to live in various parts of the Middle East until they emigrated in large numbers to the new State of Israel beginning in 1948. Today the vast majority of Middle East Jews are in Israel.

OTHER RELIGIONS. In addition to Muslims, Christians, and Jews, there are Zoroastrians, Baha'is, and other religious groups in the Middle East, each maintaining its own religious identity.

Languages

Over a dozen languages are spoken in the Middle East today. These include Arabic, Aramaic, Armenian, Greek, Hebrew, Kurdish, Iranian, and Turkish. The predominant language is Arabic, which is spoken in all parts of the region except Turkey and Iran. As a language spoken over so vast an area, stretching from the Atlantic Ocean to the Persian Gulf, Arabic has many local dialects, making it difficult for Arabic peoples from different areas to understand one another. Major Arab dialects include Egyptian, Syrian, Iraqi, Arabian Peninsula, and North African. Turkish predominates in Turkey, Farsi in Iran and northern Iraq, and Hebrew in Israel. Literary Arabic, common throughout the area, is used and basically understood by the educated classes. Standard written Arabic is the same in all regions. Increasingly, educated Arabs speak standard Arabic based on written Arabic; it is generally used on radio and television.

Population Distribution

Population is distributed unevenly throughout most of the Middle East. The largest number of people live crowded together in the villages and cities of the Nile and Tigris–Euphrates valleys. Here water for agriculture and human consumption is available throughout the year. Many people live on the Mediterranean coast and in northern and western Iran and Turkey. The interior areas, where there is little rainfall, support a sparse population of desert dwellers, or nomads, who depend on herding or hunting in order to live.

Egypt, Lebanon, and Israel are the most densely populated countries in the Middle East. Turkey (c. 43 million), Egypt (c. 40 million), and Iran (c. 35

million) have the largest populations; Qatar (c. 101,000), United Arab Emirates (c. 245,000), Cyprus (c. 700,000), and Oman (c. 840,000) have the smallest. Large numbers of foreigners have been attracted by job opportunities in Iran, Saudi Arabia, and other oil-rich nations. Kuwait and several other Persian Gulf states have more foreign workers than native-born inhabitants. The Kuwaitis are a minority in their own country, numbering about half a million in a population of 1.2 million that includes 250,000 Palestinians and also large numbers of Iranians, Egyptians, Indians, and Pakistanis.

Ways of Life

Most people in the Middle East live in small villages. A growing proportion, now over thirty percent, live in large towns or cities. There are also small numbers of nomadic or seminomadic peoples who live in thinly inhabited semiarid areas.

VILLAGE LIFE
Village life in the Middle East continues to be fairly primitive by Western standards, as is illustrated in this picture of a housewife carrying water from the local well. "Family houses" with different entrances for different generations or parts of the family are in the background. United Nations

VILLAGERS. Most villagers earn their living by farming. Others make a living by providing services and by trading.

Most of the land belongs to village landlords or absentee owners (who live in distant towns or cities). In return for giving the landowner a large share of his crop, the peasant is generally given the right to farm a small piece of land, plus seeds, tools, and work animals. (In the United States such farmers are called sharecroppers.)

The average village consists of hutlike dwellings, a school for the lower grades, and a few stores where food and goods are sold. Larger villages generally have a marketplace for the sale and exchange of goods from neighboring villages on certain days of the week.

Living conditions in most villages are harsh by Western standards. The small share of crops left for the peasant provides a mere subsistence living for the average farm family. Unsanitary, crowded living quarters, inadequate medical facilities, and poor diets have contributed to low life expectancy and high death rates. The average home lacks electricity, plumbing, and central heating. Oil lamps are used for light, outhouses serve as toilets, and water must be drawn from wells. Hospitals and recreational facilities such as movie theaters are found only in larger towns and cities.

Livestock are a common part of life. Sheep and goats are used for milk, meat, hair, wool, skins, and dung (manure used for fertilizer). The main work animals are donkeys and oxen. Camels are used in oases and semiarid areas bordering the deserts. Livestock are generally pastured in the village fields after harvests to feed on stubble, grain stalks, and leaves.

NOMADS. The number of Middle Easterners who do not have permanent homes — now less than half a million — is steadily declining. These "nomads" are called *Bedouins*, an Arabic word meaning "people who live in the open country." Bedouins keep herds of sheep, goats, and camels. Most live in tents made of camel or goatskins and move in regular patterns to find sufficient pasturage for their flocks. They rely on villagers, town dwellers, and city dwellers for things they cannot produce themselves.

Bedouins used to depend on camels and donkeys for travel and for transportation across the deserts. Today most Bedouins use trucks to travel from place to place, taking their families, belongings, and sheep with them. Although the camel is still essential for providing food (milk and meat) and shelter (hair and skins), the camel caravan has virtually disappeared. Once crossed only by camel trails, the desert is now laced by networks of motor roads.

Bedouins are fiercely proud people who consider themselves to be the only true Arabs. They are organized into clans and tribes. A clan is a group of families descended from a common ancestor. Clans combine to form tribes that may vary in size from several dozen to several thousand families (usually 400 to 500 families). Tribal leaders, called sheikhs, make decisions and settle disputes with the help of a council of elders.

The number of nomads has been declining because their function has been made obsolete by modern means of transportation and communication. There is no longer a need for Bedouin caravans to serve as the means of transportation across the vast deserts. Consequently many Bedouins have reluctantly given up their nomadic way of life and moved to the cities to find employment. Many have become oil drillers, truckdrivers, mechanics, and unskilled laborers. Others have settled down in villages to become farmers. Many have joined the new national armies or have become part of the police forces.

CITY DWELLERS. Cities have long been important in the life of the Middle East. Today they are centers of leadership and change, as well as social, commercial, and cultural centers. Their impact on the life, thought, and lifestyles of the Middle East is growing rapidly.

Many of the Middle East's largest cities were established before the rise of Islam — some in ancient times. A few have been built in the last century or two, for example, Port Said (Egypt), Abadan (Iran), and Tel Aviv (Israel).

Some of the world's largest cities are in the Middle East, including Cairo

NEW SHOPPING CENTER

The newer sections of cities in the Middle East have become increasingly modernized and Westernized. This is a new shopping center in Teheran, capital of Iran. United Nations

and Alexandria (Egypt), Teheran (Iran), and Istanbul (Turkey) — all with populations of over a million. In addition, a number of cities in the region have populations of over 100,000, for example, Ankara, Izmir, and Adana in Turkey, Damascus and Aleppo in Syria, Isfahan and Tabriz in Iran, Baghdad in Iraq, Beirut in Lebanon, Port Said in Egypt, and Tel Aviv, Haifa, and Jerusalem in Israel.

Cairo is the largest city in the Middle East. It has a population of over eight million. It is an ancient cultural center and a dynamic urban center. In its newer or modernized sections there are wide avenues, modern hotels, office buildings, and apartment houses. Beirut (Lebanon) was the Arab world's leading cosmopolitan and financial center before large sections were damaged by violent civil war in the 1970s.

Although ancient, most large Middle East cities have been modernized. As a result many consist of an "old city," often surrounded by walls, and a "new city" outside the walls. (Walls were built in ancient and medieval times for protection against enemies.) The old city is generally traditional in appearance and ways of life; the new city is often a modern urban center. In a number of Middle East cities, parts or all of the old walls have been torn down to make way for new living quarters or thoroughfares.

The older central section of a Middle East city usually contains the city's main mosque (Muslim house of worship). Also found here are the original government buildings, including a fortified palace, which are generally maintained as museums and tourist attractions today. Surrounding this area are narrow, winding streets and alleys. These include the traditional crowded marketplace or bazaar, consisting of hundreds of small shops and stalls (souks), which often stretches for miles under arcaded roofs of wooden beams or masonry. The residential areas of the older cities surround the bazaar and include food shops and public baths in addition to dwellings.

The modern sections of Middle East cities often resemble cities of the Western world. There are neon-lighted central business districts with tall office buildings of concrete and steel, including banks, government build-ings, and large hotels. Also to be found are wide avenues, tree-lined boulevards, large open squares, and Western-style stores and shopping centers, theaters, nightclubs, and restaurants. Beyond the central business district is the main residential section where most people live. There are also public and government buildings, hospitals, public schools, post offices, museums, and bus transportation systems. In addition, modern cities and sections have their own mosques, public baths, and a marketplace (usually an open square with stalls).

Housing in the cities is very varied, as in other parts of the world. For those who can afford it there are luxury apartment houses, comfortable large town houses, and suburban "villas." Middle-income groups live in smaller stone or brick dwellings. The poor live in slum "shantytown"

TEHERAN BAZAAR
The traditional market place of Middle Eastern cities, called the bazaar, consists of hundreds of small shops and stalls. Note the sharp contrast between this traditional marketplace and the shopping center shown on page 33. Both are in Teheran. Alain Keler/Sygma

districts on the outskirts of the city. Their dwellings are for the most part crude huts or shacks made of any materials that can be found, including lumber scraps, tin, and corrugated iron.

City workers include artisans, merchants, religious functionaries, government administrators, and others, who work at the occupations that have characterized urban life in the Middle East for centuries. Since the beginning of the 20th century, when Westernization and industrialization began to have a significant impact, there has been the same general range of occupations that characterizes the work forces of cities in the Western world, including unskilled laborers, office workers, technicians, and managerial executives.

Economy

An Underdeveloped Region

The Middle East is for the most part an underdeveloped region. Industry has greatly increased since World War II, but there is still relatively little industrialization in much of the region. Except in the major oil-producing states and Israel (the most technologically advanced and industrialized country in the Middle East), national income is low, life expectancy is short, and there is a high degree of illiteracy. Most people maintain what by our standards would be considered a poverty-level existence by farming or herding — or as unskilled laborers in towns and cities. Housing, diet, and clothing are substandard. Less that seven percent of the land is presently available for cultivation.

Aside from the oil-rich nations, most Middle East states are poor in spite of recent industrial growth. They rely on loans, gifts, and other forms of assistance from other countries, on foreign investments in their industries, and on spending by tourists.

Agriculture

Despite the small amount of arable land, agriculture has always been important in most of the Middle East. Among the chief crops are wheat, barley, and cotton. Also grown are rice, dates, olives, beets, tobacco, nuts, peaches, grapes, sugar cane, and citrus fruits. Three-fourths of the world's

TRADITIONAL FARMING
Although the introduction of modern farm methods and equipment is given high priority in the economic development plans of Middle East countries, farming is still largely traditional in most areas, as illustrated in this picture of a farmer tilling the soil with a wooden plow and donkeys. United Nations

dates come from Iraq. Egypt and Syria are important cotton producers. Tobacco grown in Turkey, Lebanon, and Syria and oranges and other fruit and flowers grown in Israel have worldwide markets.

Despite reliance on farming as the basic occupation, most farmers still use primitive tools and methods. Nevertheless, in recent years, many nations in the Middle East have attempted to improve agricultural conditions. Irrigation and flood control programs have been undertaken. Mechanical tools and equipment have been introduced, as well as crop rotation and other newer farming methods. The use of chemical fertilizer and pesticides has increased.

Industry

Most industry in the Middle East has long been and still is in the handicraft stage. In most urban areas craftsmen in small shops still engage in the production of textiles, rugs, embroidery, metalwork, and other articles.

In recent decades factory production has begun to replace this handicraft system in a growing number of industries, including food processing, building materials, and tile manufacture. Since World War II many factories have been built in and around the larger cities and entirely new industries have been developed, for example, auto assembly, plastics, radio and television sets, chemical production, and oil production and refining. Israel has become the most industrialized nation in the Middle East with over a quarter of its national product coming from manufacturing. Turkey and Egypt are other important industrial producers. Egypt is the most industrialized Arab nation. The largest Middle East development project in recent years has been the Aswan High Dam project in Egypt. Although it has never fulfilled expectations, it has made possible a significant increase in the amount of irrigated land and in the supply of electric power.

Middle East Oil

Middle East nations have over half of the world's known oil reserves. They produce over a quarter of the world's oil. The oil (petroleum) industry has become by far the most important industry in the Middle East. Since the early 1930s, billions of dollars have been invested in the production of this vital commodity.

Most Middle East oil is exported. Petroleum exports now make up over three-fourths of the total value of Middle East shipments abroad. Western Europe, the United States, and Japan receive over seventy percent of these supplies. Most Middle East crude oil is shipped directly to world markets on giant tankers. The rest, about fifteen percent, flows through Middle East pipelines to terminals on the Mediterranean coast.

OIL ECONOMY

The production and refining of oil has been reshaping the economies of a number of Middle East countries. Seen here is one of the world's largest oil refineries, Ras Tanura, along the Persian Gulf in Saudi Arabia, which produces oil fuels and gasoline. United Nations

The major oil-producing nations of the Middle East are Saudi Arabia, Iran, Iraq, and Kuwait. In the early 1980s Saudi Arabia, the leading oil-producing state, was producing over ten million barrels of oil per day. (There are forty-two gallons per barrel.) Iran, the second largest producer, was producing six million barrels a day until civil strife in 1978 and 1979 reduced production. Iraq was the third largest producer, yielding over two million barrels daily. The United Arab Emirates, Qatar, and Oman are also important oil-producing states.

Much of the oil profits have been invested in economic development, including the construction of industrial plants and factories, airports, dams, and harbors. Highways, pipelines, power plants, and railroads have also been built. Large sums have been spent for educational and health facilities, housing, and other social programs.

Oil income has also made it possible for Arab oil-exporting nations, particularly Saudi Arabia, to extend financial assistance to other Arab nations in need of it (for example, Egypt, Syria). Vast and growing sums have also been invested in the purchase of arms and in military training.

In addition, billions of Arab "petrodollars" have been invested abroad or placed in foreign banks. Arab oil-exporting nations have joined with other

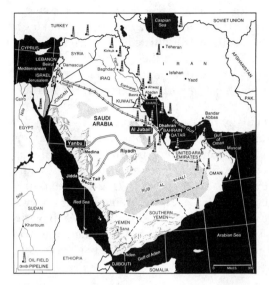

MIDDLE EAST OIL FIELDS
The map gives a clear picture of where the leading Middle East oil fields are located. With its oil profits Saudi Arabia, the world's leading oil producing nation, is building vast new industrial complexes at Yanbu and Al Jubail.
New York Times

oil-exporting countries to form the Organization of Petroleum Exporting Countries (OPEC) in order to regulate production and prices of oil on a worldwide basis. The growing energy needs and dependence on Middle East oil of developing nations as well as Western and other industrialized nations have made OPEC an increasingly important organization in world affairs.

Customs and Traditions

Common Culture

Because of the strong impact of the Islamic religion, Muslim customs have become the basis for a dominant Muslim culture throughout nearly all the Middle East. Within this "Muslim world," Arabs, Turks, Persians, Kurds, Jews, and other ethnic, religious, and language groups continue to maintain their own distinctive identities, customs, and traditions.

Islam is an all-encompassing way of life as well as a religion. Common beliefs and institutions link Muslims throughout the world. Although they are under different governments and in different regions, Muslims the world over feel they are part of one family or "brotherhood." Despite political, social, economic, and sectarian differences there are broad, pervasive, and common cultural patterns, shaped largely by Islamic beliefs and traditions. Muslims share the basic belief that nothing on earth happens without God's will and that "there is no God but Allah and Mohammed is His messenger." They are guided by the Koran and the Islamic code of justice and morality based on it (the Shari'a). They accept the basic obligatory duties of all followers of Islam (for example, praying, fasting, making a pilgrimage to Mecca) and the doctrines formulated by certain Muslim religious leaders ("teachers") to direct them in their religious, moral, and social behavior. Although styles of mosques vary from one country to another, mosques are usually the most important structures in a Muslim town. Muslims also look back with pride to the cultural greatness of Islam during the Middle Ages (particularly the 7th to 9th centuries).

The Islamic faith embraces more than the Arab world. Only ten to fifteen percent of the world's 700 to 800 million Muslims are Arabs with Arabic as their first language. Nevertheless, Arab influences throughout the Islamic world have served to maintain the Arabic character at its core. Arab tastes, outlooks, and traditions have in differing degrees become part of the cultural life of societies that have remained separate. Although the Arab world is by no means all of Islam, it is the symbolic heart of a vast community. The influence of Arabic is based in large part on the fact that the Koran is in Arabic and it is not supposed to be translated.

Traditions and Family Structure

Although important changes have taken place in the 20th century, traditional and religious ways still dominate the lives of many people of the Middle East. Since tradition is strong, most Middle Easterners live in large "extended" families. Three generations (children, parents, grandparents) often live under the same roof. Family ties are close and great respect is paid to parents and elderly people. Patriarchal rule prevails, with the father the unquestioned decision-making head of the family. Marriages are still generally arranged by the families in more conservative communities and preferred marriages among cousins are encouraged.

Religion helps bind together the members of the communities. Hospitality is considered essential and guests are well received. Women are often veiled and wear plain dark clothing when they appear in public. Most women still play an inferior role. Children begin to assume family responsibilities at an early age and child labor is common.

A stern attitude is taken toward crime and severe punishment is not unusual. In certain instances traditional Muslim practices permit such penalties as public whippings of criminals, cutting off the hands of thieves, and stoning adulteresses. In Saudi Arabia and other more conservative Muslim states, motion pictures and the use, sale, and promotion of alcohol and tobacco are banned.

Loyalties to faith, family, and tribe have been important unifying forces throughout most of Middle East history. The idea of loyalty to a nation (nationalism) is relatively new, and is often not as strong as other ties.

WOMEN AND CHANGE

Both the traditional and the modern in women's dress can be seen in this picture of one section of a Kuwaiti shopping center. Since it became an oil-rich kingdom, the former British protectorate of Kuwait has developed one of the world's highest standards of living. People living and working in Kuwait may receive free medical service, free education through the university level, and subsidized housing. Apesteguy/Gamma-Liaison

Change and Modernization

In the 20th century, ways of life in the Middle East have begun to change markedly. Middle East peoples have been caught up in a "revolution of rising expectations." They have become conscious of the fact that modernization and change can improve their lives and living standards.

Middle East leaders have recognized the need to modernize their countries in order to gain strength and prestige. In varying degrees they have taken steps to meet increasing demands for land reform, agricultural improvements, industrialization, emancipation of women, and better transportation. In recent years there has been increasing opposition to modernization and Westernization, particularly by Muslim "traditionalists" who believe that rapid Westernization and modernization corrode and corrupt Islamic values and must be prevented. As a result of these conflicting beliefs, changing the traditional outlook of society has become one of the greatest challenges faced by Middle East peoples and their leaders. A return to strict adherence to Islamic tradition was a major rallying point in the Iranian revolution which was masterminded by a fundamentalist religious leader, the Ayatollah Khomeini, in the late 1970s. Khomeini and many of the fundamentalist Islamic leaders blame the evils and problems that beset their countries on Western imperialism, which, in their judgment, is especially symbolized today by the United States.

Changing Family Structure and Role of Women

Under the impact of Westernization the traditional family structure has begun to break down. Older forms of personal contact are being replaced by new, more impersonal family relationships. Polygamy — the practice of one man having several wives — has been declining, though it still prevails in some communities.

Although women still occupy a place in Muslim society that is subordinate to men, the emancipation of women has been slowly spreading. Most Middle East nations have given legal rights to women, including the right to vote. Interest in women's rights has grown, particularly in the larger cities.

STREET SCENE IN ABU DHABI
Americans will recognize this example of Western influence in Abu Dhabi, one of the seven states on the eastern Arabian Peninsula comprising the United Arab Emirates. Since the discovery of vast oil reserves, Abu Dhabi and Dubai, another of the UAE sheikdoms, have accumulated untold wealth. Salhani/Gamma-Liaison

Westernization

Many aspects of Western culture have been adopted. Education for the young, improved sanitation, and improved medical facilities are spreading. Motion pictures, radio, and television have become common forms of communication and entertainment.

Agricultural Improvements

Greater agricultural output has resulted from the adoption of newer methods and farm machinery. With government aid, farmers have begun to use tractors and other mechanized tools and equipment. In Egypt, Iran, and several other countries many former estates have been broken up and the land distributed to peasants at little or no cost.

In addition, major water development programs have been undertaken by Egypt, Iraq, Jordan, Israel, Lebanon, and other Middle East governments. Particularly important have been projects for flood control, expansion of irrigation, and generation of electric power (through the construction of dams).

EGYPTIAN INDUSTRY

The development of modern industry and transportation in the Middle East is evidenced by this modern repair shop for diesel locomotive trains in Egypt, where diesel locomotives are replacing steam engines. United Nations

Industrial Development

All Middle East nations have undertaken economic development programs. Industrial development and progress have largely been a result of state encouragement, planning, and investment. Foreign technical and financial assistance and loans have helped considerably. In many cases governments have "nationalized" or "socialized" new or existing industries. The percentage of national income invested in oil production, mining, and transportation has increased greatly. Industrial output has grown rapidly, as has highway and road construction. Industrial change and growth have been most noteworthy in the oil-rich states and in Lebanon and Israel.

Population Growth and Distribution

As a result of economic development and contact with the West, the death rate in the Middle East — particularly infant mortality — has been reduced. This has contributed to population growth in both rural and urban areas. Drawn by the hope of greater job opportunities and the attractions of city life, people from the countryside have been moving into the cities in growing numbers.

Problems of Change and Modernization

Change and modernization have created serious problems and challenges for the peoples and governments of the Middle East.

Growing Population

Population growth in the Middle East has tended to offset the gains of industrialization. Many people have left the countryside because, with modernization of agriculture, there are not enough farming jobs for an expanding population, and the land can no longer support them. The bigger cities, particularly the already teeming capitals, have become even more crowded.

Unemployment and Other Economic Dislocations

Economic "progress" has often had serious harmful effects. Hundreds of thousands of peasants have left their native villages for more profitable work in the cities. But because these people are unskilled, too few have been able to find jobs. At the same time, large numbers of foreign workers compete for jobs in the cities. Urban unemployment has become a major problem. Sporadic protests and riots against insufficient food, rising prices, and lack of jobs have erupted in some of the major cities.

Need for Capital

Aside from oil revenues, there is little capital in the Middle East for investments that will stimulate the building of factories and other projects that offer economic development as well as job opportunities. Traditionally, wealthy Middle Easterners have invested their savings in land — and they still prefer to do so.

Lacking private capital, political leaders have tried to raise capital by taxing the rich, setting limits on land and property ownership, and — more importantly — by obtaining large grants or loans from other nations. For example, since World War II Turkey has received over $3 billion in U.S. aid (in the form of grants and loans); Iran has received over $800 million. Since 1973, Egypt has been getting over a billion dollars a year in economic assistance from the United States. Increasing amounts of financial aid have been given by oil-rich Arab nations to such oil-poor Middle East nations as Syria, Jordan, and Egypt.[1] Israel has also received generous aid from the United States.

Need for Leadership

Economic development has been handicapped by a lack of skilled managers and technicians and by inefficient government administration. To overcome these deficiencies, Middle East regimes have developed their own training programs, often with Western assistance. They have also sent young men to Western countries to learn modern managerial techniques. Attempts have been made to eliminate corruption and inefficiency in government.

Need for Improved Education

Educational levels in Middle Eastern countries are generally still low, though efforts to improve them have been increasing. How to achieve sound education in the many new schools that have been built throughout the Middle East is a real problem. To this end, secondary schools and colleges are emphasizing careers that help stimulate industry and raise standards of living, including the sciences, engineering, and mechanics. In the lower schools, stress is being given to basic skills such as reading, writing, and arithmetic, as well as to skills necessary to improve agriculture and home living.

Traditional Attitudes

Modernization has gone hand in hand and has offered incentives for such things as personal initiative and ambition, hard work, and resourcefulness.

[1] To "punish" Egypt for signing a peace treaty with Israel in 1979, Saudi Arabia cut off its financial assistance to Cairo.

STUDENTS AT RIYADH UNIVERSITY

The rulers of Saudi Arabia are making strenuous efforts to improve education at the college and university levels in order to develop a trained managerial and technician corps for their growing industry. Here we see students at work in a modern laboratory in Riyadh University, the oldest and largest in Saudi Arabia. Aramco Photo

These values have not traditionally been stressed in Muslim culture and religion. Since people cannot easily change traditional lifestyles and customs, developing such traits poses a major problem for modernization in the Middle East.

Social Strains and Dilemmas

Attempts to achieve modernization and rapid economic development have produced serious social strains and dilemmas, resulting from the conflict between the traditional and the modern.

Educated Middle Easterners want the science and technology of the West. At the same time they would like to preserve the Middle East cultural heritage and values, which they fear are being diluted or debased by Westernization. Increasing doubts have arisen as to whether both are possible.

In most Middle East nations the younger generation has been most affected by the tides of change. As a result of their new ways of thinking and doing, a wide and deep "generation gap" has emerged in the Middle East — as in other developing regions. Closely related to this problem is the growing concern with the status of women.

Although opposed to Western values, many students attending colleges and universities have become disturbed by censorship and by the use of force to repress opposition in some Middle East nations. They have actively protested against what they consider to be cruel forms of punishment and torture by the military and secret police. Students have also opposed corruption in government and business as well as restrictions on the formation of political parties and unions. Many have become Marxists or have joined with leftists to demand political, social, and economic reforms. Some have actively organized to overthrow repressive regimes.

Additional social strains have resulted from the growing insistence in some Middle East countries that first loyalty be given by their citizens to the national government rather than to a religious sect or ethnic minority.

Muslim leaders, objecting to modernization and industrialization as interference with religious doctrine and tradition, oppose such things as increased women's rights (including coeducation and removal of the veil in public) as well as dancing and drinking in places of public entertainment. Since the power of religious leaders is very real and extensive among Muslims, most people are torn between the desire for change and their holy men's insistence on tradition.

The question of whether Muslim society can industrialize without altering traditional social and political structures is basic and fundamental. It is particularly applicable to Iran as well as to countries like Saudi Arabia, the United Arab Emirates, and Oman, where theocratic (religiously dominated) systems of government prevail.

Government and Political Trends

There are several types of governments in the Middle East today. Most countries are either monarchies or military dictatorships. Only one — Israel — is a Western-style democracy. A number of Middle East regimes have undergone periodic military coups or takeovers.

Monarchy

Two types of monarchy prevail. Nations like Saudi Arabia, Kuwait, and the sheikhdoms of the Persian Gulf (for example, Oman, Qatar, Bahrain) are *traditional "feudal" monarchies*. The ruler (king, sheikh, or emir) generally has absolute power and dominates the government completely. Tribes, families, and religious groups support his rule and authority. Citizens have few political rights or individual liberties. Political parties as we know them do not exist. There are no elections. The leading government officials usually come from the ruling family.

Jordan is a *constitutional monarchy* — as was Iran until 1979, when the

MONARCHY
King Khalid and Crown Prince Fahd of Saudi Arabia. Rulers of Saudi Arabia and other Arab kingdoms are among the world's few remaining absolute monarchs. The King rules with un- limited power, assisted by members of the royal family. He is also considered to be the chief defender of the faith (Islam). Aramco Photo

monarchy was overturned. A constitution places limits on the king's powers and there is an elected legislature. Actually the ruler has dominated such governments and, though permitted by the constitution, political parties are often outlawed. The legislatures in such monarchies have tended to be dominated by representatives of the wealthy landowning families.

Role of the Military

The military has played an important role in the history of the Middle East. Army service continues to be a respected career and a way to improve one's status in life. The army, generally speaking, is the one group that has discipline, authority, and weapons. This has given it an important advantage over other groups.

Military leaders in most Middle East states have, in recent years, been more accepting of the need for change and modernization than other traditional groups and sects. In a number of instances pressures from the army have forced traditional rulers to undertake political, economic, and social reforms, including curtailment of the power and holdings of wealthy landowners, distribution of land to peasants, and reform of legal and criminal codes.

Military Regimes

Since they have become independent, many nations in the Middle East have come under military domination or rule as a result of coups or takeovers. Nevertheless, most continue to call themselves republics. In a number of these countries, for example, Syria, Iraq, and Southern Yemen, Marxist regimes have been established. They consider themselves "revolutionary" or "radical" and stress socialist-type economic planning by the government.

In 1980 Turkey's military leaders took control of the country in an effort to prevent extremists of the left and right as well as religious fanatics from destroying the Turkish Republic.

The army also plays an important role in countries that have not recently experienced military takeovers, for example, Egypt, Jordan, and Saudi Arabia.

Other Types of Government

Turkey, Lebanon, and Israel have governmental structures that are neither traditional monarchies nor military-dominated regimes.

TURKEY has been a republic since 1923. It is the only Muslim country in the Middle East where there have been peaceful changes of government through elections in which there have been rival political parties. In 1980 the armed forces took over the government in a bloodless coup. The military command said they did this because the country's political parties were failing to deal with Turkey's economic problems and with political terrorism. It was expected that civilian rule would be restored when the National Assembly drafted a new constitution strengthening the major political parties and reducing the influence of minority "splinter parties."

LEBANON is an Arab state whose political system has collapsed as a result of bloody fighting among rival political, religious, and economic groups (sectarian violence). Until civil war broke out in the 1970s its governmental system was unique among the Arab nations of the Middle East. It had an elected legislature and president. Governmental power was shared by Christians and Muslims.

ISRAEL is a republic and parliamentary democracy, with a government modeled on West European patterns. It has a president, a prime minister, a cabinet, a regularly elected one-house legislature, and a number of active political parties. Its government is the most democratic in the Middle East, with a free press, open political dissent, and guaranteed civil liberties.

Mastery Activities

1. Consult a good encyclopedia about Egypt, Iraq, Iran, and Saudi Arabia. Explain one important way in which the history and development of each has been influenced by the geographic feature italicized next to its name.

Egypt — *Nile River*
Iran — *mountains and plateaus*
Saudi Arabia — *deserts*
Iraq — *location*

2. Explain or identify each of the following names or terms used in this chapter:

Northern Tier countries	Nomads
Greenbelt	Bazaars
Tigris–Euphrates River	Underdeveloped region
Jordan River	Extended families
Arab world	Feudal monarchies
Copts	Oil-rich nations
Kurds	Revolution of Rising Expectations

Questions for Homework and Discussion

1. On the basis of the information given in this chapter state (a) two ways in which the geography of the Middle East is like that of the United States, and (b) three ways in which it is different.

2. In a recent poll of public opinion on the Middle East over sixty percent of those polled thought that the following statements about the Middle East were true. Explain the extent to which you agree or disagree with their judgment in each case:
   (a) The Middle East is an Arab world, with a common background and culture.
   (b) Like Christianity, Islam has major branches of belief.
   (c) Standards of living in the Middle East are low because of the lack of change.
   (d) The largest cities in the Middle East are ancient and run-down.
   (e) Israel has the highest standard of living in the Middle East.

3. Westernization and industrialization have brought both progress and problems to the Middle East.
   (a) Discuss three ways in which this trend has benefited the peoples of the Middle East.
   (b) Explain three problems that have resulted.
   (c) Give two reasons that help explain why the Middle East is still an underdeveloped region.

4. List three characteristics of democratic government and explain the extent to which these are present in most countries in the Middle East.

3

Close-Up Studies of Middle East Countries

The Middle East is a varied and diverse region. Although there are many basic similarities among most Middle East nations, there are also important differences. Sometimes these differences make it difficult to "generalize." The following case studies illustrate this point. Selected for brief "close-up" studies are Egypt, Iran, Israel, Lebanon, Saudi Arabia, Jordan, Syria, and Turkey.

Egypt is a Muslim Arab republic with a strong military influence. The government is moving away from socialist programs adopted in the 1950s and 1960s. Syria is a military-dominated Muslim Arab socialist republic. Jordan is a Muslim Arab state governed as a constitutional monarchy. Saudi Arabia is a Muslim Arab monarchy organized along more authoritarian lines. Lebanon, until its recent civil war one of the more stable Middle East nations, is a Christian–Muslim Arab parliamentary republic. Israel is a democratic Jewish republic with a large Arab minority.

Turkey and Iran are non-Arab Muslim states. Until fairly recently Turkey has been a stable republic; it has many Western democratic institutions. Until the overthrow of the Shah, Iran was a traditional monarchy, experimenting with Western-type political institutions to a far greater degree than Saudi Arabia and other conservative Muslim nations. It is now an Islamic republic. Unlike most of the Arab states where independence was acquired relatively recently, Turkey and Iran have had long traditions of sovereignty, independence, and experience with self-government.

Egypt

History

More than 5,000 years old, the birthplace of an important culture and civilization, Egypt has been dominated for centuries by foreign invaders.

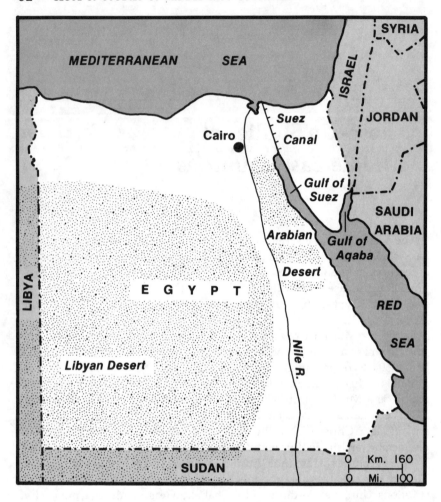

After the Arab invasion in the 7th century A.D., Egypt became part of various Arab empires. Between 1517 and the end of World War I it was part of the Ottoman Empire. However, throughout that period it maintained its own identity under local rulers who pledged allegiance to the Ottoman Sultan. In the 19th century, the ruler assumed the title of khedive (monarch's deputy) and later king.

After Napoleon's invasion of Egypt in 1798, European influence grew during the 19th century. The British dominated Egypt from 1882 until 1922, when it was given limited independence in response to several decades of growing Egyptian nationalism. British troops were not fully removed until 1956.

In 1952 the Egyptian monarchy was overthrown by a coup d'etat, and a

THE ASWAN HIGH DAM

Abdel Nasser became President and popular leader of the Arab Republic of Egypt, shortly after the overthrow of the monarchy in 1952. The Aswan High Dam, completed in 1971, was built under his auspices to provide irrigation, reclamation, and electric power facilities. It was constructed with Russian financial and technical assistance after the United States and the United Kingdom withdrew their support. Egypt Government Tourist Office

republic was established. One of the leaders of the coup was Colonel Gamal Abdel Nasser who became the key figure in Egyptian life from 1954 until his death in 1970. Nasser undertook programs of modernization, industrialization, and agricultural reform along socialist lines, but failed to raise standards of living for most Egyptians.

Nasser was also a charismatic leader who mobilized Arab sentiment against Western imperialism, particularly after he nationalized the Suez Canal in 1956. His attempts from 1958 to 1961 to unite Egypt and Syria into a single nation (the United Arab Republic) failed. His failure to improve Egypt's economy plus his foreign policy failures — especially Egypt's humiliating defeat by Israel in the War of 1967 — contributed to a decline in his influence among other Arab states, although he remained popular within Egypt.

Anwar el-Sadat, who succeeded Nasser as president in 1970, has become a major figure on the world scene despite early predictions that he would not last long as leader of Egypt.* Sadat has become a strong national leader.

* President Sadat was assassinated October 6, 1981, by Muslim extremists, just as this book went to press. He was succeeded as President by his protege, Vice President Hosni Mubarak. See p. 257.

He has reversed Nasser's program of state socialism, broken Egypt's formerly strong ties with the Soviet Union, and has recently developed closer relations with the United States. Even though he is immensely popular with the masses, Sadat has been unable to solve Egypt's pressing economic problems, particularly rising prices and large-scale unemployment.

To remove the financial and military burdens of war with Israel so that he could concentrate on improving the sorry state of Egypt's economy, he initiated peace talks with Israel, with whom Egypt had fought four wars since 1948. President Sadat's most effective move was his dramatic trip to Jerusalem in November 1977 which led to the rapprochement between Egypt and Israel, the signing of the Camp David peace treaty in March 1979, and a joint Nobel prize for Sadat and Prime Minister Menachem Begin of Israel.

Geography

About one-eighth the size of the United States, Egypt is largely desert, with only a little more than three percent of its land under cultivation, particularly in the Nile River Valley and Delta and in a few oases.

People

Egypt is the most populous nation in the Arab world. Most of its forty million people live in Nile Valley villages and in several major cities. Cairo, Egypt's capital, is a center of culture and industry (population over eight million) and the largest city in Africa. Alexandria is another intellectual and economic center (population over two and a half million) and Egypt's largest port. Egypt's urban population has been increasing at an alarming rate, bringing in its wake serious problems of overcrowding and unemployment.

Islam is Egypt's state religion. Ninety percent of Egyptians are Muslims (mostly Sunni). About six million Egyptians are Christian Copts. Arabic is the official and generally used language.

Economy and Way of Life

Although there has been considerable industrialization and modernization in recent decades, Egypt is still mainly an underdeveloped agricultural nation with a meager per-capita income of less than $300 a year.

Standards of living remain low despite improved public health services, increased welfare services, and the increased availability of modern communications and recreational facilities, including radio, television, and motion pictures. Although more schools have been built and educational opportunities increased, illiteracy still runs high.

Egypt's serious economic problems have resisted ready solutions. In addition to few natural resources and little arable land, there is a serious lack of capital for investment, an unfavorable balance of trade, inflation, large-scale unemployment, and a swollen government bureaucracy with many unproductive workers. Large military budgets have also drained the economy. As a result the country has had to rely on large infusions of foreign aid.

Egypt is a major producer of cotton textiles. In recent years there have been gains in cement, chemicals, food processing, and tourism.

Government

Contemporary Egypt is a republic with a president, prime minister, and an elected People's Assembly. The president appoints the vice-president, cabinet, and governors of Egypt's twenty-five provinces. President Nasser abolished political parties. Only candidates from the single mass political organization which Nasser formed were permitted to run for office. President Sadat has permitted the return of some competing political parties. However, laws have been passed barring political activity by Communists, Muslim extremists, and people who held office before the ouster of King Farouk in 1952. In 1978, Mr. Sadat's National Democratic Party won over eighty-five percent of the seats in parliament.

In Egypt, as elsewhere in much of the Middle East, the government depends on the loyalty of the leaders of the armed forces.

In September 1981, responding to rising militancy by Muslim fundamentalists and violence between Muslims and Copts, President Sadat ordered the most severe purge of his eleven years in office in an effort to eliminate religious interference in political affairs and to stifle opposition to his regime. The more than 1,500 Muslims and Christians detained included Muslim clergy, Coptic priests, journalists, politicians, attorneys, and professors whom Mr. Sadat held directly or indirectly responsible for the strife between the Muslim majority and the Christian minority. The Coptic Pope, Shenuda III, was stripped of his authority and placed under house arrest in a desert monastery. A number of Muslim and Christian societies were banned and opposition publications were shut down. The Sadat government also announced its intention to supervise 40,000 mosques to make sure they were used solely for religious purposes.

Iran

History

Iran, formerly called Persia (until 1935), is a non-Arab Muslim state. Its history as a nation goes back to the 6th century B.C. when Cyrus the Great

united the Medes and the Persians and built a great empire. The empire later fell to a series of invaders. In the 7th century the Arabs conquered Persia and introduced Islam. Later the Persians were conquered by the Turks and Mongols. The Mongols lost control in the 1500s. Thereafter Persian Safavid, Turkmen, and Afghan rulers controlled the country.

In the late 19th and early 20th centuries Iran came under British and Russian influence. In 1907 an Anglo–Russian agreement divided Iran into spheres of influence. In the early 1900s the British Anglo-Persian Oil Company began to develop the oil fields of southwestern Iran.

In 1925 Prime Minister Reza Kahn Pahlevi, an ex–army officer who wished to end foreign interference and to modernize his country, forced Ahmed Shah to abdicate and became Iran's ruler and military dictator. Assuming the royal title of Shah, Khan improved the police force, established a national bank, encouraged industry, built many new schools, promulgated new law codes, expanded the transportation systems, and ended special rights for foreigners.

Early in World War II, Britain and the other Allies were concerned with the activities of German agents in Iran. This concern, combined with Reza Khan's refusal to permit an Allied supply route to Russia through Iran, led to occupation by British and Russian forces and to Reza Khan's abdication in favor of his son Mohammed Reza Pahlevi in 1941. The young Shah served for twelve years until a nationalist movement led by Mohammed Mossadegh forced him to flee the country temporarily. The Shah's supporters in Iran, aided by the U.S. Central Intelligence Agency (CIA) and British intelligence, helped to overthrow Prime Minister Mossadegh in 1953 and to restore Shah Mohammed Reza Pahlevi to his throne.

During the nearly forty years of his reign and before a popular revolution forced him to leave the country in 1979, the Shah tried to modernize and industrialize Iran, to the consternation of religious Muslims. Many large estates, including land formerly held by religious foundations, were broken up and given or sold to peasants at low prices. Large sums were spent on industrial development. There was also a large military buildup. Many social reforms were undertaken, including the granting of increased rights for women, the construction of many new schools, and increased social, welfare, and health benefits. The Shah also encouraged Western forms of dress and entertainment. The vast and growing oil wealth of Iran, the Middle East's second largest oil producer (next to Saudi Arabia), made possible the financing of these programs.

SHAH OF IRAN
The wealth and opulence of the Iranian monarchy before its overturn by a popular revolution in 1979 is shown in this picture of Shah Mohammed Reza Pahlevi and Queen Farah before the royal family left the country. Gamma-Liaison

When the British withdrew their troops and planes from the Persian Gulf area in the late 1960s as part of their military withdrawal from east of Suez, the Shah, bolstered by imports of American and British weapons, became the "policeman" of the area. Iranian forces helped put down Communist disturbances in Oman. In addition, the Shah's ambition to make Iran the paramount power in the Persian Gulf area and his forcible takeover from the British, in order to control oil supply routes, of three small but strategically important islands (Abu Musa and Big and Little Tonb) at the mouth of the Gulf antagonized the nearby Arab states, particularly Saudi Arabia, Iraq, Kuwait, and the United Arab Emirates. To placate the Arabs Iran dropped its ancient claim to the large Gulf islands of Bahrain.

After World War II Iran established cooperative relations with the West without antagonizing the USSR, with which Iran shares a frontier over 1,200 miles long. Particularly close relations were developed with the United States. European nations and the United States participated heavily in designing and building Iran's new industrial plants and projects. The USSR built Iran's first steel mill. Several thousand Soviet technicians and even larger numbers of American and European technical experts (nearly 50,000) worked for or served as advisers to the Iranian government.

Under the Shah, Iran did not share in the Arab hostility to Israel and remained the major source of Israel's oil. The more than 70,000 Iranian Jews as well as Zoroastrians and Armenian Orthodox Christians were given a large measure of religious freedom.[1]

Mounting and violent opposition by most Iranians to the dictatorial methods of the Shah and to the cruelties of his secret police, the SAVAK, as well as opposition of Muslim leaders and others to his economic and religious policies brought on a general strike and much bloodshed and caused the Shah to flee the country in early 1979.[2] The new government quickly fell to supporters of the Ayatollah Khomeini, a Muslim religious leader, who had been living in exile in France.

The new Khomeini-dominated regime has established an Islamic republic based on strict interpretation of the Koran, the 7th century Islamic holy book. Western music and art, liquor, and mixed bathing have been banned. Women have been ordered to wear the traditional head-to-toe veil (the chador) to work. Some have been stoned to death for adultery. Real power has passed from the hands of the civil parliamentary government to religious leaders, local Islamic governing committees, and revolutionary militias. Even more than during the Shah's regime, dissenters have been

---

[1] Many Jews fled during the violence that led to the overthrow of the Shah in 1979.

[2] The Shah died of cancer in 1980 after several months of exile, first in the United States for medical treatment and then in Panama and finally Egypt.

tried without due process. Almost a thousand were executed as enemies of the state during the first year of the Islamic revolutionary regime.

Failure of the new government to manage the economy has resulted in a rapidly deteriorating situation bordering on chaos. Industrial production has slumped, oil production has had to be cut back, and there is galloping inflation. Businessmen and merchants charge that under Khomeini corruption is as bad as under the Shah.

Economic problems have been paralleled by serious ethnic, political, and social tensions. Rebel Kurdish and Azerbaijan minorities seeking autonomy have battled Islamic guardsmen. Under the leadership of the Ayatollah Shariat Medari, one of the most powerful ayatollahs in Iran, the five million Azerbaijanis boycotted the November 1979 election for an Islamic Republic, objecting to the proposed constitution on the ground that it put too much power in the hands of the Ayatollah and eliminated any viable opposition.

Many in the middle and upper classes, segments of the military, Islamic Marxists, and other leftist groups have formed a growing opposition to the government. In July 1980 an attempted military coup was crushed. There have been frequent terrorist bombings.

Reflecting the bitterness against the United States for supporting the Shah and his regime, Ayatollah Khomeini has whipped up feeling against the United States and denounced it as an imperialist aggressor responsible for the evils of modernization and Westernization that had corrupted the Islamic way of life in Iran. Iranian revolutionaries also blamed the United States for having supported the regime of the late Shah, in order to protect U.S. oil imports.

Fifty-two American hostages, seized by Iranian militants from the American embassy in Teheran in November 1979 as ransom for the deposed Shah and his wealth, remained captive for 444 days from November 4, 1979 to January 20, 1981, despite all efforts to free them, including condemnation by the United Nations and all of the Western world. They were finally freed on January 20, 1981 at the approximate hour that Ronald Reagan was sworn in as president of the United States. Shortly thereafter former President Carter flew to the American air base at Weisbaden, West Germany to greet the former captives, who soon returned to a heroes' welcome in the United States the likes of which had not been seen since World War II.

Under Khomeini Iran has become increasingly isolated in world affairs. The seizure of the American hostages and their captivity for over fourteen months resulted in strained relations with most Western nations and Japan. Leaders of Saudi Arabia, Jordan, and other Muslim states are worried about the possibility that Iran's Islamic revolution could spread to their own countries. Khomeini has also antagonized much of the Arab world. In 1980

IRANIAN REVOLUTION

Before Iranian militants broke into the United States Embassy in Teheran in November 1979 and seized American hostages, there were growing demonstrations against the United States for supporting the Shah's regime. Shown above are demonstrators in front of the Embassy shortly before the hostages were taken. The pictures are of the Ayatollah Khomeini, leader of the revolution that overturned the Shah and established an Islamic republic headed by Khomeini. J. Isaac/United Nations

open warfare resulted from Iraq's invasion of Iranian border territories in an attempt to gain full sovereignty over the Shatt-al-Arab waterway, which separates the two countries at the head of the Persian Gulf and through which most exported Iranian oil is carried by tankers. Iraq also demanded a redefinition of their joint border to the north that would give Iraq several pieces of land it considers to be rightfully its own.

Iran's attitude toward the Soviet Union, one of its few supporters, has also been cool. A Russian diplomat has been expelled for espionage. Moreover, in spite of lessened trade with the West in 1980 resulting from economic sanctions imposed as a result of the seizure of the American hostages, Iran has decreased rather than increased its trade with the Communist superpower.

In view of Iran's strategic importance geographically and as a major source of Middle East oil, these developments were being carefully watched by the United States, the Soviet Union, and other Middle East countries, all of whom had a good deal to lose or gain from the swift and drastic changes in Iran.

Geography

Iran is a land of topographical and climatic contrasts. At about two and a half times the size of Texas, it is one of the largest countries in the Middle East. For the most part it is made up of mountains, which cover nearly half of the country, and desert plains. Only thirty percent of the land is inhabited and farmed. Iran's southern desert is one of the hottest regions on earth. Other sections of the country have had below-zero temperatures in winter. Although much of the country is arid with little rainfall, some areas, particularly along the Caspian seacoast, are fertile and rainy. Oil is Iran's chief natural resource.

People

With a rapidly growing population, now over thirty-five million, Iran is, after Egypt and Turkey, the third most populous nation in the Middle East. Well over ninety percent of the population is Shiite Muslim, which is also the official state religion. Among the largest religious minorities are 300,000 Christians (mainly Armenian Orthodox), 35,000 Jews (70,000 until the Khomeini-led revolution), and 10,000 Zoroastrians.

Most Iranians are Muslims but not Arabs. Persians make up the largest segment of the population. Important ethnic minorities include Kurds and Turks. There are also some 600,000 Arabs in Iran.

The official, dominant language in Iran is Persian (Farsi), an Indo-European language related to ancient Sanskrit, containing many Arab words and written in the flowing Arabic style and alphabet. Kurdish and Arabic are also spoken.

Economy and Way of Life

As a result of the ex-Shah's determination to modernize Iran, there was rapid economic development prior to his downfall. Industrial and oil-producing centers were developed and many steel, petrochemical, cement, auto assembly, and other plants built. The textile industry was rapidly expanded and large-scale production methods were introduced.

Oil became Iran's most important industry and source of income. The industry is operated by the government-owned National Iranian Oil Company. Before the overthrow of the monarchy, annual oil profits had risen to over $20 billion a year. In addition to oil wells and refineries at older oil centers such as Abadan, at the head of the Persian Gulf, Iran has been producing oil from Persian Gulf offshore oil centers since the 1960s. Oil has accounted for ninety percent of the value of Iranian products sold abroad.

Large sections of cities had been Westernized, with modern shopping centers, office buildings, wide boulevards, and new transportation systems.

Teheran, the national capital, with a population of over four million, was a bustling center of trade, manufacture, and culture. Isfahan (population over 800,000) was another important urban and cultural center.

Standards of living had been rising, particularly among city workers and a growing (though still relatively small) middle class of urban workers, until the Khomeini-led revolution disrupted the economic and commercial structure of Iran. (At the beginning of 1981 the economy of Iran under the militant anti-Western Ayatollah Khomeini was near collapse.) Under the Shah there had been increased attention to the social needs of the people through improved medical, housing, educational, communication, and entertainment facilities.

Despite significant past progress, standards of living for most Iranians remain low and modernization has barely touched the bulk of the population. Most villages still lack sewers, piped water, electricity, and medical facilities and doctors. Most production is still done by craftsmen working in their homes or small shops, often with the help of young children.

Economic development and social changes encouraged by the Shah led to serious social strains. Islamic priests (mullahs) and other religious leaders, whose influence on the people is still strong, were antagonized by the loss of their properties and their declining domination in education and law. They opposed modernization and Westernization as being destructive to Islamic traditions. In addition, there was considerable resentment over the high wages paid to the thousands of foreign advisers, technicians, and workers brought in to help develop and work the oil and other industries. The poverty-stricken multitudes resented the growing gap between rich and poor. In recent years and both before and since the Shah's overthrow, inflation, shortages of food and electric power, corruption, and mismanagement have become major problems and causes of discontent.

Iranian students were angered at what they felt to be too slow a pace of economic and political change. They considered the Shah "a tool of U.S. corporations" and criticized his reform program as being far from adequate. They also were incensed by his denial of basic human rights. At the same time, this did not prevent them from denying the human rights of others, as illustrated by the treatment of the American hostages. (See Chapters 7 and 8).

Much of the economic and — by Western standards — social progress of recent decades seemed to be jeopardized by the mismanagement of the Khomeini regime. Signs of what by 1981 could be considered a seriously disintegrating economy included rapidly growing inflation, sharp drops in industrial and oil production, decreased exports, and soaring unemployment. Meanwhile the city poor remained as poverty-stricken as before. Internal resentment against the regime was clearly mounting. Compounding the entire problem was Iran's war with Iraq, with the latter country occupying valuable oil-rich parts of Iran.

Government

The Shah ruled despotically, often ignoring the constitution and parliament. Since the revolution of 1978–1979, which resulted in the overthrow of the Shah, Iran has become an Islamic state dominated by the Ayatollah Khomeini. Its new constitution is based on strict Muslim law as pronounced by the Prophet Mohammed in the 7th century and collected in the Koran, the Muslim holy book.

The constitution of the new Islamic Republic puts ruling authority into the hands of a Council of Guardians and a *Faqih*, or Guardian of the Islamic Republic. The Council of Guardians, made up of religious leaders, must approve measures passed by an elected legislative assembly. As leader of the republic the *Faqih* (Ayatollah Khomeini) is all-powerful. He can declare

AZERBAIJANI GRIEVANCES UNDER THE ISLAMIC REPUBLIC
Minorities in Iran and other Middle East states have long sought greater autonomy and increased rights. Since the revolution in Iran, Baluchis, Azerbaijanis, Kurds, and others have also protested against new controls imposed by the new Islamic regime of the Ayatollah Khomeini. Here we see Azerbaijani Mullahs (clergy) presenting their grievances to a new central government official in Tabriz.
Peress/Magnum

war, dismiss an elected president, and appoint jurists who may veto the laws of an elected parliament. Shiite Islam is named Iran's official religion and Muslim mullahs are given complete domination over all aspects of Iranian life.

It was clear that under Ayatollah Khomeini an authoritarian political tyranny had been imposed on Iran. Political opposition had been outlawed. Political opponents of the new regime had been tried and jailed or executed. Western-oriented university professors had been dismissed. The army had been purged. A new feared secret police, the SAVAMA, had been created, replacing the former Shah's SAVAK. SAVAMA "agents" had assassinated Iranian exiles abroad. Ethnic and religious minorities were being harassed or were in revolt against the non-compromising attitude of the regime. Many middle-class Iranian citizens had fled before a ban on foreign travel was imposed.

In 1981 the real governing power was exercised by a supreme revolutionary council and military guardsmen ruling in the name of Ayatollah Khomeini, who had been declared guardian of the republic for life. Events reached a flashpoint in June when President Abolhassan Bani-Sadr, the first president elected under the new constitution, was impeached by the parliament and removed from office by Khomeini. Bani-Sadr went into hiding to avoid prosecution and later fled to France. His ouster climaxed a two-year power struggle between his Muslim fundamentalist enemies in the Islamic Republican Party (Khomeini's official party) and a coalition of his supporters (moderate secularists, Western-educated liberals, and Marxists). Hundreds of Bani-Sadr's followers were executed by the regime, and a wave of terrorist acts cut down many of Iran's political leaders. A powerful bomb explosion that destroyed the headquarters of the ruling Islamic Republican Party killed at least seventy-four cabinet and parliament members and others, including Chief Justice Ayatollah Mohammed Beheshti, who had been considered the second most powerful man in Iran.

In a special election former Prime Minister Mohammed Ali Rajai was elected president to succeed Bani-Sadr, but little more than a month later he and his prime minister were among those killed in an explosion that wrecked the prime minister's closely guarded headquarters. State funerals turned into mob demonstrations against the United States, which was blamed for the death of Rajai and his colleagues. New elections were to be held, as the wave of assassinations and executions continued to undermine Iran's stability. The most serious opposition to the Khomeini regime appeared to come from the People's Mujahedeen (Crusaders), a guerrilla movement of young well-educated leftists who combine fidelity to Islamic traditions with Marxism and who had been active in the struggle to depose the Shah.

Israel

History

The history of the land that is the State of Israel today goes back to ancient biblical times, before the days of King David and King Solomon and the Hebrew prophets. By 1000 B.C. the scattered Jewish tribes that lived in Canaan (later called Land of Israel) had united to form a flourishing kingdom. After Solomon's death, revolt split the land into two kingdoms — Israel and Judah — and there followed conquests by Babylonians, Persians, Greeks, and others. The Romans conquered Israel in the 1st century B.C. and renamed the country Palestine. In the 1st century A.D. they forced most Jews to leave Palestine, from where they scattered to many lands. This dispersion is referred to as the "Diaspora." Other Jews and their descen-

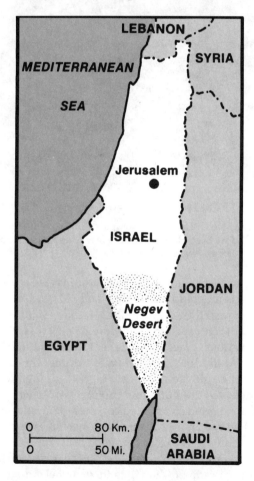

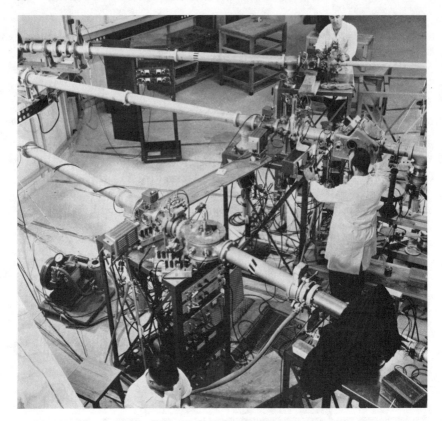

ISRAELI TECHNOLOGY
Israel's technological and scientific development has given it the highest standard of living in the Middle East. Here we see nuclear scientists working with a Van der Graf nuclear accelerator. Israel Consulate

dants remained in Palestine, frequently enduring persecution and poverty as different groups fought to control the land.

The Arabs conquered Palestine in the 7th century and controlled it until the end of the 11th century. European-dominated Crusader kingdoms were established at various times during the 11th, 12th, and 13th centuries. Thereafter, non-Arab Muslims ruled Palestine until the 20th century. Four centuries of Turkish rule came to an end in 1917, during World War I, when British forces defeated the Turks and captured Jerusalem.

During this long period of repeated conquests, Palestine was increasingly neglected and became an arid, swampy wasteland with a declining population.

Although scattered all over the globe, Jews, as part of their faith, continued to regard Palestine ("Zion") as their homeland and to express the hope that one day they would return. Over the years small numbers traveled to Palestine to pray or to study or to die. They joined the small community of Jews who had continued to live in Palestine after the start of the Diaspora.

Palestine became a British mandate in 1922. During the period of the mandate (1922–1948) thousands of Jews from many different countries settled in Palestine on land purchased from the Arabs by Jewish groups. They were helped by the Zionist movement, which had as its goal the reestablishment of a Jewish state in Palestine. A number of agricultural colonies had been established beginning in the 1870s and 1880s. After World War I, Zionist pioneers established additional farm settlements and improved the land by draining swamps, irrigating deserts, sinking wells, and planting forests. As the country began to develop and flourish, factories, towns, and cities were also established.

The Zionist movement helped to bring about the Balfour Declaration, issued by the British government in 1917, which pledged support for the establishment in Palestine of a national home for the Jews.

In 1922 Britain divided the Palestine mandate into two parts: the larger part east of the Jordan River became the country of Transjordan (now Jordan), while the smaller part west of the Jordan River continued to be called Palestine. There were large migrations of both Jews and Arabs to Palestine as the country became revitalized and productive.

As the number of Jews increased, Arab opposition to Jewish immigration grew and anti-Jewish riots and attacks occurred. The Haganah (a Jewish self-defense underground organization established in 1920 to defend Jews against Arab attacks) and later more militant Jewish groups like the Irgun became active in responding to Arab attacks and terrorism.

In the late 1930s Jewish immigration to Palestine increased with refugees from Nazi Germany. The British tried to curtail Jewish immigration and land acquisition. Jewish underground groups fought this policy by organizing "illegal" immigration.[3]

After World War II, the British were no longer willing to cope with the mounting Arab–Jewish friction and growing resistance to their rule. They decided to give up their Palestine mandate and turned the problem over to the United Nations.

In 1947, the United Nations voted to partition Palestine into an Arab state and a Jewish state. In accordance with this plan the independent State of Israel was proclaimed in May 1948. Unwilling to accept the partition plan, armies from five Arab states invaded Israel but failed to destroy the new

---

[3] It should be noted that only a small portion of European Jewry was saved in this fashion. Six million Jews perished in the savage extermination program known as the Nazi Holocaust.

state. Jordan took over the area of the West Bank intended as part of the Arab state under the U.N. partition plan and ruled it until the Six Day War of 1967.

Since its establishment, Israel has been a country on the alert. For most of its history it has either been at war with its Arab neighbors or living under often-violated cease-fires and truces. Although the Arabs have been unable to destroy Israel, they have continued to talk about and prepare for additional attempts, believing that their greater numbers, resources, and international bargaining power will bring them victory in the end.

Despite this unending pressure, Israel has made great economic, scientific, and cultural progress and has become a modern industrial and agricultural nation. Among the Israeli political leaders who have helped Israel move in this direction have been Chaim Weizmann, renowned scientist and Zionist leader who became the first president of the new nation, as well as David Ben-Gurion, the first prime minister, and his successors, Levi Eshkol, Moshe Sharett, Golda Meir, Yitzhak Rabin, and Menachem Begin.

As a result of remarkable military victories, Israel has gained additional territory. During the war of 1967 Israel took control of the Sinai Peninsula and the Gaza Strip from Egypt, the Golan Heights from Syria, and the West Bank of the Jordan River and Old City of Jerusalem from Jordan. (See Chapter 4 for an account of the Arab–Israeli wars.)

The United States has been a firm supporter of Israel's existence and has given it economic and military aid, particularly since the 1970s. At the same time a great challenge to U.S. diplomacy has been its desire to remain on good terms with Arab states, though not at Israel's expense. The United States, too, played an increasingly important role in Egyptian–Israeli peace talks. In March 1979, these efforts were climaxed on the White House lawn in Washington, D.C. by the signing of a peace treaty that provided for the return of the Sinai to Egypt by Israel in return for normalization of relations between the two countries, and also for the establishment of processes for granting autonomy to West Bank and Gaza Strip Palestinians.

The Soviet Union voted for the partition resolution and at first granted recognition to Israel. Since the early 1950s, however, it has opposed Israel and has given active support to the Arabs.

Geography

Israel is a tiny land, a little larger than the state of New Jersey. It extends about 260 miles from north to south and varies from nine to seventy miles in width. About half of the country is made up of a narrow coastal plain along the Mediterranean and a hilly region in the north. The Negev Desert in the south makes up the rest of the country. The major cities are the capital, Jerusalem, the commercial center, Tel Aviv, and the port city of Haifa.

ISRAELI KIBBUTZ
The kibbutz is a unique feature of Israel's economy. The kibbutzim are cooperative villages in which the members jointly own the land and other means of production and share in the farming and other duties and responsibilities of communal living.
Israel Consulate

People

Israel's population is now nearly four million, as compared to 800,000 on the eve of statehood in 1947. It has increased rapidly as a result of immigration from many parts of the world. Jews constitute about eighty-five percent of the population. Arabs make up most of the remainder. About half of the Jewish population was born in Israel. Most of Israel's Jews have either come from or are descendants of immigrants from Arab countries of the Middle East. From 1948 to the late 1970s nearly a million and a half Jews came to Israel from more than forty countries, including approximately 750,000 who fled as refugees from Arab countries of the Middle East. (It should be noted that estimates of the number of refugees from Arab countries differ widely.)

Judaism is Israel's predominant religion. The Arab minority is mainly Sunni Muslim. There are also smaller numbers of Christian Arabs, mostly Greek Catholic and Greek Orthodox. In addition there are a number of smaller denominations and religious groups, including the Druze, Circassians, Baha'i, and Samaritans.

Israel has two official languages, Hebrew and Arabic. Many Israelis are fluent in both. English is understood widely and often spoken. It is the principal foreign language taught in school.

Economy and Way of Life

In less than forty years the Israelis have developed a way of life that is unique and a society that is in some ways different from that of any other country.

Western lifestyles predominate in dress, sports, recreational pursuits, entertainment, and political activity. At the same time architecture, food, popular music, and other aspects of Israeli life reflect Mediterranean and Eastern influences. The Arab minority lives in villages and in city quarters that are Eastern and Muslim in appearance. Arabs continue to wear the typical Arab headdress and to speak the Arab tongue, though many can speak Hebrew fluently.

The people of Israel have the highest standard of living in the Middle East — one that is close to that of leading industrial nations. The average Arab in Israel earns an income three to four times more than Arabs in neighboring countries. There is compulsory education through high school. Enrollment has risen rapidly in the nation's continually expanding system of elementary and secondary schools, colleges, and universities. Literacy rates are high. Free medical care is provided for over seventy percent of the nation's population, together with other important social security benefits. Women have played an active role in every sphere of life in Israel. Much stress is given to literature, theater, music and the arts. Advanced scientific and technical institutes have been established. There is also a lively and provocative free press representative of all opinions in Israel from the right to the left. Over twenty daily newspapers are published.

The population of Israel has become increasingly urban. More than four-fifths live in cities and towns. The largest cities are Jerusalem and Tel Aviv, each with a population of over 350,000, and Haifa, another leading economic and cultural center, with over 225,000.

Israel's rapid economic development has made possible its high living standards. Modern production methods have been introduced and advanced technology applied, making possible industrial development in such fields as food processing, textiles, metalworking, chemicals, and diamond cutting. Oil refineries and storage tanks in Haifa help serve Israel's needs. Israel produces over seventy-five percent of its arms and ammunition. Leading exports include diamonds, citrus fruit, chemicals, and textiles.

In addition to the application of advanced technology, Israeli economic development has been made possible by the skilled manpower and know-how brought by many immigrants from abroad and by large amounts of economic assistance, particularly from the United States. It has also been helped by charitable contributions from Jewish communities outside of Israel, particularly the United Jewish Appeal in the United States, and by

West German reparations payments to victims of the Holocaust and to the State of Israel.[4]

Agriculture is still a very important economic activity. In recent years an ambitious irrigation program has converted increasing portions of the Negev Desert region into fertile land. The application of scientific methods and extensive irrigation to farming has led to improved and expanded agricultural output. Most of the Jewish population who rely for a living on agriculture live in cooperative farm villages. The *kibbutz*, whose members own property jointly and share farming and other duties and responsibilities, is the most widely known kind of farm settlement. A number of small outposts and settlements have been established in border and occupied areas for military and economic reasons.

Despite its economic and social progress, Israel has faced and continues to face a number of serious problems, including the need to absorb new immigrants and overcome the "culture gap" that exists between European and American immigrants and the poorer, less educated, and culturally different immigrants from Africa and other Middle Eastern countries. Israel has also been confronted with problems in dealing with a large and increasingly restless Arab minority, as well as with unemployment, high inflation, and an unfavorable balance of trade. It has had to divert the largest part of its budget to military preparedness. An especially difficult problem has been the ongoing controversy between Orthodox Jews and others over the role of religion in Israeli public life.

Government

Israel is the only working democratic republic in the Middle East. It has a president, an elected legislative body called the Knesset (which includes seven Arabs), and an independent court system. The government is administered by a cabinet, headed by a prime minister. All men and women over the age of eighteen may vote.

Because of its system of proportional representation Israel has many active political parties, including several labor and religious parties. Coalition cabinets have been necessary to give the prime minister a parliamentary majority. Israel's major parties have been Ma'arach, a labor coalition, and Likud, a coalition of conservative parties. The Labor Party

---

[4] In September 1952 West Germany and Israel signed a restitution and reparations agreement in which the federal government of West Germany attempted to atone in some measure for the horrors of World War II perpetrated by the Nazi regime. Under this indemnification agreement, which led to improved relations between the two countries, over $822 million was paid to Israel.

KNESSET

The Knesset is Israel's Parliament or legislative body. Under a democratic parliamentary system many parties are represented according to a system of proportional representation. A number of Israel's outstanding leaders in the first decades of its history are shown in this picture of the Israeli Knesset in session. Can you identify David Ben-Gurion? Golda Meir? Others? Zionist Archives

was defeated for the first time in twenty-nine years in 1977. As leader of Likud, the winning party, Menachem Begin became prime minister. He was reelected in a very close race in 1981, but some people predicted that Israeli voters would have to go to the polls again within a year because the loss of even one member on a vote of confidence would bring down Begin's right-of-center coalition.

Israeli citizens of all faiths and ethnic groups enjoy freedom of religion, expression, and assembly. In 1979 a U.S. State Department report on human rights stated: "Israel is a full-fledged parliamentary democracy with extremely high standards of justice and human rights." Israelis enjoy full freedom to participate in the political process. There are strong guarantees against arbitrary arrest and imprisonment. Citizenship is granted to every Jew who wishes to settle in Israel, and Israelis are free to travel abroad or emigrate. Separate religious courts handle problems related to marriage, divorce, burials, and wills.

Lebanon

History

The area that is now Lebanon was in ancient times the home of Hittites, Arameans, and Phoenicians. The region was later conquered by Assyrians, Persians, Greeks, and Romans. Thereafter it became part of the Byzantine and Ottoman empires.

Maronite Christians established themselves in the area during the early Byzantine period, around the 6th century. Even after the spread of Islam in

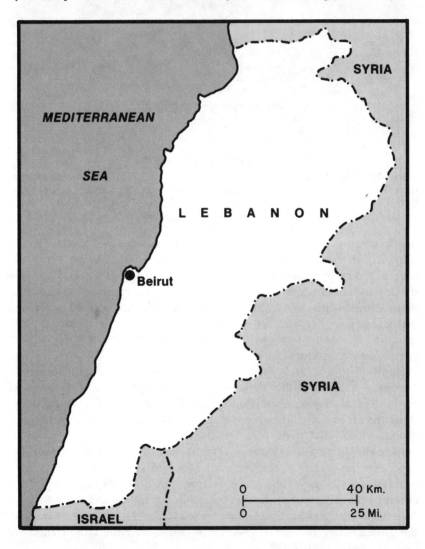

CIVIL WAR IN LEBANON

Since 1975 Lebanon has been shattered by civil war between Muslims and Christians. That certain aspects of life go on as usual, even during wartime, is illustrated by this 1979 photo of fashionable sun-bathers in Beirut relaxing in the shadows of the city's war-ravaged buildings. Salhani/Gamma-Liaison

the 7th century and until fairly recently, Lebanon remained predominantly Christian. In the 1860s, after massacres of Maronites by Druze (probably encouraged by the Ottomans), France and Britain forced the Turks to give the province of Lebanon a special government headed by a Christian (but non-Lebanese) governor. In addition the Maronites received many privileges. Together with other Lebanese Christians they revived Arab literature and helped spread nationalist sentiment among the Arabs in opposition to continued Turkish control.

Before World War I, much of Lebanon was part of predominantly Muslim Syria within the Turkish empire. After the war, Lebanon was established as a French mandate, separate from the rest of Syria, to satisfy the demands of the Christian population. It was administered as a French mandate until 1941. The Free French (the French government in exile, outside of Vichy France, during World War II) declared Lebanon independent in 1941 after the Germans occupied France. All powers were transferred to the new Lebanese government in 1945, but Lebanon did not become truly free until the last French soldier left at the end of 1946.

As an independent nation Lebanon tried to develop close ties with both the United States and the Arab world. It joined the Arab League and later took part in the invasion of Israel in 1948.

In 1958 civil war broke out, with Syrian-encouraged Muslim leftists leading the opposition to the Maronite Christian government and its pro-Western policies. At President Camille Chamoun's request, the United States sent troops to Lebanon. They were withdrawn several months later, after the formation of a new government and the restoration of order.

Beginning in the late 1960s, Palestinian guerrillas began to use Lebanese territory as a base for terrorist attacks on Israel's northern settlements. The Lebanese government disclaimed responsibility for the assaults but was powerless to stop them. Israel retaliated by attacking terrorist camps and villages. In early 1978 a strong Israeli force entered southern Lebanon, destroyed terrorist bases, and pushed the Palestinian guerrillas northward. The Israelis withdrew when a U.N. force was sent in to replace them and police the border between southern Lebanon and northern Israel. Palestinian guerrillas continue to attack Israeli settlements, and Israeli forces continue to retaliate.

In 1975, bloody civil war in Lebanon broke out again between Muslims and Christians largely because of Muslim discontent with their share of political and economic power and also because of Maronite Christian discontent with the growing Palestine Liberation Organization (PLO) presence.[5] Perhaps as many as 120,000 lives have been lost in the violence and devastation that have taken place.

Before the civil war Lebanon was considered an exception among Arab states. It had freely elected officials, a sound economy, and a highly literate and worldly population. The Lebanese are struggling to restore the order that formerly prevailed. Whether or not they will be successful or even survive as a nation is yet to be seen.

Geography

Lebanon is a tiny country, four-fifths the size of Connecticut. It is made up largely of a narrow coastal plain and two sets of mountains that extend from north to south, with a fertile valley in between.

People

Three and a half million people live in Lebanon. Over ninety percent are Arabs; perhaps fifty to sixty percent of them are Muslims. The remainder are mainly Christians (Maronite, Greek Orthodox, Armenian, Greek and Roman Catholic). There are also about 90,000 Druze. The Jewish population dwindled from 5,000 to approximately 400 in the late 1970s when many fled to escape the civil strife in Lebanon. Arabic is the official and predominant language, though English and French are widely used.

[5] For details of the civil war in Lebanon see Chapter 4.

Economy and Way of Life

Lebanon is a nation of farmers and traders. Although its people have had a standard of living higher than most of the Middle East peoples, the civil war of the 1970s has seriously disrupted the economy. As a result the Lebanon of the 1980s is not the Lebanon that existed before the civil war tore the social, political, religious, and economic fabric of the country apart.

Although the largest part of Lebanon's work force is engaged in agriculture, over sixty percent of the population is urban. Beirut is the nation's capital and largest city, with a population of over a million. Before the civil war it was an important cosmopolitan and cultural center, as well as the financial hub of the Middle East. It has since become a war-ravaged, divided city, paralyzed by Muslim and Christian antagonism. Tripoli is Lebanon's second largest city.

The largest part of Lebanon's national income comes from trade and services. Leading agricultural products include citrus fruits, vegetables, and tobacco. Food processing, textiles, cement and oil refining are leading industries. Pipelines from Saudi Arabia and Iraq have made Lebanon a center of East–West oil trade.

Government

Lebanon is a parliamentary republic. It has a one-house legislature elected on the basis of religion (*confessional representation*). Each Christian or Muslim sect elects representatives to parliament (the Chamber of Deputies) on the basis of size.[6] The president has always been a Maronite Christian. In 1981 Elias Sarkis served in that position. The less powerful positions of prime minister and president of the Chamber have traditionally gone to Sunni and Shiite Muslims, respectively. In the past all qualified citizens, including women, were required to vote and many political parties were represented in parliament.

Saudi Arabia

History

Although the present kingdom of Saudi Arabia was not established until the early 1930s, the land it occupies has a long history.

In ancient times Arab tribesmen roamed the desserts or lived in trading centers such as Mecca and Medina, along well-established caravan routes. In the 7th and 8th centuries Mohammed and his followers united the Arabs and founded a great empire.

---

[6] In order not to upset the delicate political balance between Christians and Muslims, no complete census has been taken since 1932.

In the 16th and 17th centuries the Turks, as part of the Ottoman Empire, established loose control over the coastal area along the Red Sea (known as the Hejaz) in which are located Islam's holiest cities, Mecca and Medina.

In the 18th century the Saud family, members of the very puritanical Wahabi Muslim sect, gained control over large portions of the other provinces of the Arabian Peninsula. In the 19th century the Rashid dynasty gained control of central Arabia and expelled the Saud family.

In the early part of the 20th century, Abdul Azziz Ibn Saud returned from exile. He consolidated Wahabi control over most of the peninsula and successfully challenged the authority of Sharif Hussein, a member of the Hashemite family (Mohammed's family) who was the religious leader of Mecca until he declared his independence in 1916 with the help of the British and declared himself king of the Hejaz. Saud gained control of virtually the entire country in the late 1920s and early 1930s, after the breakup of the Ottoman Empire. He became its absolute monarch and

MECCA, SAUDI ARABIA

Thousands of pilgrims gather at El Haram, the Great Mosque, during the annual gathering of Muslim faithful in Mecca, the most sacred of Muslim holy cities. Mecca is the birthplace of Muhammed. Religious News Service

changed its name to Saudi Arabia in 1932. Since Ibn Saud's death in 1953, his successors have been his sons Saud, Feisal, and Khalid. Khalid ascended the throne in 1975 after a royal nephew assassinated Feisal.

Saudi Arabia took no part in World War II. Although friendly to the Western Allies, it did not declare war on Germany and Japan until near the end of the hostilities.

Oil was discovered in Saudi Arabia near the Persian Gulf in 1932. The rapid development of its oil resources since World War II, particularly by the Arabian American Oil Company (ARAMCO), has brought vast wealth to the country. Saudi Arabia has become the richest and perhaps the most influential state in the Middle East.

Saudi Arabia has joined other Arab states in opposition to Israel but has played only a limited role in the past fighting. It has granted billions of dollars in aid to Jordan, Syria, Egypt (until the Camp David peace accords), and other Arab nations to replenish their military arsenals and help bolster their sagging economies. It has been an active and influential member of the Organization of Petroleum Exporting Countries (OPEC) and in 1973 used its oil as a political weapon by withholding it from nations friendly to Israel, including the United States. In recent years the tremendous financial power made possible by Saudi Arabia's oil wealth has enabled it to exert diplomatic pressure and play the role of mediator in a number of conflicts in the Arab world.

Saudi leaders are anti-Communist and view with suspicion the radical regimes of Iraq, Syria, South Yemen, and Libya. They have supported and given economic and military aid to the Yemen Arab Republic in its continuing struggle with Marxist South Yemen (which is Soviet-backed). Before the Shah of Iran's overthrow in the late 1970s, the Saudis worried about his ambitions in the Persian Gulf area and his attempts to become protector of the Persian Gulf oil routes. They likewise view with suspicion the new Muslim regime in Iran and the ambitions of Iraq in its war with Iran begun in 1980.

For the most part, relations between Saudi Arabia and the United States have been close, although the Saudis have made clear their displeasure at American support for peace negotiations between Israel and Egypt. The United States is respected by the Saudis because of its role as leader of the non-Communist world, because of its technical know-how, and because of the leading role that ARAMCO, the world's largest oil-producing company, has played in developing the Saudi economy. The United States also has been the world's leading consumer of Saudi Arabian oil and has sold large quantities of arms to the Saudis. The Saudis are hopeful that the United States will play a greater role than before in defusing crises that threaten the stability of the Persian Gulf region, particularly in view of the destabilizing effects of the revolution in Iran in 1979 and the war between Iraq and Iran in

1980 and 1981. Indeed, the Reagan administration has made the defense of the Persian Gulf area one of the major priorities for American foreign policy in the Middle East.

Geography

More than three times the size of Texas, Saudi Arabia covers most of the Arabian Peninsula. Aside from coastal plains and rugged mountains in its western portions, it is made up mainly of arid plateaus and wastelands and trackless desert.

Apart from oil, there are few important natural resources in Saudi Arabia. Only one percent of the land is arable.

People

Territorially the largest Middle East country, Saudi Arabia's population is estimated at seven million, nearly all of whom are Muslim Arabs. However, only about half are citizens.

The majority of Saudis are members of the very conservative Wahabi sect of Sunni Islam. They believe in strict adherence to Mohammed's teachings, including a ban on luxuries, decoration of mosques, and the use of tobacco and coffee. Wahabis believe that they practice the purest form of Islam.

Saudi Arabia is looked on with special reverence by the world's 700 to 800 million Muslims because it contains Mecca, the birthplace of Mohammed and holiest of Islamic holy sites, and Medina, the burial place of Mohammed and second most sacred city of Islam. Half a million Muslims from all over the world make a pilgrimage to Mecca each year.

Islam is still the Saudi state religion, but religious leaders have slowly been losing some of their power and influence to leaders trained in modern technology and ways of life. Some Saudi leaders fear that the growing religious revival in the Muslim world could affect this trend.

Arabic is the official and commonly spoken language.

Economy and Way of Life

Saudi Arabia's population is three-fourths rural. Most Saudis live in farm villages or oasis communities and follow a traditional, simple way of life. About a quarter of this number are Bedouin nomads and semi-nomads whose numbers are steadily decreasing as more and more settle down to become farmers or move to urban areas to get jobs in the oil industry.

Approximately a quarter of the people in Saudi Arabia live in urban areas. The country's largest cities are Riyadh (670,000) and Jidda (565,000).

WEALTHY SAUDI FAMILY

At the same time that they have been distrustful of Western imperialism, many Middle East rulers have tried to Westernize and industrialize their economies. Here we see a wealthy Saudi family watching a Western program on T.V. Saudi Arabia's great oil wealth has made it the most influential of Arab states in the Middle East. Aramco Photo

Conservative Islamic traditions continue to influence most aspects of life in Saudi Arabia. Family ties are strong. The father is considered the head of the household, with unquestioned authority. Women wear veils outside the home. Alcohol is forbidden. By Western standards, punishment of criminals is very harsh. There are sometimes public floggings and executions for moral and sexual offenses.

Saudi education is by-and-large traditional (Koranic religious), but modern elementary, secondary and higher education is being developed. Education is free but school attendance is not compulsory.

Side by side with the still-prevalent traditional ways of life are growing signs of change and modernization, particularly in the larger cities and especially in newly developed, oil-related industrial cities along Saudi Arabia's Persian Gulf coast. In these areas modern transportation and communication systems are being developed. Cities are being transformed by modern highways (complete with rush-hour traffic jams), new Western-style office buildings, modern health facilities, and newer forms of entertainment (radio, television, motion pictures).

As yet only a small portion of Saudi oil profits have "seeped down to the masses." Much of the population is still poor, and living standards for the average citizen are low. Nevertheless the government has used some of its vast new wealth for social welfare purposes. Free medical services have been made available and new universities, colleges, and technical institutes have been built. Adult-education programs have been established to improve the low literacy rate.

The oil industry is Saudi Arabia's great source of wealth, with revenues now exceeding $90 billion a year. It has made possible large monetary reserves, increasing overseas investments, and the development of new industrial centers comprising petrochemical, steel, aluminum, fertilizer, oil-refining, and other plants. Some forty to fifty thousand Americans are working in Saudi Arabia as industrial and military advisers and specialists. Increasing numbers of unskilled foreign workers are also flocking to industrial centers from other Muslim countries.

In addition, dams have been built to hold valley floodwaters. Irrigation systems are being developed and fishing facilities are being modernized.

Government

Saudia Arabia is an absolute monarchy based on the laws and customs of Islam. There is no formal constitution or parliament in the modern sense. The king is the all-powerful political and religious leader. In matters not covered by Islamic law, he issues royal decrees that have the force of law. A Council of Ministers assists him in managing the government.

Political parties do not exist. The royal family, consisting of several thousand people (children, grandchildren, and great grandchildren of the late King Ibn Saud), is the chief political group. The king is selected by leading members of the royal family. Close relatives hold important government positions.

Religious courts headed by judges handle both civil and criminal cases. There are no juries. The king is the highest court of appeals.

Jordan

History

What is now Jordan has a long history, going back to ancient times. Largely desert, for much of its history it was part of Syria and Arabia. It did not achieve statehood until modern times.

In biblical times Jordan was part of various civilizations and empires. During the Bronze Age (3000–1000 B.C.) several small states developed east of the Jordan River. The Hebrew states of Judah and Israel developed along the west bank of the Jordan. Later the area became part of the Greek, Roman, Arab, and Turkish empires.

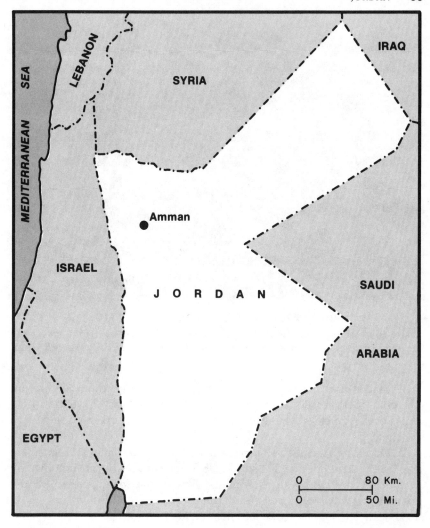

In 1922, after 400 years of Turkish rule, Palestine, the area comprising present-day Jordan and Israel, was given to Britain as the League of Nations Palestine mandate. Britain promptly divided the Palestine mandate. The territory east of the Jordan River, which was four-fifths of the mandate, became the independent Emirate of Transjordan under the rule of Emir Abdullah, but still subject to British control. The other one-fifth — the western portion — remained under the jurisdiction of a British high commissioner and retained the name of Palestine.

In 1946 Britain granted Transjordan full independence, with Abdullah as king. During the Arab–Israeli War of 1948, the West Bank and the Old City

THE MIDDLE EAST'S ANCIENT HERITAGE
These ruins of the Temple of Artemis in Jerash, Jordan, are reminders of the ancient backgrounds of the Middle East. The ruins show Greco-Roman influence. Alia Royal Jordanian Airlines

of Jerusalem (East Jerusalem) were occupied by Jordan and added to the kingdom. (Both territories were lost to Israel in the War of 1967.) In 1949 Transjordan officially changed its name to the Hashemite Kingdom of Jordan.

In 1951 King Abdullah was assassinated by a Palestinian extremist. He was briefly succeeded by his son Talal. Talal was removed from office by parliament in 1952 because of mental illness, and for the next year the country was ruled by regents until Talal's son Hussein turned eighteen in 1953. King Hussein has been Jordan's ruler ever since.

Jordan has been a troubled state. It has at times engaged in border clashes and other disputes with other Arab states. Far more significantly, a major problem has been the presence of vast numbers of Palestinians who left Israel and territories that were to be an Arab state under the U.N. partition plan. They and their descendants now constitute about half of Jordan's population. After the War of 1967, the Palestine Liberation Organization used Jordan as a base for terrorist attacks on Israeli communities. In 1970 the PLO, with Syrian support, also sought to overthrow King Hussein and establish a single Palestinian state for all of what was formerly Jordan (including the West Bank). The Jordanian army attacked the Palestinian terrorists, crushed the PLO strongholds, and expelled its leaders and troops.

ARAB REFUGEE CAMP
Several hundred thousand Arab refugees continue to live in United Nations
supported refugee camps in Jordan, Syria, Iraq, Lebanon, the West Bank, and the
Gaza Strip. The camps are supervised by UNRWA, the United Nations Relief and
Works Agency. Here we see children lining up for a meal in the Marka Refugee
Camp near Amman, the capital of Jordan. Nasr/UNRWA

Many Palestinians then crossed the Jordan River to enter the Israel-
occupied West Bank rather than risk the wrath of Jordan's Bedouin-led
army.

In the late 1970's, however, King Hussein attempted to moderate his
position toward the PLO and Syria and thus gain more acceptance in some
parts of the Arab world. More recently this relationship soured as Jordan
moved closer to Iraq, Syria's bitter enemy. In December 1980, Syria even
massed several divisions of its armed forces on the Jordanian border, almost
provoking a war with the Hashemite Kingdom. Jordan has continued to
gain more acceptability in the Arab world, especially the Persian Gulf Arab
kingdoms led by Saudi Arabia, as well as with Iraq.

The possibility of a self-governing Palestinian authority on the West
Bank linked to Jordan has been suggested by some as the most feasible way
of settling the problem of the Palestinians. Israel rejects this opinion.

Although Jordan has not recognized Israel, it has generally been more
moderate toward the Jewish state than most Arab states, and until recently

was generally pro-American in its foreign policy. Since the Camp David Accords paving the way for peace between Egypt and Israel, which Jordan opposed, Jordan has been viewed as becoming increasingly nonaligned and less pro-American. It has also become a center of inter-Arab activities.

Geography

Jordan is a small kingdom about the size of Indiana. It largely consists of arid deserts, rocky plains, hills, and mountains. The Jordan River forms a natural boundary on the west.

Today, Jordan consists of the East Bank. Once called Transjordan, it is a region of barren, rocky desert plateaus and uplands. Jordan's capital and largest city, Amman, is in the East Bank.

Jordan is a nearly landlocked nation, with a tiny sixteen-mile coastline on the Gulf of Aqaba, where its only major port, Aqaba, is located. Jordan and Israel share the Dead Sea, the lowest point on earth, 1,300 feet below sea level.

People

Jordan has a population of less than three million, nearly all of whom are Arabs and approximately half of whom are Palestinian. There are also small numbers of Armenians, Circassians, and Kurds. About ninety-five percent are Sunni Muslims and approximately five percent are Christians. Almost all speak Arabic, the official language of the country.

Economy and Way of Life

Jordan is one of the poorest Middle East countries. It is an agricultural nation with few natural resources. Only about eleven percent of the land is arable. Less than half of its people live in farm villages. A declining number, now less than six percent, are nomadic or semi-nomadic Bedouins. More than half the people (about fifty-six percent) live in cities. Many live along the Jordan River, where there is sufficient water for agriculture. Amman, east of the Jordan River, the largest and capital city, has a population of about 750,000.

Standards of living in Jordan are low and there is a lack of fuel and raw materials. Although more schools have been built in recent years, it is estimated that about sixty percent of the population still cannot read or write. Most still do not have the benefits of electricity. Although there have been attempts to expand the economy and encourage trade and industry, economic development has been limited, in part because of the devastation resulting from the civil war in 1970. Jordan has had to depend on extensive economic aid from the United States, other Arab countries, and the United Nations (for care of Palestinian refugees).

In recent years shipping and port facilities have been developed at Aqaba, phosphate deposits in the Dead Sea have been exploited, and there have been attempts to encourage tourism.

Government

Jordan is a constitutional monarchy, with a legislative body and a court system. Nevertheless, there are no political parties. The king is the dominant figure. He selects members of the upper house of parliament. He approves and promulgates laws, commands the armed forces, declares war, concludes peace, and signs treaties. He also orders the holding of elections, convenes or adjourns the National Assembly, and appoints judges and district governors. There have been no elections since 1967.

Although there is a regular court system, religious matters are handled by special religious courts.

Syria

History

The land that is present-day Syria has been a center of many cultures and civilizations since ancient times. Before becoming part of the Arab empire and later part of the Ottoman Turk empire, the region was dominated or occupied in whole or part by Egyptians, Hebrews, Phoenicians, Assyrians, Greeks, Romans, Persians, and other peoples. Because it is strategically located between Europe and Asia, its merchants and traders were able to move goods back and forth between the Mediterranean and Far Eastern worlds for thousands of years. Syria was a province of the Ottoman Empire before World War I. It became a French mandate between World Wars I and II and gained its independence in 1944. Britain and France withdrew their military forces in 1946.

Since its independence, Syria's history has been marked by political instability and a number of governmental changes engineered by the military. General Hafez al-Assad, Syria's present strongman, came to power in 1970 as a result of a military coup. He has since ruled as president and head of a one-party-dominated state (the Baath Party).

Although Syria has been united with most Arab countries in its opposition to Israel, its relations with its neighbors have often been hostile. Recently Syria has been on unfriendly terms with Iraq, which it has opposed in the war between Iraq and Iran. In the early 1970s Syria's relations with Jordan were very strained because Syria supported PLO guerrillas who were seeking to overthrow the Jordanian government. Later

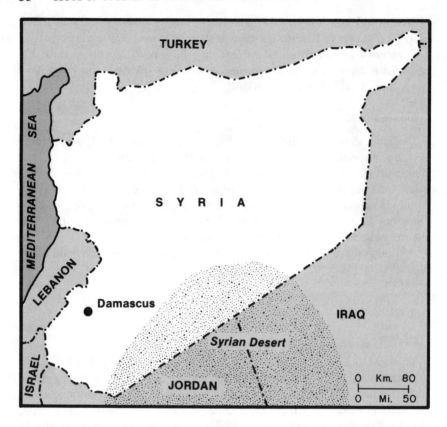

Syria and Jordan attempted to patch up their differences, but since the two countries took opposite sides in the Iraq–Iran war, they have come to the brink of war themselves. Syria has also denounced Egypt's President Sadat for making peace with Israel. Diplomatic relations with the United States were broken off during the 1973 war because the United States gave aid to Israel. Although relations have since been restored, coolness still prevails between the two nations.

In 1976 Syria sent troops into Lebanon, thus directly intervening in the civil war between Christians and Muslims. A large "peacekeeping" force from several Arab nations (mostly Syrians) has been caught up in the seemingly unresolvable Lebanese civil war.

Syria has aligned itself with the Soviet Union and has received much Soviet military and economic aid. At the same time, it has outlawed the Syrian Communist party.

A serious crisis erupted in 1981 when Syria put SAM-6 and SAM-9 Soviet missiles in the Beka valley in Lebanon. Israel interpreted this as a threat to her security and threatened to blow them up if they were not removed.

PRESIDENT ASSAD AND MILITARY GUARD (SYRIA)
Like other rulers of Middle East states, President Hafez al-Assad of Syria came to power as a result of a military coup. Heads of state like strong man Assad depend on the support of the military as well as upon outside economic and military assistance, in this case the Soviet Union. Syria's relations with its neighbors have often been strained. Abbas/Gamma-Liaison

Geography

Syria is about as large as South Dakota. It has a variety of physical features, including lowlands, fertile river valleys and plains, mountains, and deserts.

People

Syria has a population of approximately eight million, ninety percent of whom are Arabs. The Kurds are the largest non-Arab ethnic group. There are also smaller numbers of Armenians, Turks, and Bedouins.

Most Syrians are Sunni Muslims. Other Muslim sects include the Alawites, of which President Hafez al-Assad is a member. Approximately ten to fifteen percent are Christians, largely of the Greek, Syrian, and Armenian Orthodox churches.

Arabic is the official and predominant language in Syria. French and English are also spoken. The Armenians and Kurds speak their own languages.

Economy and Way of Life

Like most states in the Middle East, Syria is still underdeveloped. Despite land reform and land improvement and irrigation programs, less than half of the land suitable for farming is being cultivated. Education has become compulsory for children from six years up to the age of fourteen and more schools have been built, but many Syrians still cannot read or write.

Syria's urban population is increasing. Leading cities include Damascus, the capital and center of trade, industry, and culture (population approximately 900,000), and Aleppo, another independent commercial and industrial center (population approximately 625,000). Many Syrians are poor farmers or shepherds, living in rural villages and communities.

Unlike many other Arab nations, Syria grows enough to feed itself. It is also a major Middle East trade center, with more miles of surfaced roads, highways, and railroads than most other Middle East nations. Although there have been serious efforts to promote industry, less than a fifth of the work force is so engaged. The oil-refining, cement, flour-milling, and textile industries have grown rapidly. Since the discovery of modest-size oil deposits in the 1950s, Syria has been able to meet most of its own oil needs.

Under its program of Arab socialism, which includes government planning, control, and ownership of industry, most of Syria's foreign and domestic industries, including American- and Dutch-owned oil companies, were nationalized in the 1960s. More recently, under President Assad, private ownership of smaller industrial and commercial firms and businesses has again been encouraged.

Syria's economy is strained because of the failure of overambitious economic programs and because of large military expenditures. Consequently, in recent years Syria has had to depend increasingly on outside aid, particularly from Saudi Arabia and other oil-rich Arab states. The United States and European nations have also given assistance.

Government

Syria is a military-dominated Arab republic. Although the constitution provides for separate executive, legislative, and judicial branches, most power is given to the president and the socialist Arab Baath Party. The state controls the press, radio, and other media. A number of other parties are allowed to exist, but the Baathists have clearly been in control since 1963.

In spite of its influential position, the Baath Party is split into rival factions, including moderate and extremist groups; and there has been an ongoing struggle for power. Muslim and conservative elements resent the "secularization" of the economy by the creation of civil law codes and courts, with jurisdiction in non-religious matters. In their judgment, Islam should be the only legal acceptable code for all social, political, and cultural as well as religious matters.

After the regime of Iranian Shah Mohammed Reza Pahlevi was overthrown in 1979 and replaced by an autocratic Islamic republic headed by Ayatollah Khomeini, tensions and outbursts of violence developed in Syria between the minority Shiite Muslims who are dominant in the government of President Assad and the majority Sunni Muslims.

Turkey

History

The region occupied by present-day Turkey is one of the oldest inhabited areas in the world. The home of ancient peoples like the Hittites and Lydians, it later came under Greek and Roman influence. The Byzantine Empire, established after the fall of Rome with Constantinople as its capital, lasted a thousand years until, in the 15th century, it fell to the Ottoman Turks, an invading people from the East.

The Ottomans built a great empire in the 15th and 16th centuries, stretching across the Balkan Peninsula and parts of southern and eastern

Europe, Asia Minor, the fertile crescent of the Middle East, and North Africa. Years of growth were followed by a longer period of decline, particularly in the 19th and early 20th centuries. By 1914 the empire had lost most of its possessions in Europe and Africa. In the Middle East, however, it continued to rule over territories that have become present-day Iraq, Israel, Jordan, Lebanon, Syria, Yemen, and parts of Saudi Arabia.

Wishing to restore the greatness of the empire through reform and the elimination of corruption, a reform party called the Young Turks revolted and overthrew the sultan in 1908 and forced his successor to yield considerable power. Under Young Turk leadership Turkey entered World War I on the side of Germany and Austria-Hungary in an effort to gain back lost territory. The Treaty of Sevres, which the sultan signed in 1920, marked the end of Ottoman power. It stripped the empire of its remaining possessions and territorial claims. In the Middle East, Syria, Palestine, and Mesopotamia (Iraq) were assigned as mandates to Britain and France.

Turkish nationalists led by Mustafa Kemal (later known as Kemal Ataturk, "father of the Turks") were very dissatisfied with the Treaty of Sevres, particularly since it also provided for the ceding of eastern Thrace to Greece, for Greek rule over the province of Smyrna (Izmir) for five years, for reduction of Turkish armed forces, and for control of Turkey's finances by an Allied commission.

Under Kemal's leadership, the Greek troops were defeated and expelled in 1922 and the Allies were forced to negotiate a new treaty, the Treaty of Lausanne, recognizing full Turkish independence and returning much disputed territory. Also in 1922 the last sultan was expelled and was replaced by a purely religious leader as caliph; he in turn was ousted and in 1924 Turkey became a secular republic, with Kemal Ataturk as its president.

Until his death in 1938, Ataturk ruled with dictatorial power. But he was widely respected and admired for modernizing Turkey along Western lines, carrying out an ambitious program of social, economic, and political reforms, and gaining a position of respect for his nation.[7]

Under Kemal's leadership Turkey gained stature as a nation. It was admitted to the League of Nations and given the right to govern and militarize the Turkish Straits (the Bosphorus and the Dardanelles).

Turkey remained neutral during World War II until close to the end of the war, when it declared war on the Axis. It became a charter member of the United Nations in 1945.

Since World War II Turkey has built up powerful armed forces and has become an important NATO "linchpin" in the Middle East. As an ally of the United States and the West, it has received considerable economic and

[7] See Chapter 4 for details of Kemal's reforms.

military assistance from the United States. It has also outlawed its Communist party.

Turkey's chief recent foreign concern, in addition to the presence of the Soviet Union as its neighbor, has been its differences with Greece over the rights of the Turkish minority on the island of Cyprus, leading to an invasion of Cyprus by Turkish armed forces in 1974.[8]

The United States cut off arms sales to Turkey from 1975 to 1978 as a result of Turkey's refusal to withdraw its forces from Cyprus. Relations between the two countries cooled and Turkey closed down military surveillance bases which the United States had used to monitor Soviet military and nuclear activities. Although arms sales and use of the bases have been restored, Turkey has sought to improve relations with Russia and has signed economic-assistance and friendship pacts with the Soviets.

Since the late 1950s, growing dissatisfaction with economic conditions in Turkey, particularly over rising prices and unemployment, has caused considerable unrest and political discontent. Bitterness among religious and ethnic minorities has increased. Martial law and military controls have often had to be imposed.

In 1978, Turkish armed forces put down bloody turmoil resulting from the feuding of religious and political extremists in eastern Turkey. Most victims were members of a minority Shiite Muslim sect known as the Alevis who have complained of discrimination by the majority Sunni sect.

In 1980 military leaders took control of the government in an attempt to prevent political and economic collapse. They promised to restore civilian rule after a new constitution was drafted that would make possible greater stability.

Geography

Turkey consists of two parts, Asiatic Turkey and European Turkey. Asiatic Turkey, or Asia Minor, occupies the Anatolian Peninsula between the Mediterranean and Black seas. It is twice the size of California and makes up ninety-seven percent of the country's total area. European Turkey, or Thrace, is about the size of Massachusetts. It makes up the other three percent of Turkey's area. European Turkey is separated from Asia Minor by the Dardanelles, the Sea of Marmora, and the Bosphorus.

Most of Asiatic Turkey is an arid, rugged plateau, ringed by high mountains on all but its western side. There are broad coastal plains in the north, west, and south, suitable for agriculture. The Mediterranean coastal plain is the most fertile section. There is a forested area in the north. The European section of Turkey mainly consists of rolling plains and hills suitable for agriculture, and low mountains in the northern sections.

[8] See Chapter 4 for details.

People

Turks make up 90 percent of the population of Turkey (presently approximately 43 million). The largest minority is the more than 7.5 million Kurds (about seven percent of the population). There are also smaller numbers of Greeks, Armenians, and Jews. Nearly all Turks are members of the Islamic faith (98 percent Sunni Muslim). The official language, spoken by over 90 percent of the population, is Turkish. Kurdish and Arabic are also spoken.

Economy and Way of Life

Reforms initiated by Kemal Ataturk have changed Turkish life in many ways. Western styles in dress, entertainment, and other areas of living are more evident. The public school system has expanded and is free. Women play a greater role outside the home than they used to. Turkey's political system has been Europeanized.

Despite the fact that the government has been promoting industrial expansion, Turkey's way of life is still mostly rural and agricultural. Standards of living are low from a Western standpoint, though somewhat higher than those of other Middle East countries (aside from Israel and the oil-rich Arab states). Only about thirty percent of the land is under cultivation. Although education has been improved, and an estimated two-thirds of the

ATATURK
Mustapha Kemal, affectionately admired and respected as "father of the Turks" (Ataturk) by his people, led in the creation of the present republic of Turkey in the early 1920s, after the collapse of the Ottoman Empire. Kemal began the modernization of Turkey along Western lines. He ruled as president for many years. Here we see a well known Turkish sculptress, Mrs. Zerrin Bolukbasi, working on a massive head of Ataturk. Turkish Ministry of Tourism and Information

urban population is literate, more than two-thirds of the rural population is still unable to read and write. In some villages there still are not enough schools.

Backward conditions in many rural areas have prompted a rapid drift to Turkey's cities, where living conditions are generally better than in the countryside. About half of the population now lives in urban communities. However, this has led to overcrowding, growing unemployment, and an increasing demand for goods and services. Istanbul (formerly Constantinople), with a population of over 2.5 million, is the country's largest city and the center of industry, trade, culture, and religion. Ankara, the nation's capital, is another important urban center (population over 1.5 million).

More than half of the Turkish labor force is engaged in agriculture. The government has made extensive efforts to improve and modernize farming. Tobacco, cotton, fruits, nuts, and olives are important crops. Next to India, Turkey is the world's largest producer of opium. It has cooperated with the United States and the United Nations to control opium cultivation in an effort to prevent illegal smuggling and sale of the drug.

Turkey has rich but as yet largely unexploited natural resources (coal, iron, copper, chrome, manganese). Iron, steel, textile, paper, glass, sugar, and cement industries have been established or expanded with government assistance.

To finance ambitious development programs in industry and agriculture, Turkey has had to borrow heavily. The burden of loan repayments, plus large trade deficits, have strained the economy to the point of near collapse. A population that has been doubling every twenty-seven years has imposed additional burdens.

Government

Turkey is a republic with a parliamentary form of government. It has a president, an elected legislative body, a civil and criminal court system, and a written constitution. The prime minister is the key figure in government. There are many political parties. All Turkish citizens over the age of twenty-one may vote.

Turkey's economic, religious, and social problems have caused serious political instability. In recent years there have been a series of short-lived coalition governments. On several occasions the military has intervened to cope with serious internal crises.

In 1980 leaders of the armed forces took control of the government in a military coup, in order to prevent political collapse brought about by the government's inability to solve its political, social, and economic problems. The ruling military junta, formally known as the National Security Council, indicated it would call an assembly to write a new constitution and draft

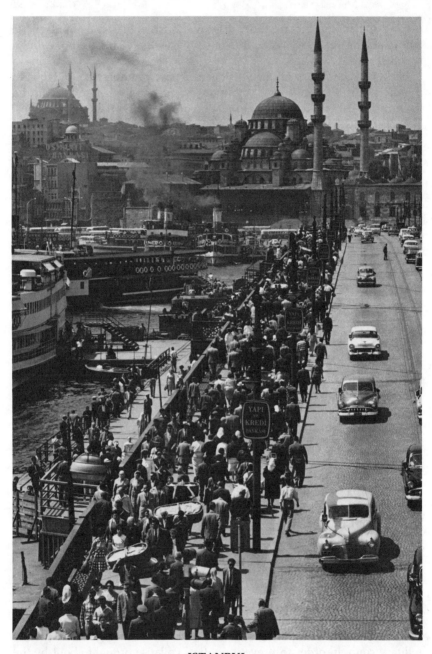

ISTANBUL

Istanbul, capital of Turkey, is one of the world's great cities. In the background we see the famous Blue Mosque. Other signs of the "meeting of East and West" are also visible. Can you see them? Turkish Ministry of Tourism and Information

new laws on elections and political parties. Their stated aim was to return power to civilian authorities when weaknesses of the existing political system would be corrected.

Mastery Activities

1. Identify each of the following Middle East countries by placing, on the line to the left of its name, the letter that locates it on the map below.

_____1. Egypt   _____5. Saudi Arabia
_____2. Syria   _____6. Turkey
_____3. Lebanon   _____7. Israel
_____4. Jordan   _____8. Iran

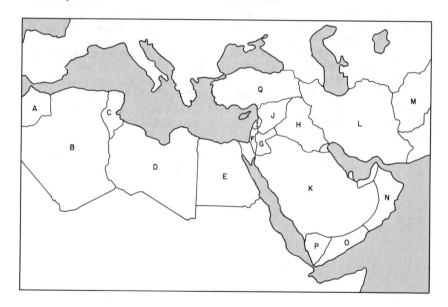

2. Identify each of the Middle East countries discussed in this chapter by printing its name to the left of the correct statement.

_____This country became an Islamic republic as a result of a revolution that overturned its ruler in the late 1970s.

_____This Arab state directly intervened in the civil war in Lebanon in the 1970s and sent a large peacekeeping force to preserve the truce between Muslims and Christians.

_____Over half a million Palestinian refugees live in this tiny Arab monarchy or in territory it once occupied.

_____This kingdom has become one of the most influential Arab countries in the Middle East as a result of its vast oil wealth.

_____This Middle East country, located partly in Asia and partly in Europe, is an important NATO member.

_____To preserve its independence and survival this small Middle East state has had to fight several wars with its Arab neighbors.

_____This nation, which has the largest Arab population, was the first Arab nation to sign a peace treaty with Israel.

_____This formerly stable Middle East state has suffered severely as a result of civil war between its Christian and Muslim populations.

Questions for Homework and Discussion

1. Select two Middle East nations discussed in this chapter in which you are most interested. For each, list five important facts or ideas about each of which you have become aware for the first time.

2. Explain why you feel each of the following statements is true or false.
(a) Egypt has been able to negotiate peace with Israel because it has had few economic problems to divert its attention from this goal.
(b) Saudi Arabia's oil wealth has made it possible for it to become one of the most "Westernized" nations in the Middle East.
(c) Britain's inability to successfully govern its Palestine mandate paved the way for the emergence of Israel as an independent Middle East nation.

3. Explain the role played by each of the following in the history of his country: (a) Gamal Abdel Nasser, (b) Kemal Ataturk, (c) Ayatollah Khomeini, (d) Ibn Saud, (e) David Ben-Gurion

4. "Although it is a Middle East nation, Israel is very different from other countries in the region." Explain fully the meaning of this statement.

4

The Middle East Since World War I

World War I and the two decades that followed brought about major changes in the Middle East. There was greater international involvement in the area, as evidenced by the establishment of the mandate system, increased big-power interests and rivalries, and the growing importance of oil. In addition, following the dissolution of the Ottoman Empire, new nationalistic states and aspirations challenged the old Islamic order.

Since World War II the Middle East has been a region of crisis and tension. Among the more important causes of this instability have been the social and economic changes taking place as a result of the area's transition from traditionalism to modernism, the increased nationalism that has been part of this change, the growth of Communism, and increasing national and international rivalries. These basic factors have brought about a number of significant developments, including: (1) growing Arab nationalism, (2) continuing conflict between Arab states and Israel, (3) inter-Arab and other regional rivalries and conflicts, and (4) attempts by the Soviet Union to take advantage of tensions and crises to achieve its goals in the Middle East.

A full understanding of the role and policies of the United States in the Middle East in the 20th century must take into account these important developments.

The Growth of Arab Nationalism

Arab nationalism is a complex set of feelings and attitudes. It includes the desire for political independence and freedom from foreign occupation or domination. It also takes the form of "pan-Arabism" (or pan-Arab nationalism) — the feeling that all Arabs should be united, a form of nationalism that cuts across frontiers. Intermixed with both is the sense of an Islamic brotherhood. Arab leaders share contradictory feelings of rivalry and community. Regardless of what they believe to be the need for loyalty to their individual nations — and their national interests — they cannot or dare not totally ignore the often conflicting but always compelling bonds of religion and Pan-Arabism.

Origins of Arab Nationalism

In the 19th and early 20th centuries — and for several centuries before this — Arab lands in the Middle East were part of the Islamic Ottoman Empire. In addition, in the 19th century many came under the control or influence of Britain, France, Italy, and other imperialist European powers.

The origins of modern Arab nationalism can be traced back to this period. Arab intellectuals and scholars began to stress the common Arab cultural heritage. Muslim Arab nationalists began to call for increased rights of self-government within the Ottoman Empire.[1]

World War I

The establishment of separate, politically independent Arab states did not become an important force or popular idea among Arabs (except in Egypt) until after World War I, with the breakup of the Ottoman Empire. This development had its beginnings during the war itself.

Early in the war the British persuaded the Arab leader, Sharif Hussein of Mecca, and his sons to join in the war against the Turks. Hussein hoped to establish an Arab state in the Arabian Peninsula and in Syria and Iraq. In return for a pledge in October 1915 by Sir Henry McMahon, Britain's chief representative in Egypt, that Britain would "recognize and support the independence of the Arabs," Hussein and his four sons waged guerrilla war against the Turks in the Hejaz, Syria, and Palestine. Arab attacks and raids on a number of key railways and towns held by the Turks, including Aqaba on the Red Sea, helped pin down Turkish troops who otherwise would have been available to oppose the British in Palestine.

In their revolt, Hussein and his son, Feisal, received support and advice from Colonel T. E. Lawrence ("Lawrence of Arabia"), a young Englishman who closely identified himself with the Arab cause and helped secure assistance from the British army in Egypt. After the British took Damascus in October 1918, they permitted Feisal and his troops to make a "triumphant" entry into the city.[2]

---

[1] Although the idea is foreign to Islamic concepts, it should be noted that Arab nationalist movements derived much from European influence and example.

[2] The extent of the "Arab Revolt" has often been exaggerated. Beyond the limited role of Hussein, there was no general Arab uprising. Arab support for the Turks was also limited. Lawrence's role has often been overemphasized and romanticized.

LAWRENCE OF ARABIA
Colonel Thomas E. Lawrence, or "Lawrence of Arabia" as he came to be called, was a young British officer sympathetic to the Arab cause, who helped secure British assistance for the Arabs in their fight to overthrow Turkish rule during World War I. The Arab revolt helped the British in their campaign to wrest control of the Middle East from the Turks during the War. Lawrence, at the right, is conferring with Arab leaders. New York Public Library

World War I to World War II

Between World Wars I and II (1918–1939) Arab nationalism became a growing force in the Middle East. The Arab nationalist movement attracted a growing portion of the Arab world.

Turkey (the Ottoman Empire) had entered World War I on the side of the Central Powers (Germany and Austria-Hungary) against the Allied nations (Britain, France, Russia). The defeat of the Central Powers led to the dismemberment and final dissolution of the Ottoman Empire, of which many Arab territories had been part. Turkey gave up all claims to her non-Turkish territories, including much of the Middle East.[3]

During World War I the British had promised Arab leaders that they would support Arab independence after the war. Instead, because of the reluctance of the imperialist powers to give up their controls, the former Ottoman Empire was divided into a series of newly created states and

[3] The student should note that, although the Turkish-dominated Ottoman Empire died after World War I, a new, strong, nationalist Turkish republic arose from its ashes, led by the able Mustapha Kemal.

assigned by the League of Nations to Britain and France as *mandates*. The British and French were to administer and develop their mandates until they were ready for independence. Palestine and Iraq became British mandates; Syria and Lebanon became French mandates.

Arab nationalists fought against British and French domination, as well as against the Jews in Palestine. They strongly resented the mandate system and felt cheated that full independence had not been granted. Their openly stated goals were independence of all Arab peoples and freedom from external influence or domination, particularly in the form of Western (European) imperialism.

Although it continued to play an important role as the most influential European power in the Middle East, Britain was forced to respond to growing demands of Arab nationalists. France was forced to make similar concessions.

In 1923 Britain recognized Egypt's independence. Britain also recognized the establishment of the kingdom of Saudi Arabia in 1927 under the leadership of King Ibn Saud. Saud was an ambitious Arab chieftain who had subjugated nearly all of the semi-independent chieftains of the Arab Peninsula.[4] Iraq was given independence in 1932.

In addition, Britain divided its original Palestine mandate into two parts. The portion east of the Jordan River became Transjordan, an Arab state. Transjordan included four-fifths of the original mandate. It remained under British control until 1946 and continued to depend on British military and financial support. The small remaining portion of the original Palestine mandate (all land west of the Jordan River) was retained as the British mandate under a British high commissioner.

As a result of mounting resistance to its continuing control of Syria, France signed a treaty with Syria in 1936 promising gradual withdrawal of French troops and Syria's eventual admission to the League of Nations as an independent state. To ease growing friction between Muslims and Christians in Lebanon, the French helped draft a new constitution in 1926 providing for a sharing of representation in government and public office.

Continuing British Influence

Although Britain began to make concessions to Arab nationalism in the Middle East in the period between World Wars I and II, it continued to play a dominant role in the region. Britain maintained its right to keep troops in

---

[4] As previously indicated, Britain was originally committed to support the Sharif Hussein of Mecca. It had to accept Hussein's defeat and expulsion from the Arabian Peninsula by the Saudis. Britain appointed two of Hussein's sons as rulers in the mandates that Britain administered — King Feisal in Iraq and Emir Abdullah in Transjordan.

ANGLO-SOVIET OCCUPATION OF IRAN DURING WORLD WAR II

Pro-Axis activity in Iran plus its unwillingness to grant a supply route through Iran to the Allies during World War II, led to the Anglo-Soviet occupation of Iran in 1941 and the deposition of the Shah. Above are seen Indian riflemen in the British army entering the main gates of the Abadan oil refinery at the head of the Persian Gulf, to assure its continued functioning. Wide World

Egypt to protect the Suez Canal Zone and was permitted to keep military and air bases in Iraq. It also maintained financial and military controls in its newly formed mandate of Transjordan, ruled by the Emir Abdullah.

In addition, Britain maintained its sphere of influence and relationship with many small emirates, sheikhdoms, and sultanates around the fringes of the Arabian Peninsula, along the Red Sea, the Arabian Sea, and the Persian Gulf. British-owned companies played a leading role in developing oil resources in Saudi Arabia, Iran, Kuwait, Bahrain, Qatar, and the "Trucial States" (later called the United Arab Emirates). British advisers often played an important advisory role in the governments of such states.

The Arabs and World War II

Generally speaking, most of the Arab world was either neutral or uncooperative with the Allies during World War II because of their unhappy experiences with imperialist controls exercised by the British and French in the prewar period. Although it officially broke off relations with the Axis in 1939, Egypt did not declare war on Germany until 1945, after Allied victory had become certain. Iraq did not declare war against the Axis until 1943, after British forces had put down a coup by pro-German military leaders. Although it indicated its sympathy for the Allied cause, Saudi Arabia remained neutral until 1945, when without declaring war, Ibn Saud proclaimed his country's support of the Allies.

In addition to not giving active assistance to the Allies, many portions of the Arab world were openly sympathetic to the Axis during the war. As a result of being actively "wooed" by the Germans and Italians in the 1930s, the Arabs hoped for an Axis victory that would end English and French control of the Middle East. Many favored the Nazis because of German anti-Semitic propaganda and Arab–Jewish friction in Palestine. During the war, two pro-German Arab leaders, Rashid Ali al-Gailani, premier of Iraq (until ousted by the British in 1943), and Haj Amin al-Husseini, the former grand mufti of Jerusalem, escaped to Germany, where they helped spread Nazi propaganda.

The Legacy of World War II

World War II changed the balance of power in the Middle East. Britain and France were exhausted by the war. France had been easily conquered and overrun by the Germans. The British had suffered costly and debilitating defeats even though Britain itself had not been invaded. Italy lost its colonies in Africa, including Libya.

The prestige of Britain and France plunged to a low ebb after the war. In the postwar era, each gave up or lost most of its colonial holdings and dependencies in the Middle East. France reluctantly gave up control of its mandates in Syria and Lebanon in 1946, shortly after the war. Britain surrendered its mandates in Jordan in 1946 and in Palestine in 1948. In 1956 it removed the last of its troops from Egypt and the Suez Canal Zone.

In the 1960s, beset by economic problems at home, the British reluctantly decided to reduce their military commitments "east of Suez" in order to ease the financial strain of maintaining an empire. Accordingly, in the late 1960s and early 1970s, they relinquished their remaining protectorates over Aden, Qatar, and the Trucial States on the Persian Gulf.

As Britain and France gave up their formerly influential role in the Middle East, the United States and the Soviet Union became more active in the area.

Arab Nationalism Since World War II

In the post–World War II years, Arab nationalism became an increasingly important force in the Middle East.

Arab nationalists have increasingly emphasized the importance of eliminating all remaining evidences of foreign domination and of playing an independent role in world affairs. Many Arab leaders have stressed the need for modernization and the development of Arab political, economic, and military strength as a means of achieving a respected position in the world. They have demanded and obtained increasing shares of ownership and control of their valuable oil resources, formerly exploited almost exclusively by Western colonial powers.

Peasants and the urban poor have become aware — through radio, television, films, and other media — that there is a better way of life possible and have made demands for social and economic improvements. In several Arab nations, notably Iraq and Syria, there has been emphasis on the establishment of "radical revolutionary socialist economies" as a means of building strong Arab states. Oil-rich Arab nations have nationalized all or most of formerly Western-owned oil properties and have used the oil and huge oil revenues to reshape their economies and relationships with the rest of the world.

Although many Arab nationalists still dream of an overall, united Arab state or world, the many divisions in the Arab world have defeated and rendered futile all attempts to create such unity, despite a number of unifying bonds. Opposition to Israel has become perhaps the most unifying force among Arab nations. Other unifying forces include the Islamic religion and bitterness and anger on the part of much of the Arab world against former Western imperialist domination and control of Arab lands and oil resources.

The Arab League

In 1945 the Arab League was established to promote the pan-Arab goals of unity, solidarity, and cooperation among Arab nations. Today its membership includes Algeria, Bahrain, Djibouti, Egypt, Iraq, Jordan, Kuwait, Lebanon, Libya, Mauritania, Morocco, Oman, Qatar, Saudi Arabia, Somalia, Sudan, Syria, Tunisia, United Arab Emirates, Yemen, South Yemen, and the Palestine Liberation Organization (PLO). Egypt's membership was suspended after President Sadat signed the peace treaty with Israel in 1979.

The Arab League has served as a clearinghouse and meeting ground for inter-Arab discussions. It has also directed and supervised the Arab economic boycott of those trading with Israel. Nevertheless, its effectiveness has been limited by the division and fragmentation of the Arab world. Its members have been unwilling to subordinate national or individual rivalries to a united "federal" ideal.

A loosely organized body with no power over member states, the Arab League has been weakened by bitter personal and national feuds and rivalries. In a small number of situations, the League has taken united political action. For example, in 1976 it helped organize a truce-observation force during the civil war in Lebanon; it also helped negotiate a cease-fire in the dispute between North and South Yemen in 1979.

For the most part, however, the Arab League has been unable to prevent or arbitrate the many inter-Arab conflicts that have taken place. Most major crises in the Arab world have been discussed at special "summit" meetings of heads of states and governments outside of Arab League channels. The League's principal role has been to serve as a powerful propaganda instrument and common political front against Israel.

Attempts at Arab Unity

In recent decades the ideal of *pan-Arabism* — the ideal that all Arabs should be united — has remained largely unfulfilled. Arab disunity, rather than unity, has become characteristic of today's Arab world. A number of attempts have been made at political unity among two or more Arab states; but aside from the United Arab Emirates the only inter-Arab framework that has survived has been the Arab League.[5]

The most noteworthy attempt at Arab political unity since world War II occurred when Egypt and Syria established a political union called the United Arab Republic (UAR) in 1958. The UAR was dissolved by Syria in 1961 because it felt that its interests were being subordinated to those of Egypt. Among other efforts at political unity that were discussed, tentatively agreed to, and abandoned were those between Iraq and Jordan in 1958; Egypt, Iraq, and Syria in 1963; Egypt and Yemen in 1964; Egypt, Libya, and Syria in 1971; and Syria and Jordan in 1975 and 1978. A brief and completely abortive attempt by Syria to form a military alliance with Iraq in 1979 in the aftermath of Egypt's peace overtures with Israel got nowhere because of deep-rooted mutual hostility and a bitter feud between the rival

[5] The United Arab Emirates, a union of seven small Arab kingdoms, was formed in 1971 when Britain gave up its "protector" status over them. Before the establishment of the UAE, the emirates were known as the Trucial States or Trucial Oman because of their links to Britain based on truces and treaties. The UAE consists of the sheikhdoms of Abu Dhabi, Ajam, Dubai, Fujairah, Ras al-Khaimah, Sharjah, and Umm al-Qaywayn. These extend along the southern edge of the Persian Gulf from the Qatar Peninsula to the Gulf of Oman.

ARAB SUMMIT CONFERENCE
Arab leaders meet from time to time to discuss common strategy. Above is King Hussein of Jordan presiding at one such summit meeting of Arab heads of state.
Francolon/Gamma-Liaison

wings of the socialist Baath Party which rule both Syria and Iraq. In 1980 Syria and Libya agreed to a merger but did not indicate how and when it would take place.

In the name of pan-Arabism, rival Arab states have at times justified interfering in the internal affairs of brother Arab states. This has worked against Arab unity. Several noteworthy examples of such interference include Egypt's sending troops to Yemen in 1962 to back leftist rebels, Syria's invasion of Jordan in 1970 to help Palestinian guerrillas who were trying to overthrow the government, and Libya's support of groups attempting to overthrow the Tunisian, Sudanese, and Egyptian regimes in the middle and late 1970s.

Control of Middle East Oil

Since the 1950s, the growing determination of oil-producing Arab nations to control their own destinies has resulted in significant changes in policy with respect to the ownership, control, and profits of the oil resources of the Middle East.

Under concessions granted at various times between 1901 and World War II, foreign oil companies were given the right to develop the oil resources of the Middle East. After World War II, Arab nations began to demand a greater share of oil profits as part of their determination to regain from Western powers control of a resource that they considered rightfully their own. In response to their demands — and sometimes in order to avoid

OPEC CONFERENCE

OPEC, the Organization of Petroleum Exporting Countries, was formed in 1960 to coordinate and establish oil prices to consuming nations. Decisions made at OPEC conferences, such as the one above, have often led to sharp price increases, which have had a profound impact on the world economy. Gamma-Liaison

nationalization (takeover) of foreign oil properties by the Arab countries — Western oil companies negotiated agreements providing for increased royalties of up to fifty percent of the selling price of each barrel of oil.

Beginning in the late 1960s, a number of oil-producing nations escalated their demands by calling for ownership of oil-producing facilities and a share of all profits *in addition to royalties*. The Arab oil-exporting nations were able to negotiate for and receive new "participation formulas" giving them an increased share in the management and ownership of all existing Western oil concessions.

As a result of the joint bargaining efforts of members of the Organization of Arab Petroleum Exporting Countries (OAPEC), an organization formed in 1968 to look after common interests, the share of Arab nations in the ownership of the oil industries within their borders has already risen to sixty percent or more. Complete 100 percent takeover is expected to come before the end of the century.[6] OAPEC members include Algeria, Bahrain, Egypt, Iraq, Kuwait, Libya, Qatar, Saudi Arabia, Syria, and the United Arab Emirates.

[6] In 1979 Saudi Arabia, for example, controlled sixty percent of Aramco, which runs the Saudi oil fields, with the oil companies — Texaco, Exxon, Mobil, and Standard Oil of California — controlling the remaining forty percent.

In Iraq, Libya, and Iran (until the overthrow of the Shah in 1979), where foreign oil properties have already been taken over (nationalized) by the governments, foreign oil companies and interests have been permitted to continue to provide managerial and technical services because of the need for foreign technical know-how and expertise.

Arab nations play a determining role in another and more important group — the Organization of Petroleum Exporting Countries (OPEC). OPEC exercises a major role in international affairs through its ability to influence oil prices and production in major oil-producing nations. OPEC was organized as an oil cartel in 1960 to look after the interests of oil-exporting nations by making joint decisions on international trade and development with industrialized countries, including oil production and oil prices, and by pressing for elimination of allowances to foreign-owned oil companies.[7] Its membership has grown from five to fourteen oil-producing and -exporting nations: Algeria, Bahrain, Ecuador, Gabon, Indonesia, Iran, Iraq, Kuwait, Libya, Nigeria, Qatar, Saudi Arabia, United Arab Emirates, and Venezuela. Since its formation OPEC has raised oil prices on world markets from less than two dollars a barrel to over thirty-four dollars a barrel. Prices rose most sharply after the Arab–Israeli War of 1973 and after the overthrow of the Shah of Iran in 1979. They were expected to rise further in the 1980s, not only because of the prolonged Iraq–Iran war but for other economic and political reasons as well. This has contributed significantly to worldwide inflation and international monetary strain. At the beginning of the decade, some OPEC members were charging as much as $40 a barrel. However, prices began to drop in the early 1980s when stepped up production in Saudi Arabia and conservation measures in the United States resulted in an oil glut.

Use of Oil as a Weapon

In addition to increasing the price of oil, the Arab nations have used oil as an economic weapon. To "punish" the United States and the Netherlands for extending aid to Israel during the 1973 war, the Arab states totally embargoed oil shipments to them and curtailed exports to the rest of the world as well.[8] Their aim was to let oil-purchasing nations know that unless they adopted pro-Arab or anti-Israel policies, such treatment would con-

[7] A cartel is a combination of independent business organizations, or a bloc of nations, formed to regulate production, pricing, and marketing of goods by its members. The Arab states operate through both OAPEC, the Organization of Arab Petroleum Exporting Countries, and OPEC, the Organization of Petroleum Exporting Countries. The policies of the two organizations are largely the same.

[8] The embargo on shipments to the United States was lifted in March 1974 and to the Netherlands in July of that year.

tinue. As a result, because of the need for Arab oil (as in Japan) or in the hope that the oil-rich Arab nations might give them financial assistance, a number of nations formerly friendly to Israel have severed relations with the Jewish state or have persistently taken pro-Arab positions.

The huge investments of Arab "petrodollars" in commercial and industrial firms and real estate in the West have become a source of mounting concern and growing controversy in the United States and elsewhere. There has also been controversy over the Arab boycott of blacklisted banks and businesses in Western countries that do business with Israel. Many people in the United States, concerned that Arab investments are being used to achieve the political goals of Arab oil-producing states, have stepped up pressure for the adoption of a comprehensive energy program to make the United States less dependent on OPEC nations.

Opposition to Israel

Deep-seated and serious disagreements among Arab nations and leaders have made it impossible for the Arab world to achieve unity on most issues, including the issue of unity itself. On one issue, however, there had been agreement — opposition to Israel — until Egypt and Israel signed the 1979 peace treaty. This opposition, often expressed by Arab nations and leaders as antagonism to the very existence of Israel as a nation, has been an important factor in bringing on four wars between the Arabs and Israel since Israel's establishment as an independent state. It has also been one of the main stumbling blocks in the search for an overall peace settlement in the Middle East. The leaders of Syria, Iraq, South Yemen, Libya, and Algeria, the so-called "rejectionist front," have held to the position that the Arabs should not come to terms with Israel under any condition and should continue to fight for its destruction. In contrast, President Sadat of Egypt, courageously defying Arab opposition, has made peace with Israel.

Leadership in the Arab States

No single Arab leader or group has emerged to unite the entire Arab world. Nevertheless there have been a number of Arab leaders and organizations, in addition to OAPEC and OPEC, that have attracted Arab support beyond national borders.

Gamal Abdel Nasser

The foremost champion of Arab unity and pan-Arabism in the post–World War II world was Gamal Abdel Nasser, president of Egypt from 1956 to 1970. Nasser was leader of a group of military officers who overthrew the Egyptian monarchy in 1952. He dominated the Arab state for nearly two decades. Nasser gained tremendous popularity in the Arab world by advocating greater independence from Western economic and political influence and nonalignment. By nationalizing the Suez Canal, by leading opposition to Israel and the West, and by concerning himself with the social and economic improvement of his people, he emerged as a distinctly Arab and popular leader.

Despite the fact that his military and political ventures and economic programs generally ended in failure, Nasser was revered by the Arab masses and is still a great hero in the Arab world. He was the leading force in the short-lived union of Egypt and Syria from 1958 to 1961. Pro-Nasser groups led revolts in Yemen and Syria and attempted coups in other parts of the Arab world. Nasser's popularity among other Arab leaders declined as a result of his attempts to interfere in the affairs of other Arab nations. A leading force in bringing about the 1967 war with Israel, he was humiliated by Egypt's rapid defeat in that war. Thereafter Nasser's influence in the Arab world declined. Since Nasser's death in 1970, no other figure has served as a comparable symbol of Arab unity.

Anwar el-Sadat

Anwar el-Sadat succeeded Nasser as president of Egypt. Nasser had looked on himself as an Arab first and had claimed leadership of the Pan-Arab movement. Sadat, although an Arab, looked on himself as an Egyptian first and believed that his first priority must be the economic development of Egypt and the improvement of the desperately poor living conditions in his country. He felt that peace with Israel would make it possible for him to concentrate on this task. His attempts to negotiate a peace treaty with Israel led to his bitter denunciation by the leaders of most Arab nations.[9]

The Baath Party

The Baath or Arab Socialist Resurrection Party has been militant in advocating Pan-Arab unity. Although Baathist leaders have disagreed on many important issues, their goal is the same, namely, the establishment of Marxist socialist governments based on the principle of secularism (non-religious control) throughout the Middle East. The Baath Party dominates the governments of Syria and Iraq.

Saudi Arabia, the United Arab Emirates, and other more conservative

---

[9] Only a few Arab nations, for example Sudan and Oman, supported Sadat's efforts.

states have viewed with great suspicion the leftist Baath regimes in Syria and Iraq and their pro-Soviet orientation and contacts. They have opposed efforts of the Baath Party to export "revolutionary socialism" to other countries, including their own.

Although the Baath Party favors Arab unity, the extreme ideas of many of its leaders have aroused more suspicion than unity in the Arab world. There have been strong differences and antagonisms between the Baathist parties of Syria and Iraq, where the party has had its greatest strength.

The Palestine Liberation Organization

The PLO, headed by Yasser Arafat, was founded in 1964 to coordinate the activities of anti-Israel terrorist groups. The PLO's proclaimed aim is the destruction of Israel, and for this reason Israelis refuse to have any dealings with it. However, all Arab states and the United Nations recognize the PLO as the representative of the Palestinian Arabs. Since its formation, the PLO has claimed credit for scores of terrorist attacks and raids on Israeli citizens and settlements. It has also opposed all efforts of Egypt to negotiate peace with Israel.

THE PLO

The Palestine Liberation Organization is an Arab terrorist organization that supports the establishment of a Palestinian state. It refuses to recognize the existence of Israel and has pledged to destroy it. Here we see the PLO celebrating its tenth anniversary. Poster being carried shows Yasser Arafat, head of the PLO.
Lapousterle/Gamma-Liaison

The Palestinian Issue

A major stumbling block to peace settlements in the Middle East and an issue interwoven with feelings of Arab nationalism has been the question of establishment of a separate Palestinian Arab state on the West Bank of the Jordan River and the Gaza Strip, two territories regained by Israel in its defensive War of 1967.

This issue had its origins in the refusal of the Arab states to accept the U.N. Partition Resolution of November 29, 1947, which proposed the establishment of an Arab and a Jewish state in Palestine. The creation of the State of Israel on May 14, 1948 was followed within hours by the invasion of Israel by the military forces of Egypt, Jordan, Syria, Lebanon, and Iraq. The war resulted in a major reshuffling of the population. During and after the hostilities an estimated 600,000 Palestinian Arabs moved from Israel to Gaza, the West Bank, Jordan, Syria, and Lebanon. Many left during the early fighting to avoid harm, encouraged by overconfident Arab leaders that they would soon be able to return. Later, other Arabs fled because of rumors and stories of Jewish violence. Some said they were ousted by the Israelis. Whether the majority were compelled to leave or left of their own accord has been a matter of controversy.

At the same time, an estimated 750,000 Jews who had been living in the Middle East left the surrounding Arab states to go to Israel. The majority were forced to flee because of stepped-up Arab pressure, persecution, and acts of violence against them.

The uprooted Jews were integrated into Israeli society. The Arab refugees, however, were not absorbed or integrated into the societies of surrounding Arab countries. They were forced to live in refugee camps financed by the United Nations. Except for Jordan, no Arab nation granted them citizenship.

The Issue of Palestinian Refugees

With little opportunity or encouragement to resettle in Arab lands, most Palestinian Arab refugees continue to live under squalid conditions in villages and U.N.-established refugee camps in Lebanon, Syria, Iraq, the Gaza Strip, Jordan, and the West Bank (seized by Jordan in 1948; occupied by Israel since 1967). Several hundred thousand refugees (about twenty percent) have found permanent homes or have been resettled in Arab states, where they have been integrated into Arab society.

Most of the money to support the Palestinian refugees has come through the United Nations Relief and Works Agency (UNRWA), which receives contributions from governments. The United States has made the largest contribution for this purpose (approximately seventy percent). The Arab states have contributed relatively little (less than five percent). The USSR has contributed nothing.

ARAB REFUGEES

During the Arab-Israel wars many Arabs left Israel to go to surrounding Arab countries. At the same time most Jews in Middle East Arab states fled to Israel. This picture shows Arab refugees from Israel crossing a bridge over the Jordan River, to enter Jordan. Religious News Service

The refugee villages and camps have remained an obstacle to the solution of the Arab–Israel conflict. Most proposals for resettlement or compensation have been rejected or blocked by the Arab states. In addition, the Arab refugee villages and camps have become breeding grounds and bases for anti-Israeli hatred and terrorist activity.

The complex issue of Palestinian refugee repatriation or resettlement continues to be debated. Meanwhile, the Arab states have refused to assimilate the refugees and Israel has refused to reabsorb them. Many people believe that the refusal of the Arab states to absorb the Palestinian refugees is political. They say the Arabs want to keep the problem alive in order to stir up anti-Israeli feeling. They argue that the less populated Arab countries such as Saudi Arabia, Syria, and Iraq could easily accommodate thousands of Palestinians without endangering national stability.

One reason for Israeli refusal to permit the return of all Arab refugees (tens of thousands have already returned) is that the refugees are violently anti-Israel and would pose a serious threat to domestic security if allowed to return. Israelis also fear that refugee resettlement in Israel could lead to an Arab majority in the 21st century.

The Question of a Palestinian State

Arab states have been seeking the return of all the territory occupied by Israel since the 1967 war. They also insist on the creation of a Palestinian state on the West Bank and the Gaza Strip.

Israel has opposed the creation of an independent Palestinian state on the ground that it would be taken over by the PLO and endanger the very existence of Israel. The PLO National Covenant categorically calls for the destruction of Israel and the creation of a new Palestinian state in its territory. Under a peace plan agreed to by Israel and Egypt in September 1978, later reaffirmed by a peace treaty in March 1979, both nations pledged to work out the details of a "Framework for a Peace in the Middle East" that would enable the inhabitants of the West Bank and Gaza to obtain full autonomy and self-government at the end of five years. This was one of two major agreements negotiated at Camp David in the United States, with the active involvement of President Jimmy Carter of the United States. Although Egypt and Israel took steps to work out the details of the plan, the PLO denounced the agreements and continues to oppose the peace treaty signed six months later.

The Arab–Israel Dispute: Backgrounds

Since the birth of Israel in 1948, Israel and neighboring Arab states have fought four major wars. To fully appreciate the nature of this conflict one must have essential background knowledge, including an understanding of Zionism, of Arab attitudes toward Zionism, and of the British mandate in Palestine before World War II.

Zionist Backgrounds

Following the destruction of the second Jewish commonwealth by Rome in the 1st century B.C. and the Jews' exile from Palestine in the 1st century A.D. after several attempts to rebel against harsh Roman rule had been crushed, most of the Jewish people in Palestine scattered to many parts of the world. For two thousand years, during the Diaspora (state of dispersion), Jews kept alive as part of their religious beliefs the hope of one day reestablishing a Jewish state in the land of their forefathers. Throughout the period a number of Jews continued to live in Palestine.

Toward the end of the 19th century, the Zionist movement was organized to establish and support a Jewish national homeland in Palestine. The term "Zionist" comes from the word "Zion," a biblical name for one of the hills of ancient Jerusalem. Zionism combined the traditional religious yearnings of Jews with an effort to escape the hostility to and persecution of Jews (anti-Semitism) that was increasing in Europe during the last half of the 19th century, particularly (though not exclusively) in Russia, Rumania, and Poland.

Theodor Herzl, a Jewish journalist living in Austria, was the leading figure and founder of the modern Zionist movement. Herzl came to believe that the only solution to the problem of anti-Semitism was the exodus of Jews from their Diaspora and their ingathering in a sovereign state in Palestine. (The Hebrew name for the ancient homeland of Jews in Palestine is "Eretz Israel," or "Land of Israel.") Under Herzl's leadership Zionism became a political movement of worldwide importance. The first Zionist Congress, held in Switzerland in 1897, declared that the goal of Zionism was "to create for the Jewish people a home in Palestine secured by public law."

ZIONIST PIONEERS
The difficult physical conditions under which they had to live is suggested by this picture of early Zionist immigrants to Palestine eating in the fields outside their tent village. It was from Palestinian beginnings of this kind that the modern state of Israel was later to develop. Zionist Archives

Although they failed to secure a charter for a separate Jewish state in Palestine from Turkey (the Ottoman Empire), which ruled Palestine at that time, Zionists encouraged Jews to move to Palestine. Zionist "pioneers" began returning in small numbers in the last decades of the 19th century. The first settlers came mainly from Czarist Russia, where they were victims of organized attacks on Jews, called pogroms. Thereafter there was a small but increasing stream of Jewish immigrants to Palestine. By 1914, when World War I broke out in Europe, there were approximately 85,000 Jewish settlers in Palestine. Many lived in small agricultural settlements supported or assisted by contributions of Jewish philanthropists such as Sir Moses Montefiore and Baron Edmund Rothschild.

Balfour Declaration

In 1917, during World War I, the British foreign minister, Lord Balfour, addressed a letter to Lord Rothschild stating that he had been authorized by the British government to release a statement indicating that "His Majesty's

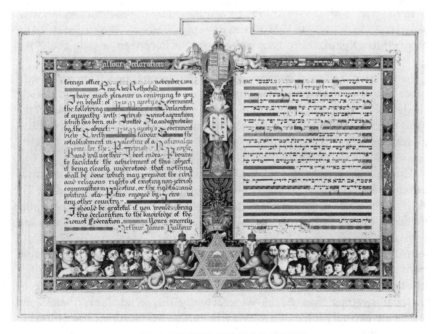

THE BALFOUR DECLARATION

Reproduced above is the famous Polish artist Arthur Szyk's illuminated drawing of the famous Balfour Declaration. The Declaration stated that the British government favored the establishment of a national homeland for the Jews in Palestine. Zionist Archives

Government view with favour the establishment in Palestine of a national home for the Jewish people, and will use their best endeavours to facilitate the achievement of this object." The declaration stated that nothing would be done "which may prejudice the civil and religious rights of existing non-Jewish communities in Palestine."

Dr. Chaim Weizmann, a leading British scientist and Zionist, helped negotiate the declaration. The British hoped that a statement in favor of Zionism would help obtain Jewish support for the Allied cause, particularly in the United States. They also felt that a Jewish population in Palestine sympathetic to Britain would enable the British to better protect the Suez Canal and the route to India.

Zionists everywhere were very encouraged by the Balfour Declaration.

Palestine under the British Mandate

The history of the British mandate in Palestine after World War I was affected by differing Zionist and Arab views about growing Jewish settlement.

In the period after World War I, encouraged by the Balfour Declaration, Jews began to migrate to Palestine in growing numbers. They were aided by the Zionist Organization. Nazi persecution of European Jews in the 1930s greatly stimulated this movement.

As a result, and also because Jews were often banned from settling in other countries because of stringent immigration quotas, from 1914 to 1939 the Jewish population in Palestine increased from 85,000 to 450,000. In the same period, the Arab population of Palestine also increased greatly to about a million. When World War II began in 1939, Jews made up over one-third of Palestine's total population.

The Jewish settlers established many agricultural colonies on lands purchased from the Arabs and built several modern cities, including Tel Aviv. They reclaimed deserts, drained swamps, introduced new farming methods, started industries, and raised living standards for both Arabs and Jews.

In 1929 there were serious disputes and riots over increased Jewish land purchases and questions of access to the holy places in Jerusalem. Since most of the land bought by the Zionists consisted of empty wastelands or malarial swamps, few Arabs were actually displaced. Nevertheless the Arabs increasingly felt that the Jews who settled in Palestine were a threat to their existence.

In the 1930s, when the Jewish population of Palestine increased sharply, largely as a result of the immigration of refugees from Hitler's Germany, the Arabs began to oppose further immigration vigorously and violently. Arab nationalist leaders received money, supplies, and other forms of help from

JEWS TRY TO ENTER ISRAEL DURING WORLD WAR II

During World War II Zionists worked hard to smuggle Jewish refugees from Nazi occupied Europe into Palestine, then a British mandate. Since this violated a British ban on such immigration, those caught were sent to Cyprus, where they were interned in detention camps, or back to Europe. Here we see British soldiers escorting an "illegal" from the ship Exodus, after it had been forced to take its passengers to Cyprus. Zionist Archives

neighboring Arab states (particularly Iraq and Syria). There was frequent incitement to acts of violence, including massacres of Jewish settlers and bloody riots in Jerusalem and rural areas. This opposition to the increased Jewish presence in Palestine reached a climax between 1937 and 1939 when the Arabs mounted a wholesale campaign of terror, often referred to as the Arab rebellion.

Upset over what it considered to be the failure of the British authorities to adequately protect Jewish interests, the Jewish Agency organized its own defense force, the *Haganah*, whose motto was "self-defense."[10] The Haganah repulsed Arab raids and built fortified settlements and outposts. In addition, as Arab terrorism increased, the *Irgun* was formed, a "dissident"

[10] The Jewish Agency was a Jewish representative body recognized by the British mandatory government as a kind of cabinet, managing agency, and spokesman for Jewish interests. The British also set up a Supreme Muslim Council to help manage Muslim affairs.

Jewish underground movement committed to illegal immigration and a policy of active response to Arab terror. The Irgun's primary object was to oust British rule from Palestine.

In the late 1930s, the British government tried to gain Arab support in anticipation of possible conflict with Nazi Germany. To appease Arab sentiments, it severely restricted Jewish immigration.

The Arabs in Palestine were opposed to the creation of a homeland for the Jews in what they considered to be *their* homeland. Encouraged by British policy, they bitterly resisted Zionism. They claimed that Palestine was rightfully theirs since they made up the large majority of the population. Some expressed fears that Palestine would someday become a Jewish state with the Arabs relegated to the position of minority, second-class citizens. They argued that they should not be penalized because of Nazi anti-Semitism in Europe. They pointed out that the Balfour Declaration also stated that "nothing shall be done which may prejudice the civil and religious rights of existing non-Jewish communities in Palestine." They demonstrated for the preservation of Palestine as an Arab homeland.

The Jews argued that they had continuously lived in Palestine even before the Arabs — from ancient times to modern times. They pointed out that Britain was obligated to fulfill its League of Nations mandate to facilitate Jewish statehood. They emphasized that as a result of Arab pressures four-fifths of Palestine had already been taken away from them and renamed Transjordan. Moreover, they insisted that Palestine was a necessary refuge from Nazi persecution.

The British government was caught in a dilemma of conflicting nationalisms. Its primary aim was to protect its own interests, and in this connection it often took the Arab side. In the period between World Wars I and II it often changed policies — to the dissatisfaction and anger of Jews, Arabs, or both. The Balfour Declaration had promised to help establish a Jewish homeland in Palestine for the Jews at the same time that it promised to protect the rights of non-Jews. Its implementation by the British led to conflicting feelings of hope and frustration among both Arabs and Jews. The Jews were eager to make Palestine *theirs* and wanted continued immigration without restriction. The Arabs wanted to keep Palestine *theirs* and demanded that immigration stop completely. The Arabs also called on Britain to abandon the idea of a Jewish national home and to terminate the mandate.

Jews and Arabs were hostile not only to each other but to the British mandatory administration as well. The Arabs rejected British recommendations for establishment of a Palestinian parliament within which the Jews would have a guaranteed minority status. In 1937, a royal commission (the Peel Commission) recommended partition of the mandate into a Jewish and an Arab state — a plan that the Jews reluctantly accepted, but that the Arabs rejected.

ISRAEL IS BORN

In May 1948 the State of Israel came into being as a result of the U.N. decision to divide Palestine into two independent countries. The headlines above marked this occasion, as well as two other important events with which it was linked. Can you identify them? Anti-Defamation League Bulletin

After the Nazis invaded Czechoslovakia in March 1939, Britain decided that in case of war it would need the oil and access routes of the region. It tried to regain Arab support by issuing a "White Paper" (policy statement) that reversed its previous intention to partition Palestine and create a Jewish state. The White Paper limited Jewish immigration into Palestine to 15,000 people a year for the next five years, and provided for freezing the ratio of population in its Palestine mandate at one Jew to three Arabs. It also limited Jewish land purchases. The plan was rejected by both sides. The Jews were particularly incensed that the doors of Palestine were closed to them at the time of Nazi genocide (mass murder) of the European Jewish population. Immediately before and after World War II, they actively worked to bring Jewish refugees to Palestine despite the British ban on such entry.

Opposed as they were to British policies in Palestine under the mandate, and particularly to the White Paper of 1939, the Jews in Palestine were firmly pro-Allies during the war. They felt that whatever their differences with Britain, defeat of Nazi Germany was the number one consideration. An estimated 50,000 Jewish Palestinians volunteered to fight with the Allied forces. In 1944 the Jews were permitted to establish their own Jewish Brigade.[11]

Israel Becomes an Independent State

In 1947 Britain indicated it intended to give up its Palestine mandate. The U.N. General Assembly voted by more than a two-thirds majority — and over Arab opposition — to divide Palestine into two independent countries. On the day that the British withdrew, May 14, 1948, the Jewish National Council proclaimed the State of Israel. Within hours of this declaration of independence, Israel was attacked by the combined armies of Egypt, Jordan, Syria, Lebanon, and Iraq.

The Arab–Israel Wars

Since 1948 a state of war has existed between Israel and most Arab nations in the Middle East. The existence of Israel has been a unifying cause and bond among Arab nations. Nearly every Arab state has spent money, lives, or both in the continuing struggle against Israel.

Roots of the Conflict

There are a number of important "roots" or causes for the fighting between Israel and its Arab neighbors. At the heart of the conflict is the issue of Israel's existence.

The Arabs consider the establishment of the State of Israel an infringement on the rights of the Arab population living in the region. They feel that the creation of a Jewish state dispossessed them of their land and created the refugee problem. They have therefore insisted on the liquidation of the "Zionist entity."

The Israelis feel that the establishment of their state is the fulfillment of their historical rights to their ancient homeland. They point out that Jews have lived in the region since ancient times and that even after the Romans destroyed the Jewish commonwealth 2,000 years ago there remained a continuous Jewish presence in Palestine until the birth of the modern state of Israel in 1948. They are resolved to maintain Israel as a national Jewish

---

[11] Despite their firm support of the Allied cause, Palestinian Jews were most unhappy with British attempts during the war to prevent the illegal immigration into Palestine of Jewish refugees from Nazi-occupied countries in Europe. Those caught by the British were sent to Cyprus or back to Europe (to almost certain death). Palestinian and American Zionists pleaded and argued in vain that the gates of Palestine should be opened to Jewish immigration.

ARAB OPPOSITION TO CREATION OF THE STATE OF ISRAEL

Arab militants show their disapproval of the U.N. decision to divide Palestine into an Arab and a Jewish state. This picture was taken at a meeting sponsored by the Congress of the Arab people in Cairo in December 1947, several months before the British withdrew from Palestine and the State of Israel was declared. Keystone

state, entitled to self-rule, security, and recognition by other nations.

Contributing to Arab opposition to Israel are a number of important factors, including the following:

(1) To extreme elements, the Islamic conception of Jews (as well as other minorities) is that they are a religious minority with no right of national independence. (On the other hand, Islamic tradition recognizes Jews and Christians as "people of the book" with limited rights. Under the *millet* system, in contrast to the modern territorial state, all religious groups were governed by their own laws.)

(2) The Arabs have been anxious to reverse centuries of decline in political prestige that culminated in modern times in humiliating political and cultural domination by the West. The fight with Israel is viewed as part of an Arab confrontation with the West and as a symbol of their determination to assert themselves in the modern world. Israel is seen as a symbol of the Western "imperialistic" attack on the Arab world. Radical leftist Arab regimes call Israel a tool of Western imperialism. The defeat and elimination of Israel is considered part of the Arabs' march toward fulfillment of their national destiny.

(3) Various Arab leaders often emphasize their militant posture toward Israel as a way of consolidating their power within their countries and within the Arab world.

(4) Although the United States and the Soviet Union fear the outbreak of war in the region, Soviet–American rivalry in the Middle East intensifies Arab belligerence toward Israel. In pursuit of predominance in the Middle East, the Soviet Union has gone to great lengths to offer Arab nations

extensive military and economic support. The Russians have sold arms to the Arabs, have supported them in the United Nations, and have helped train Arab armies. The United States, though championing the independence of Israel, has sold weapons to both sides in an effort to be "evenhanded." It wishes to retain Arab friendship and support particularly because of its increasing dependence on Arab oil.

Conflict between Israel and Arab States

There have been four Arab–Israeli wars since Israel became an independent nation.

1. THE WAR FOR INDEPENDENCE (1948–1949). The first Arab–Israeli war grew out of the U.N. decision to partition Palestine into an Arab and a Jewish state.

When Israel came into existence in 1948, she was attacked by the combined armies of Jordan, Egypt, Syria, Lebanon, and Iraq. Although greatly outnumbered, Israel drove back the invading Arab forces and seized additional territory. Egypt suffered major military reverses in the Negev. In January 1949, U.N. mediator Ralph Bunche (an American) arranged a cease-fire.

When the fighting stopped, Israel had increased its original territory by fifty percent, including the Western Galilee and part of central Palestine. Jordan occupied most of the territory originally designated by the U.N. partition plan as an Arab state (the West Bank), together with the Old City of Jerusalem. It ousted the Jewish population of the Old City. (Only Britain and Pakistan recognized the Jordanian seizure of the West Bank of Palestine and the Old City of Jerusalem.) Egypt occupied Gaza.

During and after the war, several hundred thousand Arabs left the areas controlled by Israel. From 1949 to 1953 an approximately equal number of Jews left the Arab countries for Israel, where they and their descendants eventually became a majority of Israel's Jewish population.

2. THE SUEZ WAR (1956). In late December 1956, Israel attacked Egypt's Sinai Peninsula in an effort to halt Arab terrorist (fedayeen) raids on Israeli territory. Israeli forces drove through the Gaza Strip and moved quickly to the east bank of the Suez Canal. Israel was also anxious to end the barring of Israeli shipping from the Suez Canal and the Gulf of Aqaba, its sea-lane to Africa and Asia. At the same time, in coordination with Israeli action, Britain and France attacked Egypt in order to regain control of the Suez Canal, seized (nationalized) by Egypt's President Nasser earlier the same year.

Intense pressure from the USSR and the United States quickly ended

THE ARAB-ISRAEL WARS
1920–1979

From The New York Times
March 27, 1979

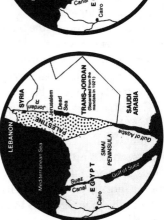

1920–48 | The British administered Palestine under a mandate from the League of Nations. In the Balfour Declaration of 1917, they promised to use "their best endeavors to facilitate" the "establishment in Palestine of a national home for the Jewish people."

1947 | The United Nations Special Committee on Palestine recommended partition into two states: one Jewish [white on the map], one Arab [cross-hatched on the map]. Jerusalem was to be an internationally administered enclave in the Arab state.

1949 | On May 14, 1948, the British relinquished their mandate. Jewish leaders immediately created the state of Israel. A day later, Egyptian and other Arab forces invaded. At the final cease-fire, Jan. 7, 1949, Israel held territory as shown above.

1956 | After the nationalization of the Suez Canal by Egypt, Israel agreed with France and Britain to an invasion. The territory taken by Israel from Oct. 29 to Nov. 6 [diagonal lines on the map] was relinquished completely by March 1957.

1967 | In the six-day war, June 5–10, Israel reached the Suez Canal and took the Sinai Peninsula from Egypt, reached the Jordan River and took the West Bank and the Arab quarter of Jerusalem from Jordan and the Golan Heights from Syria [diagonal lines].

1975 | Disengagement pacts followed the three-week war of October 1973. The first was in January 1974 along the Suez Canal, the second in May 1974 on the Golan Heights, the third in September 1975 in Sinai. U.N. zones were established in these areas.

After Sinai Withdrawal | By the terms of the treaty signed in 1979, Israel will, in steps, pull out of Sinai completely by April 1982.

hostilities in early November. A U.N. peacekeeping force was sent into the Gaza Strip and the southern tip of the Sinai Peninsula.

Under the cease-fire agreement, Egypt maintained control of the canal and Israeli, British, and French forces were withdrawn. Israel received assurances of the right to free passage through the Gulf of Aqaba (from its port of Eilat at the head of the Gulf). In agreeing to withdraw, Israel warned that removal of U.N. troops from Sharm-el-Sheikh, commanding the Straits of Tiran at the entrance to the Gulf, would constitute an act of war.

3. THE SIX DAY WAR (1967). In 1967 the United Nations withdrew its peacekeeping force from the Sinai at Egyptian President Nasser's request, despite Israeli protests. Egypt also announced it was closing the Gulf of Aqaba to Israeli shipping by banning Israeli traffic through the Straits of Tiran. Israel declared the blockade of its "back door" an act of war. Fearful that if allowed to strike first the Arabs might inflict great damage with their Russian-supplied arms, Israeli forces simultaneously attacked Egyptian, Syrian, and Jordanian bases.

In hostilities that lasted six days. Israel defeated the combined armies of Egypt, Syria, and Jordan. Israeli forces broke the Egyptian blockage by capturing Egypt's base at Sharm-el-Sheikh. They also crippled Egypt's air and ground forces. Israeli forces took the Gaza Strip and occupied the Sinai Peninsula. They also occupied the Old City of Jerusalem and the West Bank. In addition, they captured the Golan Heights on Israel's northeast frontier, from which point Syrian forces had been able to shell Israeli settlements in the valley below. The fighting came to a halt on June 10, when all parties accepted a cease-fire arranged by the United Nations and strongly supported by both the United States and the Soviet Union.

As a result of the war of 1967, Israel more than doubled the territory under its control. It occupied the Golan Heights, the West Bank of the Jordan River, all of the Sinai, and the east bank of the Suez Canal. The Old City of Jerusalem was annexed. This reuniting of Jerusalem into one city made the holy places accessible to members of all religions. (From 1948 to 1967 Jews had been denied access to the Western Wall — a site most holy to the Jews — and their synagogues and cemeteries in the Old City had been desecrated.) Israel announced it would remain in the occupied territories until decisive progress was made toward a permanent peace settlement.

On November 22, 1967 the U.N. Security Council, in an effort to bring peace to the Middle East, approved a resolution (Security Council Resolution 242) calling for withdrawal of Israeli forces from occupied territories in exchange for secure and recognized boundaries. The resolution also called for an end to the state of belligerency between Arab nations and Israel; guarantees of the sovereignty, territorial integrity, and political independence of every nation in the area; a just settlement of the refugee

RETAKING THE OLD CITY OF JERUSALEM

During the Six-Day War between Israel and the Arabs, Israel defeated the combined armies of Egypt, Syria, and Jordan and occupied the Gaza Strip, the Sinai Peninsula, and the West Bank. The Israelis also took control of the Old City of Jerusalem, which had been occupied by Jordan since the Arab-Israeli War of 1948-49. Shown above are Israeli soldiers raising their flag at the Western Wall in celebration of the re-occupation of the Old City. Israel Consulate

problem (Arab and Jewish); and a guarantee of freedom of navigation through international waterways in the area. This resolution became the basis for later peace efforts.

4. THE ARAB–ISRAEL WAR OF 1973.[12] After the Six Day War tensions remained high. The years 1967 to 1973 saw an endless cycle of attacks on Israel by Arab terrorists, followed by Israeli retaliatory attacks.

The Suez Canal remained closed to navigation as Israeli and Egyptian forces faced each other across its banks. Russia broke off diplomatic relations with Israel and accelerated its arms shipments to Egypt, Syria, and other Arab states. Although, like the United States, the Soviet Union recognized that renewed hostilities could lead to a superpower confron-

---

[12] The Arab–Israel War of 1973 has different names, including the October War, the Yom Kippur War, and the War of Ramadan. Israelis and Jews elsewhere refer to it as the Yom Kippur War because it started on the Jewish Day of Atonement. Arabs call it the War of Ramadan because it took place during Ramadan, their month of daytime fasting. The October War and the War of 1973 are considered neutral terms.

tation, it continued to encourage the Arabs. The United States stepped up military aid to Israel in order to redress the arms balance and fill the vacuum created when in 1967 the French government stopped selling arms to the Jewish state. (In the 1950s and 1960s France had become Israel's chief arms supplier.)

Open fighting, referred to as "the War of Attrition," was renewed in 1969 and 1970 after Egypt repudiated the cease-fire agreement that had ended the Six Day War. In the course of the War of Attrition there were almost daily Egyptian–Israeli artillery duels across the Suez Canal. There were also ground forays (sudden raids) and air raids, with Israeli planes penetrating deep into Egyptian territory. Palestinian terrorist raids into Israel across Syrian and Jordanian borders also occurred, and there were frequent encounters between Israeli and Syrian and Jordanian forces.

In August 1970 Egypt and Israel accepted a cease-fire agreement proposed by the United States and supported by the USSR. This agreement was immediately violated when Egypt, with Russian assistance, moved antiaircraft missiles into an agreed-upon neutral buffer zone.

After six years of mounting tension, full-scale war broke out again on October 6, 1973, when Egyptian and Syrian troops in a coordinated surprise attack crossed into Israeli-occupied territory in the Sinai Peninsula and the Golan Heights. The attack took place on the Day of Atonement (Yom Kippur), the holiest day in the Jewish calendar, in order to catch Israel off-guard and unprepared.

The Arabs were better organized and supplied than in earlier encounters. They made successful first strikes into Israeli-occupied and -defended territory on the east bank of the Suez Canal and on the Golan Heights (where the Syrians hoped to regain control of territory overlooking Israeli settlements in the valley below). The Israelis were able to counter these early Arab successes. They rallied and seized the initiative on both fronts by breaking through the Egyptian lines to the west bank of the Suez Canal and advancing to within twenty miles of the Syrian capital of Damascus.

Egypt and Syria were supplied by massive airlifts of Soviet military supplies. The United States responded with an airlift to Israel.

In late October 1973, the U.N. Security Council passed a resolution (338) calling for a cease-fire and commencement of peace negotiations. The resolution was strongly supported by the United States and the Soviet Union. Early in November 1973, Israel and Egypt signed a cease-fire agreement worked out by U.S. Secretary of State Henry A. Kissinger.

In December of that year representatives of Israel, Egypt, Jordan, the United States, the Soviet Union, and the United Nations met at a brief peace conference in Geneva and agreed on the need for peace negotiations. Following these discussions, and largely as a result of the continued efforts of Secretary Kissinger, Egypt and Israel agreed in January 1974 to disengage their forces along the Suez Canal as a first step toward permanent peace negotiations.

Disengagement Agreements

Under terms of the 1974 disengagement pact (Sinai I):

(1) Israel agreed to withdraw its troops from the west bank of the canal and to pull back from the eastern side;

(2) Egypt agreed to greatly reduce its forces in the area;

(3) a neutral "buffer zone" was established between Egyptian and Israeli forces, supervised by a U.N. Emergency Force; and

(4) the Suez Canal was to be reopened by Egypt to international trade.

In September 1975, largely as a result of American pressure on Israel, Egypt and Israel signed a second disengagement agreement (Sinai II), under which:

(1) each side agreed to continue the cease-fire for three years;

(2) an expanded buffer zone manned by U.N. troops was established;

(3) Israel yielded strategic Sinai mountain passes and two of the oil fields captured during the Six Day War of 1967; and

(4) 200 American radar technicians were to be stationed in the Sinai in the strategic Giddi and Mitla passes to monitor the disengagement.

In May 1974 Syria and Israel signed a disengagement agreement under which Israel withdrew from parts of the Golan Heights.

Results of the 1973 War

The Arab–Israel war of 1973 had a number of significant results that went beyond the terms of the disengagement agreements:

(1) The widely held belief that the Israelis could easily defeat the Arabs in any major military confrontation was shattered. The success of the initial Egyptian and Syrian strikes and the large number of Israeli casualties showed that the Arabs were closing the technological gap that had previously protected the greatly outnumbered Israelis.

(2) Although the Arabs were almost decisively defeated once again, their initial military successes in the October War of 1973 erased the sense of shame and humiliation that had followed the Six Day War of 1967. The war demonstrated that Arabs could act together to achieve military surprise and successes. They felt that their political honor had been restored.

(3) Perhaps the most important factor contributing to renewed Arab self-confidence was the realization that Arab oil could be used effectively as a political and economic weapon. The Arab oil embargo hurt the indus-

trialized West, devastated the economies of developing Third World nations, and increased the already vast wealth of Arab oil-producing nations. The use of oil as a weapon improved the ability of some Arab states to apply political and economic pressure against Western and other industrialized nations. They hoped that these nations in turn would bring pressure on Israel to be more receptive to Arab demands.

(4) Effective use of Arab oil wealth by Arab nations has in large part contributed to the growing political and economic isolation of Israel since the war of 1973. Many industrial nations such as Japan whose economic lifeblood depended on imported oil and its petrochemical derivatives, and who were formerly friendly to Israel or "nonaligned" in the conflict between Israel and the Arabs, have "tilted" toward the Arabs.

Israel also lost the support of many black African nations with which it had established friendly relations in the 1960s and early 1970s through its technical assistance programs. In the face of promises of greater economic and military aid from oil-rich Arab countries, African nations like Tanzania, Malagasy Republic, Ethiopia, Ruwanda, Cameroon, Upper Volta, and others broke off diplomatic or trade relations with Israel. Although these countries have been disillusioned by the Arab failure to keep their promises, they continue (publicly at least) to support the Arab cause.

Recent Events

Since the end of the 1973 war, the shaky truce that prevails has continued to be broken from time to time by actions of Palestinian guerrillas and reprisals by the Israelis. In June 1974 terrorist assaults on Israeli border settlements triggered three days of air bombing and rocket attacks on Palestinian encampments in Lebanon. In July 1975 Israeli forces retaliated for a series of Arab terrorist attacks, which took the lives of more than twenty Israelis and injured more than seventy, by combined sea and air assaults on Arab guerrilla bases in southern Lebanon. In November 1977 Palestinian rocket attacks that killed three Israelis resulted in the leveling of two farm villages in southern Lebanon and the death of over 100 persons.

The most dramatic Israeli reprisal was set off in March 1978 by a Palestinian terrorist attack on Herzlia, near Tel Aviv, that left thirty-four Israelis, one American, and thirteen terrorists dead. Thousands of Israeli soldiers, supported by tanks and artillery, swept across the border into Lebanon and penetrated deep into southern Lebanon to attack guerrilla bases and concentrations. Israeli jet planes bombed suspected Palestinian staging areas for commando raids into Israel. Israeli forces did not withdraw from Lebanon for several weeks, until a U.N. peacekeeping force had been established in southern Lebanon to supervise the withdrawal and keep Palestinian guerrillas from returning.

TERRORIST DAMAGE: ISRAELI KIBBUTZ

Since the end of the Arab-Israeli War of 1973, Palestinian guerrillas have launched many terrorist attacks on Israeli settlements. These have been followed by Israeli reprisals. This house on an Israeli kibbutz was damaged by a Soviet missile used by Arab terrorists in one of their attacks. Israel Consulate

In April 1980, five members of the Arab Liberation Front, an Iraqi-supported PLO group, attacked the children's dormitory on an Israeli kibbutz near the Lebanese border and took children hostage. Israeli troops retook the building, killing all five terrorists. Two days later Israeli troops entered southern Lebanon and remained there five days as a precaution against further terrorist activity.

A new crisis developed in spring 1981 when Syrian armed forces attacked the Lebanese Christian militia in the town of Zahle, causing much loss of life. To aid the Christians, Israel shot down two Syrian helicopter gunships. In retaliation, Syria brought Soviet SAM missiles into the Beka valley inside Lebanon. Israel threatened to blow up the missiles if they were not removed.

In June, a lightning and amazingly accurate air strike by Israeli jets destroyed the nuclear reactor that Iraq was building near Baghdad. Prime Minister Begin said the raid was an act of self-defense to prevent Iraq from producing atom bombs that would endanger Israel's existence. Israeli officials also pointed out that more than a year before the Israeli raid Carter administration officials had expressed concern about Iraq's nuclear ambitions to France and Italy, the two countries that were building the equipment and providing the technology, training, and nuclear substances to Iraq in order to ensure long-term access to Iraqi oil.

Many nuclear scientists agreed that the Iraqi reactor, when completed, would be fully capable of producing fuel for the manufacture of atomic weapons, but they differed in their estimates of when Iraq would be able to do so.

The United States voted for a U.N. Security Council resolution condemning Israel for the raid, after making clear that the U.S. would veto if the resolution included a call for sanctions against Israel. However, President Reagan conceded at a press conference that Israel might have sincerely believed that destroying the reactor was a defensive move.

Israel was also criticized when it bombed the PLO's headquarters in Beirut, the capital of Lebanon, in the summer of 1981, in retaliation for terrorist attacks on Israel's northern border settlements. There were conflicting reports on the number of casualties; many civilians were killed, along with PLO terrorists. Israeli spokesmen alleged that the PLO had deliberately placed its headquarters in a residential neighborhood.

ARABS IN IRAQ DENOUNCE PRESIDENT SADAT FOR SIGNING A PEACE TREATY WITH ISRAEL
The day after the signing of the Israel-Egypt Peace Treaty and while Arab Foreign Ministers were meeting in Baghdad, thousands of Iraqis demonstrated in a huge rally during which they hung an effigy of Egyptian President Sadat. Francolon/Gamma-Liaison

Other Conflicts Within the Region

Even without the Arab–Israeli conflict of the last thirty years, the Middle East would have been a conflict-ridden and conflict-producing region. Much of this instability has resulted from inter-Arab animosities and rivalries. There have also been other regional conflicts that have kept the pot boiling and made Middle East history tense, complicated, and turbulent.

Inter-Arab Conflicts

Despite ties of language, culture, religion, and a common desire for economic development and social progress, the Arab world is deeply divided. There are divisions between "leftists and rightists," between "haves and have-nots," between "traditionalists and modernists," and between "moderates and extremists." There are disagreements between Arab nations that have "leaned" toward the West and those that have "leaned" toward the East. In addition, the Arab world has been torn by struggles for leadership in the name of unity, as well as by the determination of many Arab nations to make their own decisions in inter-Arab quarrels and conflicts. Arab nations have also disagreed over boundaries and have supported efforts to overthrow the regimes of other Arab nations.

Even the PLO, which is considered to hold an important key to Arab–Israeli peace, is divided into major groups that contest for power among Palestinians. Largest and most important is *Al Fatah*, headed by Yasser Arafat, PLO chairman. Another important group within the PLO is the *Popular Front for the Liberation of Palestine*, led by Dr. George Habash, a Christian physician and Marxist. Although the PLO is united in its opposition to the continued existence of Israel, there is division regarding tactics. Palestinian "moderates," although involved in some acts of terrorism, do not exclude diplomacy in pursuing their objectives, whereas Palestinian "radicals" rely primarily on terror attacks, hijackings, and world revolution.

The following chronological list of some of the more important events in the Arab world illustrates the tension and disunity that have prevailed since the 1950s:

1955—Egypt, Syria, and Saudi Arabia join in a defense pact against Iraq and Jordan after Iraq signs a Western-sponsored defense pact, the Baghdad Pact.

1958—Lebanon experiences a civil war between Christians and Muslims. This conflict, which does not end until U.S. troops intervene, is triggered by encouragement given to a Muslim coup after the federation of Egypt and Syria into the United Arab Republic.

—In the same year, an army coup and massacre of Iraq's royal family leads to a feud with King Hussein of Jordan (a cousin of the assassinated King Feisal of Iraq) that lasts until the Arab–Israeli war of 1967.

—Iraq claims all of Kuwait, igniting a feud marked by border clashes until 1976.

1961—Syria leaves the United Arab Republic, angry over domination of the union by Egypt.

—Iraq unsuccessfully tries to annex Kuwait.

1962—A military coup in Yemen leads to civil war. Saudi Arabia breaks diplomatic relations with Cairo when Egyptian troops are sent to Yemen to back the new leftist republic.

1963—The Baath Party takes power in Iraq and Syria and the two countries join in a military union. After eight months, a new Iraqi government ends the merger.

1968—The Baathists return to power in Iraq and begin a bitter feud with Baathists in Syria. The rivalry still continues.

1969—Saudi Arabia and Marxist (leftist) South Yemen support opposing sides in a rebellion in Oman. Border clashes occur.

1970—Syrian troops invade Jordan (and then pull back) when King Hussein crushes Palestinian commandos who threatened his regime. Syria and Egypt break with Hussein.

1973—Iraqi troops cross Kuwait borders but soon withdraw under pressure from other Arab states.

1975—Egypt's signing of a second Sinai Disengagement Pact with Israel after the Yom Kippur War of 1973 angers Syria and Jordan and infuriates Palestinians.

—A second civil war breaks out in Lebanon. The fighting is temporarily brought under control by the intervention of Syrian troops in 1976, after nineteen months of turmoil in which 60,000 lives are lost and much physical damage occurs, particularly in Beirut, the capital.

1976—Tunisian, Sudanese, and Egyptian leaders charge Colonel Muammar Qaddafi of Libya with trying to overthrow their regimes. Sudan breaks relations with Libya and forms an alliance with Egyptian President Sadat. In 1977, the feud between Egypt and Libya leads to a brief but fierce border war.

1977—Egyptian President Sadat's historic visit to Jerusalem at the end of 1977, in an effort to reach a settlement with Israel, leads to severe denunciation by leaders of the radical Arab "rejectionist front" (particularly Iraq, Syria, Libya, Algeria, and South Yemen) who oppose any step toward peace until the Jewish state is eliminated.

1978—Renewed fighting breaks out in Lebanon as Syrian forces join Muslims and leftists in attacks on Lebanese Christians.

—Radical Iraq becomes involved in an increasingly tense fight with the PLO marked by assassination of PLO leaders in England, France, Italy,

IRANIAN SUPPORT FOR THE PLO

Under the Shah, Iran was one of the few Middle East states to recognize Israel. After the revolution in Iran brought Ayatollah Khomeini to power in 1979, he broke relations with Israel. Shortly thereafter Yasser Arafat, head of the PLO, visited Iran to cement relationships. Here Arafat kisses Khomeini during ceremonies marking the formal opening of PLO offices in the former Israeli Consulate building in Teheran. Wide World

and Pakistan and the closing of PLO facilities in Iraq.

—Camp David agreements, providing a possible basis for peace between Egypt and Israel and self-determination for West Bank and Gaza Strip Palestinians, are bitterly denounced by most Arab leaders. Sadat is accused of selling out the Arab world by negotiating unilaterally with Israel.

1979—Egypt's signing of a peace treaty with Israel in March 1979 leads to continuing isolation and denunciation by most Arab states.

1980—War between Iraq and non-Arab Iran splits the Arab world. Jordan supports Iraq; Syria and Libya back Iran.

—Syria and its allies in the anti-Israel Steadfastness Front — South Yemen, Algeria, Libya, and the PLO — as well as Lebanon refuse to attend the annual summit meeting of the Arab League in Amman, Jordan, arguing that the meeting would intensify inter-Arab quarrels.

—Syria begins massing troops at its border with Jordan in an attempt to divert world attention from the Amman conference and almost provokes major hostilities between the two countries.

—Iraq breaks diplomatic relations with Syria and Libya, charging that their soldiers were fighting alongside Iranian troops against Iraq.

1981—Civil strife continues in Lebanon. Syrian armed forces emplace Soviet missiles inside Lebanon in order to prevent Christian units in the north from linking up with Major Haddad's Christian forces in southern Lebanon.

—The war between Iraq and Iran continues sporadically, but without a decisive victory for either country.

—Libya invades and annexes Chad, prompting fears in adjacent African nations, especially Sudan and Tunisia, that Libyan dictator Qaddafi will next threaten them in his desire to create an African Islamic federation under his leadership.

Civil War in Lebanon

Until the mid-1970s Lebanon was considered one of the most stable and advanced countries in the Middle East. For many years political power was divided between Christians and Muslims under an arrangement that went back to the early 1930s, when their numbers were approximately equal. Thus, the presidency was reserved for a Christian, whereas the premiership went to a follower of Islam.

Muslim dissatisfaction with this power-sharing arrangement grew as the Muslim population increased more rapidly than the Christian (estimated at approximately fifty-five percent of Lebanon's population by the 1970s). As indicated earlier, no official census has been taken recently, in order to preserve the delicate balance between Christians and Muslims. Bloody civil war erupted between the two sects in 1975. Palestinian Arab refugees in Lebanon were in large measure responsible for the hostilities. By 1976, escalating violence and a very complex political situation left the country with large numbers of casualties, without effective government, and with large-scale destruction in Beirut, the nation's cosmopolitan capital and former financial center of the Middle East.

To restore order and prevent PLO-led Palestinians and leftists from seizing control of the government, in April 1976 Syrian forces entered Lebanon and occupied large portions of the country. They opened a general offensive against the Palestinians to end their attacks on government forces.[13] After several months of continued fighting, a cease-fire was

---

[13] Although Syria originally entered the conflict to restrain the PLO, its forces later joined with the Palestinians in attacks on Christians.

CIVIL WAR IN LEBANON

Bloody civil war in Lebanon between Christians and Muslims erupted in 1975. PLO-led leftist Muslims were largely responsible for the hostilities. Much of Beirut, the country's capital, was destroyed in the fighting. Taken in 1976, this photo dramatically shows the tragedy of civil strife. Demulder/Gamma-Liaison

arranged by Arab leaders of outside nations and a 30,000-man Arab "deterrent force," largely Syrian, was established. Although large-scale hostilities ceased, sporadic clashes between Christians and Palestinians continued to occur throughout 1977 and early 1978, particularly in southern Lebanon.

In 1977 the Israelis made it known that they would not permit the presence of Syrian forces near their border with Lebanon; nor would they continue to permit Lebanon to be used as a staging area for Palestinian terrorist attacks on Israel. In addition, both for humanitarian reasons and because of their desire to have an ally just beyond their northern border, Israel came to the support of Lebanese Christian militiamen in southern Lebanon who had been cut off from northern supply routes by the civil war and were under attack by Palestinian guerrillas and Muslim leftists. Under what they called the "good fence" policy, Israel provided medical supplies, training, and equipment to the Lebanese Christian forces, supplied Christians in southern Lebanon with food and water, and permitted them to cross the border to work in northern Israeli communities.

In March 1978 Israeli forces invaded southern Lebanon in strength, attacked Palestinian strongholds, and occupied portions of southern Lebanon, in retaliation for a Palestinian terrorist attack on an Israeli bus in which 48 persons, including 13 attackers, were killed and over 80 persons were injured. Israeli forces were withdrawn in June 1978, after a 10-nation United Nations interim force had been established to police the border between Lebanon and Israel. In withdrawing, the Israelis turned over more strongholds to Lebanese Christian militia forces than to the U.N. force on the ground that the U.N. force allowed PLO guerrillas to infiltrate the region.

In July 1978, Israel accused Syrian forces in Lebanon of systematically attacking and massacring Lebanese Christians in Beirut and elsewhere and warned that it would not permit their annihilation. Syrian attacks ceased in November 1978, at the request of the United Nations.

Since 1978 a shaky truce at best has prevailed, with perodic outbreaks of fighting between contending factions. By 1981 the Lebanese government had been unable to establish an effective military force to replace the feuding militias.

The United States and other countries, including most Arab states, feared that the Lebanese crisis, if prolonged, could result in either a Syrian takeover of Lebanon, a Syrian–Israeli armed confrontation, or both. Such a development would seriously affect peace negotiations between Egypt and Israel and precipitate new crises in the Middle East.

In 1981, alleging that Israel was preparing to march into Damascus, Syria mounted a siege against the Lebanese town of Zahle to drive a wedge between Christian units in northern and southern Lebanon. President Reagan's special emissary, Philip Habib, went to the Middle East to defuse the crisis, but the Syrians refused to remove the Soviet missiles they had brought into Lebanon. Ambassador Habib tried to involve other Arab states in an effort to bring an end to the civil war in Lebanon by disengaging the Syrian forces from Lebanon and strengthening the authority of the central Lebanese government.

Arab–Iranian Disputes

Iran stands at the eastern flank of the Middle East. It is a non-Arab Muslim nation. Iran has had ongoing disputes with its Arab neighbors.

For a number of years Iraq and Iran were involved in border disputes and clashes resulting from Iraq's claim to navigation rights in the Shatt-al-Arab, a river formed by the coming together of the Tigris and Euphrates rivers in southeastern Iraq and flowing southeast to the Persian Gulf, forming part of the Iran–Iraq border. In 1975 a pact was signed under which Iraq abandoned its claim in return for Iran's ending its support for a Kurdish rebellion in

Iraq. The boundary between the two countries was set in the middle of the disputed waterway. After the fall of the Shah, Iraq declared the agreement of 1975 null and void and reasserted its claim to the Shatt-al-Arab and other disputed border territories. In September 1980 full-scale warfare between the two countries broke out as over 19,000 Iraqi troops moved into Iran. Iraqi jets bombed important Iranian oil installations at Abadan and other oil centers. Iranian planes struck Baghdad and Iraqi oil fields. Throughout 1981, U.N. and other appeals for a cease-fire had not been successful.

Shah Mohammed Reza Pahlevi's attempts in the 1970s to make Iran the predominant power in the Persian Gulf area, in order to assure unrestricted passage of its oil into world traffic lanes, led to tension not only with Iraq but also with Saudi Arabia and other Arab states in the region who feared Iran's military buildup. In 1971 Iran occupied three islands at the head of the Gulf, claimed by the states of the United Arab Emirates.

Expectations that the establishment of an Islamic republic by Ayatollah Khomeini would bring Iran closer to the Arab nations have not been realized. In fact the situation seemed to be worsening. As of early 1981, strained relations with neighboring Iraq had given way to open warfare. Over and above territorial considerations, Iraqi President Saddam Hussein was angered by Khomeini's appeals for Shiite militancy and accused the Iranian holy man of being more dangerous than the Shah. (Iraq is more than one-half Shiite but the Sunni branch holds all the country's political power.) In addition there were growing signs that Saudi Arabia and the small Persian Gulf states were becoming increasingly fearful that the mounting discontent inside Iran under the Ayatollah could lead to another change of government, including the possibility of a leftist takeover, a situation that would constitute a challenge to existing regimes and further contribute to Middle East instability.

Although Saudi forces made stern reprisals, Saudi leaders believed that the brief takeover in 1979 of the Great Mosque in Mecca by Islamic extremists was directly related to the upsurge of Islamic militancy following the revolution in Iran.

Dispute between Greece and Turkey

Continuing friction between Greece and Turkey over Cyprus has contributed to Middle East tensions in recent decades.

Since it was granted independence by Britain in 1960, Cyprus has been a strife-torn nation. The island is the homeland of about 500,000 ethnic Greeks and 115,000 ethnic Turks. Greek Cypriots have traditionally favored *enosis*, or union with Greece. Turkish Cypriots want partition of the island into separate states.

Friction between the Turkish minority and the Greek majority has been constant. From time to time each has turned to Turkey or Greece for support, causing ill will between the two powers, who see themselves as guarantors of rights of their respective ethnic "countrymen" in Cyprus. Intervention and mediation by other nations (including the United States and Britain) and the United Nations have not effected a peaceful solution for the ongoing disputes and crises.

In 1974 a major crisis developed after rightist Greek officers who supported *enosis* with Greece overthrew the existing regime in Cyprus. Asserting its right to protect the Turkish Cypriot minority, Turkey invaded Cyprus by sea and air and took control of forty percent of the island. Greece made no armed response to the superior Turkish forces, but protested bitterly to the United Nations and withdrew from military participation in the NATO alliance, in which Turkey, too, plays an important role. In 1980 Greece rejoined the military alliance after a six-year absence, thereby strengthening a significant soft spot in NATO's strategic southern flank at a time of growing Russian power and instability in the Middle East.

During 1981, negotiations for a unified government remained deadlocked. The Greek-dominated Cypriot governing regime has offered self-

CRISIS IN CYPRUS

In 1974 Turkish troops invaded Cyprus to support the Turkish Cypriot demand for division of the island into two separate states, which the Greek Cypriot government refused to grant. Despite the presence of a U.N. Peace-Keeping Force, the Turks took control of 40 percent of the island. In this picture taken soon after the invasion, soldiers of the U.N. force are escorting Turkish Cypriots from an area under fire from Greek Cypriot forces. United Nations

government to the Turkish minority but refuses to recognize the separate state that has been declared for the northern forty percent of the island. Meanwhile the more than 200,000 Greek Cypriots who fled during the Turkish invasion have demanded return to their homes in the Turkish zone; and most of the 45,000 ethnic Turks in the Greek zone have crossed into the Turkish area. In spite of strong pressure by the United States, Turkey's occupation of the northern part of the island continues.

Greece and Turkey are also in disagreement over the question of control of oil-exploration rights in the Aegean Sea.

Minorities

Another complicating factor that has contributed to Middle East instability in recent years is the existence of ethnic and religious minorities of varying sizes in every Middle East country. Within their borders, for example, Egypt has Copts, Greeks, and Palestinians; Iraq has Armenians, Assyrians, Chaldeans, Kurds, and Palestinians; Jordan has Palestinians; and Lebanon has Armenians, Druze, Greek Orthodox, Maronites, and Palestinians.[14]

Traditionally, minorities in the Middle East have for the most part been treated tolerantly by the ruling regimes and elites. Religious, linguistic, and ethnic groups were usually allowed to live in semiautonomous communities (millets) where they could practice their traditional customs and ways of life. There were, of course, numerous exceptions, such as savage large-scale massacres of the Armenians in Turkey in 1915.

The millet system collapsed with the disintegration of the Turkish Ottoman Empire after World War I. The new Arab nation-states that took its place were influenced by the nationalist concept that individuals should give *first* loyalty to the nation rather than to an ethnic group or religious sect. Accordingly, when minorities or groups in some Middle East countries have since called for greater self-determination of increased rights, they have been looked on with suspicion as a threat to the state, and attempts have been made to suppress them or to force them to assimilate into the "mainstream" of Arab life.

Some minorities, like the Kurds in Iraq and the Christians in Lebanon, have fiercely resisted such attempts. Years of struggling and civil war resulted in almost total defeat for the Kurdish minority in Iraq in 1975, when Iran withdrew support after patching up border differences with Iraq. In 1977 Iraq was accused of executing and deporting Kurds in order to

---

[14] As of 1980 in Iran, a non-Arabic Muslim state, a dozen or so minorities made up about 14 million or 40 percent of the country's estimated population of slightly over 35 million.

"Arabize" Kurdistan. Recently there have been separatist movements among Kurds and other groups in Iran.

The Soviet Union has tried to use the sectarian and ethnic nature of Middle East society to its own advantage by exploiting the dissatisfactions that exist among certain minorities. For example, after World War II it took advantage of the dissatisfactions of Kurds and Armenians in the province of Azerbaijan, in Iran, by encouraging secessionist movements; and in the early 1970s it gave help to the Kurds in their rebellion for greater autonomy against the government of Iraq.

Lebanon, long an outstanding example of tolerance of minorities, has become a nation divided and more recently torn apart by suspicion and mistrust. Lebanese Christians fear losing or being forced to relinquish political power after decades of sharing authority with the Muslims. They have tried to maintain friendly relations with the United States and the West. On the other hand, some Lebanese Muslims, influenced by the Palestinians living among them, have become hostile to the West because of Israel and have sought to establish closer relations with militant Muslims across their borders in Syria, Iraq, Iran, and Jordan. Lebanese Christians have tended to be less hostile and friendlier than the Muslims toward Israel.

MILITANT MINORITIES: KURDS IN IRAN

Many minorities in the Middle East have suffered discrimination for refusing to assimilate into the mainstream of Arab life. Like the Kurds in Iran and Iraq pictured above, they have often taken up arms to defend themselves against governmental suppression and denial of rights. Wilton/Gamma-Liaison

Russian Influence in the Middle East

Russia has been interested in the Middle East since the reign of Peter the Great in the 17th century. Since World War II it has become an increasingly influential force in the region. The USSR's actions and policies have contributed to continuing tensions.

Russia's Traditional Interest

Traditionally, Russia has been interested in the Middle East for territorial and strategic reasons. Nationalistic and religious factors have also played a role in Russia's involvements.

In the 19th and early 20th centuries, Russia tried to get additional territory from the Turks in the Balkans and Near East and to obtain shipping rights through the Turkish Straits, which command entry into the Mediterranean from the Black Sea.[15] Russia wanted to restrict the rights of other states to enter the Black Sea as well as to limit the restrictions on her own rights to enter the Mediterranean. Russia claimed a "big-brother" relationship to the Slavic peoples in the Ottoman (Turkish) Empire in the Balkans and supported their efforts to obtain independence. The czars also posed as "protectors" of the Orthodox church in the Muslim Ottoman Empire.

In the 19th century Russian czars also tried to conquer the Persian Empire to attain direct control over the Persian Gulf in order to challenge Britain's position in India. In 1907, Russia and Britain settled their outstanding differences in the face of the greater German menace. The Anglo–Russian agreement divided Iran into spheres of influence.

World War I to World War II

World War I brought about the collapse of the Ottoman Empire. It also brought on the Russian Revolution (1917), the downfall of the czars, and the establishment of a new Communist state, the Union of Soviet Socialist Republics. Under its new leaders following the war, Russia's main interests centered on its own domestic problems and, in foreign affairs, on anxiety about the reemergence of Germany as an aggressive power in Europe. Little attention was given to the Middle East, where British and French interests continued to dominate through the system of mandates and preferential arrangements and alliances with Arab rulers and newly created Arab nations.

[15] Actually three small interconnecting bodies of water, often referred to as the "Turkish Straits,"—the Bosphorus, the Sea of Marmora, and the Dardanelles—lie between the Black and Mediterranean seas. Istanbul is on the Bosphorus. The Dardanelles lie between the Sea of Marmora and the Aegean Sea. A Russian vessel leaving the Black Sea goes, in order, through the Bosphorus, the Sea of Marmora, the Dardanelles, and into the Aegean before it enters the Mediterranean.

World War II to 1955

During and after World War II, Russia's renewed interest in the Middle East became apparent. During the war, in cooperation with the Western Allies, Soviet forces occupied part of Iran to help safeguard the Allied route to the USSR through the Persian Gulf and Iran, when other supply routes had been cut. After the war, Russian troops were not withdrawn, in violation of wartime agreements with the Allies. Soviet forces remained until 1946 when they were removed at the request of the Security Council, in return for Iran's promise to the USSR of increased trade and oil rights.

After World War II, renewed Soviet interest in the Middle East took the form of encouragement of a civil war in Greece and demands for military bases near the Bosphorus to control access to the Black Sea, and for the acquisition of territory in eastern Turkey. The USSR also supported separatist movements in northwestern Iran. With Western aid and encouragement Turkey, Greece, and Iran held firm and were able to counter and block the Soviet drive to extend its naval and air power into the Mediterranean and Arabian seas.

SOVIET ARMS IN THE MIDDLE EAST

Since the mid-1950s the Soviet Union has actively spread its influence in the Middle East, particularly through economic and military assistance. Here we see a military instructor posing in front of training posters supplied along with military equipment given by the U.S.S.R. to his country, Yemen. de Decker/Gamma-Liaison

Since 1955

Since 1955 Russia has been increasingly involved in the Middle East, and is now a major influence in the area.

Beginning with the negotiations for an exchange of Egyptian cotton for Czechoslovakian planes and arms in 1955, Soviet involvement has grown to major proportions. Aid to Arab nations has included the construction of industrial plants, hydroelectric facilities, and oil refineries, the grant or sale of billions of dollars in weapons (including missiles and planes), particularly to Egypt, Syria and Iraq, and the supply of large numbers of economic and military advisers. In the 1970s the USSR became the major arms supplier to Syria, Libya, Algeria, Iraq, South Yemen, and Egypt (until 1973).

Reasons for Russia's Growing Influence

As elsewhere in the world, the USSR has seized every opportunity in the Middle East to exploit difficulties for its own benefit.

The Soviet Union was an original supporter of the establishment of Israel as an independent state.[16] However, its support waned as anti-Semitism and anti-Zionism increased in the final years of Josef Stalin's regime and as Israel sided with the West on Cold War issues. Since the mid-1950s the Soviet Union — to win Arab support and take advantage of Arab–Israeli friction — has been openly anti-Israel. Whenever the Arab–Israeli controversy has been discussed in the United Nations, the USSR has taken the pro-Arab position. Massive Soviet arms aid and diplomatic support for the Arabs contributed to the outbreak of the Arab–Israeli wars of 1967 and 1973. Since 1973 Moscow has also become a heavy arms supplier to Arab nations that refuse to recognize or deal with Israel, including Syria, Libya, Algeria, Iraq, South Yemen, as well as the PLO. U.S. Secretary of State Alexander Haig has publicly accused the Soviet Union of attempting to undermine the Western democracies by supporting and training terrorist organizations such as the PLO. He has said that combating international terrorism will be a major goal of the Reagan administration.

Finally, the Soviet Union has benefited from and has tried to exploit to its advantage such developments as the withdrawal and dismantling of British bases and military establishments "east of Suez" in Asia and the Middle East; the decision of France to give up its naval bases in Tunisia and Algeria; the withdrawal by the United States from its major military base in Libya; the tensions between Greece and Turkey over Cyprus; civil wars in Yemen, Iraq, the Sudan, and Iran; and differences between Arab states. The USSR has also benefited from United States policy failures in the Middle East. (See Chapter 8.)

[16] Russian support at that time was based on its desire to weaken Britain's position in the region.

As Western states have lost influence in the Middle East, the Soviet Union has tried to move in to fill in the gap. In particular, the Russians have tried to gain influence by supplying arms when Western arms were denied and to undertake projects that the West would not fund (for instance, the Aswan Dam in Egypt). Additionally, they have aided revolutionaries with arms and technical assistance (as in South Yemen). They have also sought to establish bases in the area.

Russia's Gains in the Middle East

In return for its aid and support to leftist and other regimes in and adjacent to the Middle East, Russia has made significant gains.

At one time or another the USSR has been permitted to establish military bases and other facilities in Egypt, Iraq, Syria, South Yemen, Algeria, Libya, Somalia, and Ethiopia. These have helped expand its influence and strengthen its position in the Mediterranean, the eastern tip or "Horn of Africa," and the Indian Ocean.

Since the late 1960s the Soviets have built up their naval forces in the Mediterranean to the point that they threaten to become the dominant power in the region. Russian naval units include one or more airplane carriers, helicopter-carrying cruisers, destroyers, attack and nuclear-missile submarines, and other combat vessels. It is believed that Russia's sea power in the Mediterranean could in an emergency endanger Western control of what are called the "choke points" of the region, namely the Strait of Gibraltar, the Turkish Straits, and parts of the Aegean Sea and the Suez Canal. Only the powerful U.S. Sixth Fleet and Russia's fears of military confrontation with the United States stand in its way.

To gain their present position in the Mediterranean region the Russians have used to their advantage the Cyprus dispute, the differences among the Arab states, and even disputes between Spain and England over Gibraltar. Their strategy has challenged the position of the United States in the area.

The Soviets in the past have also had bases in Egypt and in Somalia, giving them access to the Indian Ocean, which flanks the southern sea-lanes to the Middle East. Although forced to give up their bases in both countries, the Soviets have kept naval units in the Indian Ocean since the early 1970s. They have continued to maintain naval facilities in South Yemen. As of 1981 the USSR was still hoping to obtain bases in Ethiopia in return for support in Ethiopia's war with Somalia (see below).

Russia has negotiated military and trade agreements with several Arab states. It has been increasing its exports to the region faster than any other industrialized nation. Cooperative relationships have been established with Libya, Syria, South Yemen (Aden), and Iraq. In 1980 the USSR and Syria signed a treaty of friendship and aid. Military and economic aid to leftist

SOVIET NAVAL PRESENCE IN THE MIDDLE EAST

One of the more significant developments in world affairs has been the growing naval strength of the Soviet Union. Its naval presence in Middle East waters is shown by this Soviet missile launch destroyer in the Sea of Oman. The picture was taken by a French plane that flew over the ship in March 1980. Quittard/ Gamma-Liaison

regimes in Syria and Iraq and nonhostile relations with Iran have opened the Persian Gulf to Soviet oil tankers and cargo ships. After the crisis in Cyprus between Turkey and Greece, Moscow improved its relations with Turkey in order to weaken Western ties.

Since the late 1970s Russia has extended its influence and interests to the eastern "Horn of Africa." In 1978 it threw its support behind Ethiopia in Ethiopia's war with Somalia. Establishment of one or more military bases in Ethiopia would, together with its base in South Yemen, enable the USSR to dominate the Straits of Babel Mandeb at the mouth of the Red Sea.

Russia's growing influence in Middle Eastern affairs is also evident in its increased political influence or "leverage" in the affairs of nations in the Middle East and Africa with more "radical" or leftist (Marxist) regimes, for example, Syria, Iraq, South Yemen, and Ethiopia.

Recent events in the Middle East have strongly enhanced Russia's influence and undermined America's power in the area — for example, the takover of the Afghanistan government by a Marxist pro-Soviet group in 1978, followed by the invasion and virtual takeover of Afghanistan by Soviet forces in 1979 and 1980, to support a weak Communist government;

and the destabilizing effect throughout the region caused by the Iranian revolution and civil war of 1978–1979 as well as the Iraq–Iran war of 1980–1981. The USSR has also given direct support to Ethiopia in its war with Somalia, even to the extent of using Cuban soldiers and technicians to aid the pro-Marxist military junta that now controls the country.

It is generally believed that there can be no permanent peace in the Middle East without the USSR's support or acceptance of the terms of agreements that would have to be negotiated.[17]

Soviet Goals and Strategy in the Middle East

Although there is general agreement that the Soviet Union has become one of the leading powers in the Middle East and plays an important role in regional affairs, there is no consensus as to its precise goals and strategy.

Many trained observers and analysts contend that the main goal of the USSR is to dominate the Middle East, to exclude the United States from its communications routes and other regional assets, and to use the Middle East as a means of altering the global balance of power against the West. In an interpretation sometimes called the "maximalist" point of view, Russia's interest in the Middle East is seen as part of a global objective and overall strategy of trying to outflank and envelop Europe from the south, through dominance in the Middle East and Africa, in order to separate the United States and Western Europe and bring the region under Soviet control.

According to this point of view a number of strategies are being employed by the USSR to achieve its goals, including:

(1) Establish naval dominance over the Mediterranean Sea to control this long-established route to the Middle East.

(2) Gain the favor of the Arab nations by supporting PLO and other terrorist activity against Israel, maintaining an anti-Israel position, and reinforcing or stimulating anti-Western feelings and trends by exploiting the region's tensions and instabilities.

(3) Use every opportunity to diminish United States influence by portraying the United States as a Western imperialist aggressor and friend of Israel.

(4) Gain control of the Red Sea and access to the southern exit of the Suez Canal in order to threaten Western oil routes from the Middle East.

(5) Pressure and squeeze Saudi Arabia, America's largest oil supplier and a major anti-Communist force in the Arab world, by encouraging pro-Soviet regimes in Ethiopia, South Yemen, and Iraq.

(6) Establish as many Marxist states as possible in Africa to advance the

---

[17] Although the USSR has expanded its influence in the Middle East significantly, it has come in for some criticism and has also had some reverses in Arab states, such as Egyptian President Sadat's expulsion of 20,000 Russian technicians in the early 1970s.

USSR's own interests and limit the influence of the United States in that continent.[18]

(7) Maintain working relationships with Iran to keep the Persian Gulf open as a source of oil imports.

(8) Take advantage of every failure of the United States to promote its own interests in the region.

Other observers disagree with the "maximalist" interpretation of Russia's goals and instead take a "minimalist" position. They argue that the Soviet Union is as concerned as the West with establishing stability and minimizing friction in the region. They feel that the USSR is in the Middle East not willingly but in response to U.S. moves, in order to prevent the region from being used as a base for an attack on the Soviet Union. They point out that Russia has found its Arab "client states" to be unreliable and the Arab–Israeli conflict a source of more problems than opportunities. The Soviets, like the United States, are worried that continued Arab–Israeli conflict could produce direct confrontation between the two superpowers. Accordingly, it is argued, the Soviets would really prefer to retrench rather than expand their activities in the region and to confine their interests to trade, aid, and oil.

A third interpretation of Soviet objectives falls somewhere in between the "maximalist" and "minimalist" views. According to the "targets-of-opportunity" school of thought, Soviet policy in the Middle East is part of a flexible rather than a fixed set of objectives. Those who hold this view argue that Soviet strategy in the Middle East is related to what the Soviets consider to be the status of the world balance of power. In trying to establish a balance favorable to itself, the USSR has taken advantage of the policy of détente (relaxation of tensions) with the United States and has stationed forces in the Far East along the Sino–Soviet border to contain Chinese power. At present, the USSR finds its freedom to move at will checked or limited to the west by NATO and the United States and to the east by the Chinese.

In such a situation the USSR's best opportunities for foreign policy successes are to the south — that is the Middle East (and, more recently, Africa). The Soviets believe that with relatively little effort they can keep the Middle East unstable. They hope to turn Arab–Israeli differences to the disadvantage of the United States, weaken NATO, and, by supporting OPEC oil policies, help weaken Western industrial economies. In short, the Soviets look on the Middle East as a target of opportunity for besting the United States in the superpower rivalry and tilting the global balance of power to their own advantage.

[18] Thus Russia's influence was enhanced early in 1981 when Libya's army invaded and annexed the African nation of Chad with its rich uranium deposits. Most black African countries and the Organization of African Unity were distressed by the sudden and unilateral takeover of Chad.

Mastery Activities

1. Indicate the order in which the events in each group occurred by placing a 1, 2, or 3 before them.

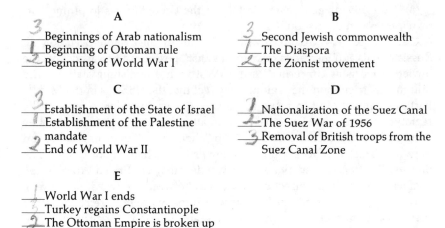

A	B
_3_ Beginnings of Arab nationalism	_3_ Second Jewish commonwealth
_1_ Beginning of Ottoman rule	_1_ The Diaspora
_2_ Beginning of World War I	_2_ The Zionist movement

C	D
_3_ Establishment of the State of Israel	_1_ Nationalization of the Suez Canal
_1_ Establishment of the Palestine mandate	_2_ The Suez War of 1956
_2_ End of World War II	_3_ Removal of British troops from the Suez Canal Zone

E

_1_ World War I ends
_3_ Turkey regains Constantinople
_2_ The Ottoman Empire is broken up

2. Identify or briefly explain each of the following names and terms used in this chapter.

Names

1. Theodor Herzl
2. Chaim Weizmann
3. Sharif Hussein
4. T. E. Lawrence
5. Reza Kahn Pahlevi
6. Henry Kissinger
7. Yasser Arafat
8. Anwar el-Sadat

Terms

1. Balfour Declaration
2. Pan-Arabism
3. Treaty of Sevres
4. OPEC
5. The Jewish Agency
6. The Haganah
7. Shatt-al-Arab
8. Trucial States
9. Anti-Semitism
10. The Six Day War
11. The Yom Kippur War
12. The War of Attrition
13. Suez Disengagement Pacts
14. The "good fence policy"
15. The Rejectionist Front
16. Sharm-el-Sheikh
17. The Golan Heights
18. The Sinai Peninsula
19. Arab refugees
20. Horn of Africa

Homework and Discussion Questions

1. Discuss two reasons for the growth of Arab nationalism in the Middle East after World War I.

2. Most Jews support and most Arabs oppose the establishment of Israel as a homeland for the Jews.
   (a) What arguments do Jews give in support of their position?
   (b) What arguments do Arabs give in support of their position?

3. Explain why Britain gave up its Palestine mandate after World War II.

4. Explain how World War II changed the balance of power in the Middle East.

5. How has each contributed to the growth of Arab nationalism since World War II?:
   (a) The Arab League
   (b) Middle East oil
   (c) The Baath Party
   (d) The Palestine Liberation Organization

6. Why has each of the following become a major Middle East issue?
   (a) the creation of a separate Palestinian state
   (b) the Palestinian refugee problem

7. Explain the following statement fully: "Since its establishment Israel has been at war, preparing for war, or recovering from war."

8. Give two reasons for agreeing or disagreeing with the following statement: "Even if there had been no Israel, the Middle East would be a caldron of tension, crisis, and unrest."

9. Discuss the causes and results of each of the following:
   (a) the civil war in Lebanon in the late 1970s
   (b) the dispute between Greece and Turkey over Cyprus

10. Explain three reasons for the recent increase of Soviet influence in the Middle East.

11. Reread carefully the three important interpretations of possible Soviet strategies discussed at the end of the chapter. With which do you agree most? Why?

5

The United States and the
Middle East Before World War II

Although the United States did not become actively involved in the Middle East until the end of World War II, its association with the region goes back approximately two hundred years to the 18th century.

18th-Century Beginnings

The earliest American contacts with the Middle East were commercial.

The Colonial Period

Toward the end of the colonial period, when the thirteen colonies still belonged to Britain, American vessels began to make voyages to the area of the southern and eastern Mediterranean, seeking trade with southern Europe, North Africa, the Levant, and Turkey.[1] This was part of the American colonists' efforts to overcome restrictions placed on their foreign commerce by Britain in the 18th century.

By the late 1700s profitable trade relationships had been developed with North Africa and the Muslim East. Thomas Jefferson estimated that North Africa received a sixth of the American colonies' exports of wheat and flour and a fourth of their dried or pickled fish. Lumber, rum, onions, and beeswax were also shipped to various destinations in the Mediterranean. Returning vessels brought back wines, salt, oil, Moroccan leather, and figs. Lesser trade contacts were developed with Persia, Syria, and Saudi Arabia.

---

[1] "The Levant" is a term that was once used to refer to countries bordering the eastern Mediterranean. It is rarely used today.

152

**FIGHTING THE
BARBARY PIRATES**
The United States had to fight
a series of wars with the
North African Barbary Pirates
to stop their seizing of
American ships and sailors in
the early 19th century. In this
picture Stephen Decatur leads
his crew in an attack on a
Tripolitanian gunboat in 1803.
New York Public Library

The Post-Revolutionary Era

America's War of Independence brought its foreign commerce almost to
a halt. After the war, the newly independent United States found itself
closed off from access to European West Indies colonies. Across the
Atlantic, to do business with those nations that were willing to trade,
American ships had to sail to the north into the Baltic, or to the south into
the Mediterranean to bypass a hostile Britain.

To gain access to the Mediterranean during the first decades of its independence, the young republic had to make special arrangements, often
amounting to bribery, with the Barbary states[2] that controlled the passages
leading into the Mediterranean through the Gibraltar Straits (the "Gates of
Hercules"). During the administrations of Presidents George Washington
and John Adams, trade treaties were negotiated with the rulers of Morocco,
Algiers, Tunis, and Tripoli. In return for recognition of their independence

---

[2] The term "Barbary states" was commonly used in the 18th and early 19th
centuries to refer to the independent and semi-independent kingdoms along the
coast of North Africa, stretching from the Atlantic to Egypt.

within the declining Ottoman Empire, these states granted American vessels entry to their ports and to the Mediterranean region.

Despite such agreements, Barbary pirates continued to capture American trading vessels and to enslave their crews. They were often encouraged by their governments. Such actions led to naval conflict with the Barbary states in the early 1800s and to their final defeat in 1816, when the United States placed a naval squadron in the Mediterranean to defend its interests.

19th- and Early 20th-Century Interests

After the War of 1812, most European countries traded freely with the United States. As a result, the need to develop economic relationships with the Middle East declined.

Trade Relationships

American trade with the Middle East did not become significant enough in the 19th century to be considered of prime national importance. One of the developments in this period was the ratification of the first United States–Ottoman "Treaty of Amity and Commerce" in 1831. It guaranteed freedom for American commerce and freedom of commercial passage through the Turkish Straits. Treaties of friendship and commerce were signed with the sultan of Muscat (1838) and the shah of Persia (1857). Nevertheless, trade relationships with the eastern Mediterranean and Middle East remained very limited. For example, from 1855 to 1913 only one American ship called at the port of Muscat in southeast Arabia. American commerce in the region during the 19th century was primarily with Turkey rather than with the Arab territories.

Other Contacts

Most American activity in the Middle East in the century before World War I took the form of educational, scientific, humanitarian, and technical programs. In the 1830s American advisers helped rebuild the Ottoman fleet after Turkish defeats in the Greek War for independence. In the 1870s former Union and Confederate officers supervised the modernization of Egyptian armed forces and carried out engineering surveys. A few tourists and scholars traveled to Egypt and other countries and lectured on published accounts of their journeys. American museums acquired artifacts (sculpture, relics, architectural remains) from archaeological explorations in Egypt, Greece, Turkey, Syria, Jordan, and Palestine.

American missionary work in the Middle East was the most sustained

AMERICAN MISSIONARIES IN THE MIDDLE EAST
(NINETEENTH CENTURY)

Protestant Missionaries were among the first Americans to work directly in the Middle East. They worked primarily with native Christian sects, preaching, teaching, establishing medical stations, and engaging in humanitarian endeavors. This picture appeared in a book on *The Origin and History of Missions,* **published in Boston in 1842.** *The Origin and History of Missions,* by Rev. Thomas Smith and Rev. John Choules, 1842.

activity of the period. Protestant missionaries went to the Middle East as early as 1821. They established schools and hospitals and translated the Bible into Arabic. Although American missionaries did not convert many Muslims or Jews and worked primarily among native Christian sects in Istanbul, Beirut, Damascus, and Jerusalem, they began work that resulted in the establishment of a number of colleges and universities with far higher standards than the local schools. These included Robert College in Istanbul (1863), the American University of Beirut (1866), and the American University of Cairo (1919).

From time to time American missionaries took the lead in creating medical stations and enlisting American aid for communities uprooted or hurt by events in the Ottoman Empire. As a result of their efforts and concern, the United States extended emergency help to Greeks during their revolt against Turkey in the 1820s, to Muslim Arab communities during the reassertion of Turkish rule in Syria in 1840, and to Armenian victims of Ottoman massacres in Anatolia (Turkey) and elsewhere in the 1890s and during World War I.

In these and other instances the United States government furnished naval transport for relief supplies. By the early 20th century, the principle that governments as well as private individuals and groups should extend humanitarian aid was well established. During World War I Congress chartered and appropriated funds for the Near East Relief Organization.

19th- and Early 20th-Century Support for a Jewish Homeland in Palestine

Biblical influence on Christian thinking resulted in support among American Christians as well as Jews for "the redemption of Zion" even before the present-day Zionist movement was established in 1897. In 1818 former president John Adams expressed in writing his desire to see the reestablishment of an independent state for "the Jews in Judea." In 1844 Mordecai Manuel Noah, an American Jew who had served as U.S. consul in Tunis, asked the Christian world to help Jews resettle in Palestine. His recommendation appeared in a pamphlet entitled *Discourse on the Restoration of the Jews*. In 1891 a petition to President Benjamin Harrison presented by the Reverend William Blackstone and signed by many leaders in public life, the church, the press, and the business world called for an international conference to "consider the Israelite claim to Palestine as part of their ancient home" and an "inalienable possession from which they were expelled by force."

Shortly after the organization of the Zionist movement, sympathy for the idea of reestablishing Palestine as a homeland for the Jews was also expressed by Presidents William McKinley, Theodore Roosevelt, and William Taft.

Lack of Active Government Interest before World War I

Despite 18th-, 19th-, and early 20th-century trade and other contacts with the Middle East, the United States did not develop a consciously formulated political or strategic policy for the region.

Before World War I the U.S. government confined itself largely to protecting the personal security and property of its nationals. Although there was little official involvement, there was some concern with Russian imperial moves toward the Turkish Straits and some interest in the struggles of the Greeks and Balkan Slavs against the Ottoman Empire. In addition, President Theodore Roosevelt helped negotiate a solution in a dispute among France, Britain, and Germany over Morocco at the Algeciras Conference in 1905–1906. (Nevertheless Roosevelt was more concerned with European and Caribbean developments than with Middle East affairs.) During World War I the U.S. did not declare war on the Ottoman Empire, which was an ally of Germany and Austria-Hungary, nor did it send troops to the region.

The World War I Peace Settlements

After World War I the United States, for the first time, began to show some official interest in the peace and security of the Middle East. President Wilson strongly influenced the postwar peace settlements. Among his wartime goals, as expressed in his Fourteen Points address in January 1918, were Turkish independence as well as self-rule for non-Turkish nationalities still under Ottoman rule. The Fourteen Points also called for free passage through the Turkish Straits for "the ships of commerce of all nations under international guarantees."

In addition, Wilson endorsed the Balfour Declaration in which British Foreign Secretary Arthur Balfour pledged the establishment of a "national home" in Palestine for the Jewish people, provided nothing was done to prejudice the interests of the inhabitants of the region. At the Paris Peace Conference, which met to draft the post–World War I peace treaties, the intelligence section of the U.S. delegation recommended that "the Jews be

PRESIDENT WILSON AT VERSAILLES
President Woodrow Wilson endorsed the Balfour Declaration and the establishment of a Jewish state in Palestine. He took an active role at the Paris Peace Conference that drew up the peace treaties at the end of the first World War. Above center, Wilson is seated at the conference table at Versailles. New York Public Library

invited to return to Palestine and settle there." It also advocated that the League of Nations "recognize Palestine as a Jewish state as soon as it is a Jewish state in fact."

Wilson's major contribution to the peace settlements was the concept of a League of Nations to keep the peace and of a system of League of Nations mandates that would eventually become independent states under the guidance of victor nations. The Middle East territories formerly under Ottoman control became British and French mandates, with Palestine (including what was later to become Jordan) and Iraq assigned to Britain, and Syria and Lebanon to France.

Role of the United States between World War I and World War II

After World War I Americans continued their educational, religious, scientific, cultural, humanitarian, and philanthropic contacts with the Middle East. In addition, in the 1920s and 1930s the United States became actively interested in the development and exploitation of the oil resources that had been discovered earlier in the century. As a result, a small but growing number of Americans became knowledgeable about the Middle East.

Contacts with the Middle East

In the period between World Wars I and II, American interests in the Middle East, aside from oil, were primarily educational, religious, scientific, cultural, and humanitarian.

EDUCATIONAL AND RELIGIOUS. Although they continued their religious work, Christian missionaries gave increasing attention to providing technical, scientific, and professional training in order to help improve the quality of Middle East life. Middle East schools attracted increasing numbers of Muslims. On the college level, increasing attention was given to the education of women. Considerable attention was also given to developing medical facilities and hospitals.

SCIENTIFIC AND CULTURAL. The interwar period has been called "the golden age of Middle East archaeology." Several leading American universities and museums sponsored archaeological expeditions. Excavations were also undertaken jointly with British and French institutions. Important "digs" by teams from Yale and Harvard and the University of Chicago were made in Egypt, Iraq, and Palestine.

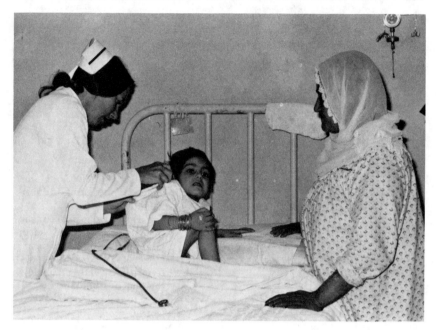

AMERICAN HUMANITARIANISM IN THE MIDDLE EAST

Between World Wars I and II the American Near East Foundation was actively engaged in humanitarian endeavors in the Middle East. In this picture we see an American nurse with one of her patients in the Foundation-supported Hamlin Hospital in Lebanon. The patient's mother is also present. Near East Foundation

HUMANITARIAN AND PHILANTHROPIC. Closely connected with archaeological explorations was the financial support given by American philanthropists who contributed liberally to museums in both the United States and the Middle East. Humanitarian endeavors took the form of work done by the Near East Foundation. In addition to trying to alleviate starvation and suffering to the extent of its limited resources, the foundation attempted to aid displaced persons and to help improve agriculture and industry as well as housing, health, and education.

Noteworthy in this period was the strong support given to the Zionist cause, particularly by American Jews. Although divided on the issue of how to pursue the goal of establishing a Jewish state in Palestine, American Jewry was united on the need to give assistance to the Jewish community living under the British mandate and to European Jews fleeing oppression. Considerable aid for immigration, land reclamation, settlement, and health care was given by both Zionist and non-Zionist organizations. Especially active were the Jewish National Fund and the Jewish Agency, which after its establishment in 1929 was recognized by the British as the official representative of the Jewish community in Palestine.

AMERICAN ARCHAEOLOGICAL EXPLORATIONS
In the 1920s, 1930s, and later, American museums and universities sponsored archaeological expeditions in the Middle East. Here Nelson Glueck, a leading American archaeologist, examines pottery artifacts dating back to the time of Abraham, that were found in Israel. Israel Consulate

American diplomatic officials intervened from time to time to protect American interests and investments in Palestine, although some State Department officials opposed the Zionist goal. In 1922 Congress passed a joint resolution endorsing a national home for the Jews in Palestine. Thereafter both the Democratic and Republican parties incorporated a pro-Zionist plank into their platforms.

Beginnings of United States Interest in Middle East Oil

By 1919 British interests controlled half the world's known oil resources outside the Western hemisphere. This was made possible by oil concessions in Iran and Mesopotamia (later to become Iraq) granted to British firms before World War I.

After the war, the U.S. government insisted that its commercial firms and citizens should have the same rights to exploit the oil resources of the Middle East as firms and citizens of other nations. In the 1920s, fears of declining domestic oil reserves and growing concern with European attempts to monopolize the oil wealth of the Middle East caused the State Department to launch a strong effort to secure participation by American oil companies in Middle East oil concessions.

American insistence and efforts paid off. By the late 1920s, United States oil companies had begun to participate in oil production and development in Iran, Iraq, and Bahrain. In the 1930s additional concessions were secured in Kuwait and Saudi Arabia. The most promising concession of all was that secured by the Arabian-American Oil Company (Aramco) in Saudi Arabia, soon to become the world's richest oil-producing and -exporting nation. Aramco was the only completely American-owned oil enterprise in the Middle East. By 1939 the American share in Middle East oil production had grown to thirteen percent (Britain's share was sixty percent; the balance was mostly French or Dutch).

Political Noninvolvement

Aside from support given to its oil interests, the United States government showed little desire for political involvement in the Middle East in the period between World Wars I and II. Although interested in the freedom of the Turkish Straits, the United States declined in the 1920s and 1930s to participate in international discussions and agreements providing for continued freedom of commercial passage through the straits.

Despite Congressional approval of the Balfour Declaration and the establishment of the British mandate in Palestine, the main interest of the U.S. government was the protection of the rights and properties of American citizens. American officials relied on Britain and France to safeguard U.S. interests. In the period between the wars, mounting friction between Arabs and Jews in Palestine was not of great concern to American authorities.

The major exception to U.S. noninvolvement in Middle East affairs in these years was the dispatch of the King-Crane Commission by President Wilson to former Ottoman territories in 1919, particularly to Palestine and Syria. The commission's purpose was to determine the views of the inhabitants on the postwar territorial decisions. Its final report recommended the establishment of an American or British mandate if necessary. The commission's report, which also advised against the creation of a Jewish state in Palestine, was never formally accepted by the U.S. government or the Paris Peace Conference.

Mastery Activities

Briefly identify each of the following as referred to in this chapter:

Barbary states	King-Crane Commission
Algeciras Conference	The American University
Fourteen Points	Near East Relief Organization
Paris Peace Conference	Aramco
Jewish National Fund	

Questions for Homework and Discussion

1. Explain what is meant by the statement: "The earliest American contacts with the Middle East were commercial."

2. How did missionaries develop 19th-century American contacts with the Middle East?

3. What evidence is there before World War II of interest on the part of Christians as well as Jews in the idea of a Jewish homeland in Palestine?

4. Discuss the role of the United States government in the Middle East (a) before World War I; (b) between World Wars I and II.

5. Why do you agree or disagree with this statement?: "Between World Wars I and II the major interests of the United States in the Middle East were educational, religious, scientific, cultural, and humanitarian rather than political."

6

American Goals and Strategies
Since World War II

Since World War II the United States has been directly involved in the Middle East as a matter of government policy. World War II and the immediate postwar years marked a turning point in its relationships with the region.

The United States and the Middle East during World War II

Beginning with World War II, political and strategic needs have caused the United States to be increasingly involved in Middle East affairs. Before the United States was drawn into the war as a belligerent, President Franklin D. Roosevelt sent a representative to the region to encourage resistance to Nazi Germany. In extending lend-lease aid to Turkey just four days before the Japanese attack on Pearl Harbor (on December 7, 1941), Roosevelt declared the defense of Turkey "vital to the defense of the United States."

The wartime role and actions of the United States in the Middle East were for the most part supportive of British efforts rather than independently initiated and implemented. In November 1942, in its first large-scale military involvement in the war, United States troops were sent to North Africa. The American forces, under General Dwight D. Eisenhower, occupied Morocco and Algeria and advanced into Tunisia. The German and Italian armies in North Africa were trapped among the American, British, and Free French forces and forced to surrender. This victory, plus the victory of General Bernard Montgomery at El Alamein in October 1942, put the Allies in control of the Mediterranean and helped pave the way for the invasion of Europe through Sicily, into Italy and southern France.

As a military theater, the Middle East did not become as significant to the United States as Western Europe and the Far East. Nevertheless it played an important role in U.S. strategic plans and operations during the war. In 1942

163

Iran was included in the U.S. lend-lease program. Shortly thereafter, U.S. forces in considerable numbers were sent to Iran to help protect Allied supply lines to the Soviet Union that ran through the Persian Gulf and across Iran. Small American naval forces were stationed in the Persian Gulf as part of a newly established U.S. Persian Gulf Command (the predecessor of the present U.S. Middle East Naval Forces in the Gulf and the Indian Ocean). Air bases, supply depots, and transportation facilities were also established in the area. In March 1944 President Roosevelt declared that the United States had a "vital interest" in the Middle East and that its peace and security were "of significance to the world as a whole."

The Changing Balance of Power in the Middle East after World War II

Before 1947 the United States did not have a clearly thought-through policy in its dealings with the Middle East. Like other Western powers, the United States relied on Britain and France to represent and protect its vital interests.

British and French influence before, during, and for several years after World War II was based on the administrative controls they had established during the mandate era. In addition, Britain maintained a strong military presence throughout the region. This took the form of troop installations, military and naval bases, naval patrols in the Mediterranean Sea, the Persian Gulf, and the Indian Ocean, and treaties and agreements with Middle East rulers and kingdoms.

After World War II it became evident that Britain and France had been exhausted and economically drained by the war. The pressing need for attention to their own domestic problems of postwar reconstruction and their growing inability to pay for the mounting costs of overseas empire made it clear that a power vacuum had developed in the Middle East. This vacuum has since been filled by the Soviet Union and the United States.

The United States Becomes Directly Involved in the Middle East

Several important developments caused the United States to become directly involved in Middle East affairs after World War II. Particularly significant were Soviet expansionism and the establishment of Israel as an independent state.

Soviet Expansionism

Russian expansionism after World War II led to America's first political, economic, and military commitments in the Middle East.

COMMUNIST EXPANSION IN EASTERN AND CENTRAL EUROPE. Even before World War II ended, the alliance between Russia and the Western powers had begun to deteriorate. After the war it fell apart quickly. The Soviet Union took advantage of the power vacuum created in Europe and Asia by the total defeat of Germany and Japan and the rapid withdrawal of United States forces from Europe. By keeping troops in Eastern and Central Europe and the Far East after hostilities ended, the Russians helped Communist parties in Bulgaria, Yugoslavia, Hungary, Poland, Rumania, Albania, East Germany, and Czechoslovakia take control of the governments of their countries. Since that time, with the exception of Yugoslavia and Albania, these Soviet-bloc countries have remained "client states" or "satellites" of the USSR, and for the most part have followed the Soviet "line" in foreign policy.

THE SOVIET CHALLENGE IN IRAN, TURKEY, AND GREECE. America's first commitments to the Middle East were prompted by Soviet expansionist pressure in Iran, Turkey, and Greece.

After World War II ended, Russia attempted to set up a pro-Soviet puppet regime in the province of Azerbaijan, in northern Iran. It also kept its troops in Iran after the fighting stopped, in violation of wartime agreements. Not until 1946, when vigorous protests were lodged by the United

RUSSIAN TROOPS LEAVING IRAN (1946)

After World War II Russian troops did not leave Iran as agreed upon during the war. In 1946, after United States and United Nations protests, Soviet forces were finally withdrawn. This photo shows their withdrawal from the city of Meshed in March 1946. Wide World

States and the United Nations, did the Soviets withdraw their forces.

Turkey, too, was under Soviet pressure. In 1945 the USSR demanded revision of the 1936 Montreux Convention, which had provided for exclusive Turkish supervision of the Dardanelles Straits between the Black Sea and the Mediterranean. Moscow called for joint Russian–Turkish administration and defense of the straits. It also demanded cession of several Turkish districts on the Russian–Turkish border. Britain and the United States rejected Moscow's demands.

In Greece, Communist guerrillas made continued attempts to take over the government after the war ended. Although Britain had previously provided aid to Greece to help put down an attempted coup, it found itself less able to do so in 1947.

Truman Doctrine

In 1947 the United States decided it was time to take strong action to stop Russian expansionism. In addition to continuing pressures on Turkey and Iran, civil war had again broken out in Greece, Communist strength was growing in France and Italy, and Communists had just taken over the government of Czechoslovakia.

In March 1947, soon after Britain notified the United States that she was no longer financially able to keep forces in Greece and the eastern Mediterranean to maintain stability, President Harry Truman asked Congress to provide military and economic assistance to nations threatened by totalitarianism. Faced with the threatened Communist takeover in Greece and the probability that the collapse of Greece would lead to further Soviet pressure on Turkey to relinquish control of the Dardanelles Straits area, Truman stressed that it must be U.S. policy to support free peoples who were resisting "attempted subjugations by armed minorities or by outside pressure."

As a result of this *Truman Doctrine*, Congress appropriated $400 million for aid to Greece and Turkey. In addition, an American military mission was sent to help advise these nations how best to resist Communist pressures and expanding Soviet influence.

In taking these steps the United States began a pattern that became clear in the postwar years, namely, the replacement of Britain by the United States as the protector of weaker states in the area.

The Cold War

The Truman Doctrine became known as the policy of *containment*. It marked a decisive break with the United States's prewar policy of isolation and noninterference in European political affairs. It also marked the beginning of the so-called *Cold War* between the Communist world, led by the USSR, and the non-Communist or "free world," led by the United States. Since the issuance of the Truman Doctrine, the Communist and non-Communist blocs (sometimes referred to as "East" and "West") have been engaged in a worldwide struggle for supremacy, short of outright war. Cold War objectives and strategies have had important effects on the Middle East.

PROTEST AGAINST UNITED STATES POLICY OF NON-INVOLVEMENT IN PALESTINE

When the horrors of the Holocaust began to be known after World War II ended, there were worldwide protests against the continuing British ban on Jewish immigration to Palestine. This demonstration in New York City reflected growing bitterness against the American policy of "non-involvement." The picture was taken shortly before the British asked to be relieved of their responsibility for governing the Palestine mandate in 1947. Zionist Archives

Establishment of the State of Israel

The United States played a major role in the establishment of Israel as an independent state after World War II. America's relationship with Israel and its concerns about friction between Israel and its Arab neighbors since that time have been important reasons for the growing role of the United States in Middle East affairs.

Before World War II began, Britain's mandate in Palestine had begun to be a heavy burden. Despite increasing Arab opposition, the Jewish population had risen under the mandate from under 100,000 to over 400,000

In 1939 the British government, responding to Arab protests and desiring to ensure Arab support should war break out, sharply reduced immigration quotas on Jews entering Palestine and restricted Jewish land purchases. Despite this British "White Paper," over a third of the 75,000 Jewish immigrants who entered Palestine during World War II were smuggled in illegally, escaping from the certain death of the Nazi Holocaust. Although mainly from Poland, Germany, Rumania, and Czechoslovakia, they also came from the Soviet Union, Bulgaria, Hungary, Austria, Yugoslavia, and Italy. By the end of the war the Jewish population of Palestine was over 600,000.

World War II wrought havoc in Europe and particularly to its Jewish population, which lost six million people in the Nazi Holocaust — approximately one-third of the world total. After the war some 60,000 homeless Russian, Polish, and German Jews living in "displaced persons camps" in Europe came to Palestine by slipping through a blockade imposed by the British to halt further immigration. Because the world was becoming aware of the horrors of the Nazi death camps during the Holocaust, worldwide protests were lodged against the British ban.

In 1945 President Truman, backed by Congress, urged the immediate admission of 100,000 Jews to Palestine. Both houses of Congress adopted a resolution urging the opening of Palestine to Jewish immigration and the establishment of a "democratic commonwealth."

Despite the presence of 100,000 of its troops, Britain was unable to maintain order or suppress the underground war against its continued occupation of Palestine. In 1947 it asked the United Nations to be relieved of its Palestine mandate. During the debates that followed within and outside of the United Nations, the United States endorsed the idea of a "viable Jewish state" in part of Palestine. In November 1947 the U.N. General Assembly voted by a two-thirds majority to partition Palestine into Arab and Jewish states, with Jerusalem to be administered as an international zone under the United Nations. Both the United States and the Soviet Union supported the resolution. With the backing of President Truman, the United States influenced other nations to vote for the plan.

Truman decided to support the concept of a Jewish state only after considerable deliberation, and despite warnings by State Department "Arabists" that support for Israel would jeopardize American relations with the Arabs and would also be contrary to America's other interests in the Middle East. Russia's support for the plan grew out of its desire to weaken British influence and, if possible, help cause Britain to move out of the region.

From November 1947 to May 1948, Arab opposition to the U.N. plan mounted and Arab terrorist attacks on Jewish settlements began. The British mandate expired on May 14, 1948. Within minutes Israel proclaimed its independence and, under President Truman's direct instruction, the United States recognized Israel within hours, becoming the first nation to do so.

Five Arab armies went to war against Israel within hours of its declaration of independence. The United States has been concerned with the instability in the region ever since.

HOLOCAUST SURVIVOR IN ISRAEL

After its establishment in 1948 the new Jewish state of Israel opened its doors to survivors of the Holocaust coming from displaced persons camps in Europe. Here a Holocaust survivor arrives in Israel. His feelings are clearly shown.
Zionist Archives

Goals of the United States in the Middle East

Since it became directly and officially involved in the Middle East after World War II, the United States has had a number of primary goals in the region. These goals are intertwined, interrelated, and overlapping. They can be summarized as follows:

—Preservation of strategic access to the Middle East and its oil resources

—Preventing outside influence — particularly the Soviet Union — from penetrating and dominating the area

—Preservation of Israel as a free, democratic nation

—Good relations with Arab nations, particularly those that are pro-Western in outlook and policy.

—Preservation of peace and stability in the region

Preservation of Strategic Access to the Middle East and Its Oil Resources

The paramount concern of the United States today is its need to prevent Soviet predominance and thus insure continued access to the oil supplies of the Middle East.

U.S. DEPENDENCE ON MIDDLE EAST OIL. Oil is vital to the economies of all industrial nations and absolutely essential to the United States, Western Europe, and Japan. Although there have been recent discoveries of oil deposits in Alaska, the North Sea, Mexico, and elsewhere,[1] the Middle East, with over half of the world's oil reserves, continues to be the largest single source of imported oil. At the end of 1980 the United States was importing forty-three percent of its oil. Approximately one-third of U.S. oil imports came from the Middle East. Arab oil comprised a total of about fifteen percent of U.S. oil consumption. Despite a search for other oil and energy sources, the need of the United States for Middle East oil has been growing. This fact underscored the need for a rigorous energy conservation program for the United States. (Such a program was a high-priority goal of the Carter administration.)

STRATEGIC LOCATION OF THE MIDDLE EAST. The Middle East is strategically located. It is an important interconnecting link among Europe, Asia, and Africa. Its more than 200 million people live close to and south of the Soviet Union, the chief rival of the United States in world affairs. Important travel routes connecting the Far East and Middle East with Europe and America pass through the Middle East.

[1] Huge oil deposits recently discovered in Mexico could, together with other new deposits being explored inside the United States and elsewhere, reduce American and Western dependency on the Middle East in the future.

U.S. DEPENDENCE ON MIDDLE EAST OIL

The United States imports about 15 percent of its total oil needs from the Middle East. Saudi Arabia is its biggest supplier. Here tugs nudge a mammoth tanker into loading position at the Ras Tanura island refinery off the Saudi coast in the Persian Gulf. Preservation of strategic access to Middle East oil is a major goal of U.S. foreign policy in the Middle East. Aramco Photo

Such trade routes could be seriously interrupted and world economies adversely affected if the Middle East were controlled or dominated by Moscow or any other unfriendly power. As indicated in Chapter 4, world economies could be disrupted by attacks on or seizures of a number of choke points, where water passages are narrowed by the terrain. These include the Strait of Gibraltar, between the Atlantic and the Mediterranean; the Turkish Straits, connecting the Black and Mediterranean seas; the Suez Canal, linking the Mediterranean Sea with the Red Sea; the Straits of Babel Mandeb, linking the Red Sea with the Indian Ocean, through the Gulf of Aden; and the Strait of Hormuz (through which ninety percent of Middle East oil supplies pass) between the Persian Gulf and the Indian Ocean. Egypt's closing of the Suez Canal to world trade from 1967 to 1975 illustrated what could occur.

Direct or even indirect control of the oil fields would by itself give the Soviet Union the power to disrupt the economies of the United States and its allies. It would also deny fuel to the military forces of the Western military alliance (NATO), thereby reducing its ability to conduct operations. Soviet domination of the Mediterranean would enable the USSR to apply military pressure to Turkey and Iran.

Soviet control of the Mediterranean, the oil fields of the Middle East and the approaches to them, as well as dominant influence in the Middle East would seriously alter the global balance of power. The position of the United States in the Middle East and in world affairs would be gravely weakened. In the event of war, the Middle East could also provide an important land passage for the Soviets to the Persian Gulf, the Indian Ocean, and the Far East.

U.S. STRATEGIES. Since World War II the United States has tried in many ways to preserve its strategic access to the Middle East in the face of increased Soviet influence and continuing tensions in this highly volatile area. The United States has attempted to limit and, where possible, decrease Soviet influence. It has taken steps to preserve Israel's independence and security. It has tried to maintain friendly relations with Arab nations particularly those that are pro-West in outlook and policy. It has attempted to promote peace and stability in the region.

To achieve its strategic goals, in the early 1950s the United States developed military alliances and established military bases in the region. With the exception of surveillance posts in Turkey, maintained to monitor Soviet military and nuclear activity, the United States has since withdrawn from nearly all of these bases. However, it continues to maintain the powerful Sixth Fleet in the Mediterranean. In addition, it has increased and strengthened its naval task force in the Indian Ocean and has moved it into the Arabian Sea because of the growing instability in the Persian Gulf region caused by the overturn of the Shah and the seizure of American hostages in Iran, the Soviet invasion of Afghanistan, and the outbreak of war between Iraq and Iran. The United States has also developed a force of highly trained and mobile army and marine-corps units that can be moved rapidly into crisis areas.

Throughout the postwar era the United States has given extended economic and military assistance to friendly Arab nations and to those threatened by Communist subversion or external aggression. The United States also maintained cordial relationships with Iran during the Shah's reign, when Iran was considered the strongest military power in the Persian Gulf. In addition, Israel has been a formidable military offset to Soviet power in the region.

More recently, Washington has persistently attempted to bring stability to the area by encouraging and taking part in negotiations to bring about a permanent peace settlement, particularly between Egypt and Israel.

These policies and strategies are described in more detail in the following sections.

UNITED STATES HELICOPTERS OVER EGYPT
The recent more positive role of the United States in the Middle East – as well as its improved relationship with Egypt – is symbolized by United States helicopters flying over the pyramids on a training flight. They are part of the rapidly growing Rapid Deployment Force created by the United States recently to make it possible for this country to respond more effectively to crisis situations in the region.
Department of Defense

Containment of Soviet Influence

Soviet–American rivalry in the Middle East is a post-World War II development. The issuance of the Truman Doctrine, as a result of Soviet pressure against Greece and Turkey, brought American security interests into the eastern Mediterranean for the first time. The United States and the USSR have been active rivals in the area ever since.

Since the mid-1950s the USSR has tried to undermine the Western political and military position in the region, to implant a Soviet presence, and to encourage a pro-Soviet attitude in nationalist and separatist movements. The United States has tried to contain Soviet expansionism and to win the support of as many Middle East states as possible. Both superpowers have had successes and failures in their competition for influence in this region of rising geopolitical importance.

TRUMAN DOCTRINE. As already indicated, the Truman Doctrine was the first official policy of the United States that was closely related to events near or in the Middle East. The United States committed itself to help Greece, Turkey, and all free peoples threatened by direct or indirect pressure or aggression from outside. The doctrine was one of *containment*, designed to limit the spread of Communism so that newly emerging or established governments would not be overthrown or subverted by Soviet pressures or aggression. Its guarantee of aid to threatened nations was designed to serve as a warning to the USSR. Bolstered by U.S. economic and military aid, Greece and Turkey were able to resist Soviet pressures.

NATO. In 1949, shortly after the United States issued the Truman Doctrine, it joined with twelve nations in the North Atlantic area to sign a military pact aimed at checking and preventing further Soviet expansion. The original members of the *North Atlantic Treaty Organization* (NATO) were the United States, Canada, Iceland, Norway, Great Britain, the Netherlands, Denmark, Belgium, Luxembourg, Portugal, France, and Italy. With the addition of Greece and Turkey in 1951 and West Germany in 1954, NATO became a fifteen-nation alliance of European and North American nations.

The NATO pact was the first important security pact signed by the United States with European nations in over a century and a half.[2] Under its terms the United States and the other members pledged to go to war in support of their treaty allies in case of an armed attack against one or more of them in Europe or North America.

In the more than thirty years since its formation, NATO has had many serious problems. There have been fears on the part of its European members that the United States might not in an emergency live up to its full military commitments to come to their immediate support. They have also been unhappy with the refusal of the United States to share with them control of its European-based nuclear weapons, which are committed to NATO in case of aggression or war. The United States on its part has been concerned with the failure of many of its NATO allies to meet their pledged military contributions to NATO forces. NATO has also not yet been able to solve such problems as the noninterchangeability of weapons and parts among the different national units under its command.

Although NATO nations outstrip Russia and its allies (the Warsaw Pact) in population and wealth, Warsaw Pact countries have in recent years

---

[2] During the American Revolution the United States signed a treaty of alliance with France. Until the NATO agreement, this was its first and only such treaty with a European nation.

UNEASY BRIDGE

MIDDLE
EAST
POLICY
DISPUTES

UNEASY BRIDGE
As an organization NATO has not taken a firm position on the complex issues of the Middle East, although most concerned with growing Soviet strength and influence. European members of the anti-communist alliance have been less supportive of Israel than the United States. New York Public Library

gained a significant edge in military strength (troops, planes, tanks, naval vessels). Since the early 1970s, NATO officials have been worried about the rapid buildup of Soviet military and particularly naval power. They are most concerned with the growing ability of Soviet naval forces to operate freely in all the world's oceans and particularly in the Mediterranean Sea and the Indian Ocean. From 1974, when Greece withdrew its military force from NATO because of the Turkish invasion of Cyprus, until 1980, when it reversed this action, the United States and the West were seriously concerned with the weakening of NATO in a most strategic region.

In addition, NATO has become increasingly concerned with the fact that, as a result of extensive Soviet aid to Ethiopia, Russia has gained access to Red Sea naval bases at Massawa and Assab. This could enable the Soviet Union to control the southern entrance to the Red Sea, which leads to the Suez Canal and Israel. NATO military analysts believe that the Soviet Union plans to establish additional military bases in or near the Middle East from which the oil routes out of the Persian Gulf and the two most important oil-producing states, Saudi Arabia and Iran, could be threatened.

Despite NATO problems and worries, the "NATO shield" has been sufficiently effective to prevent additional European territory from coming under direct Soviet control. Russia's inclusion of the Middle East and adjacent territories in her sphere of interest together with her invasion of Afghanistan has created additional fears. It has also led to a strengthening of NATO forces and greater unity among members.

BAGHDAD PACT. In 1955 the United States took a leading role in promoting the Baghdad Pact in an effort to block or forestall Soviet pressures on the Middle East. Under this treaty Britain, Iran, Iraq, Pakistan, and Turkey pledged to come to the assistance of any of the members if attacked by an outside aggressor. Like the Truman Doctrine and the NATO pact, the Baghdad Pact was aimed at the containment of Soviet influence.

Although in large measure responsible for bringing the Baghdad Pact into existence, the United States did not join as a member. It did not wish to alienate Egypt, which at the time was competing with Iraq for Arab leadership. It also did not wish to create problems in its relations with Israel. Nevertheless, the United States promised military and economic assistance to Baghdad Pact members.

Washington had miscalculated the reaction of the Arab world to its efforts in the 1950s to create a Middle East shield against Communism. Egypt and Syria denounced the Baghdad Pact. Egypt, then under the militant leadership of Nasser, tried to counter the Western buildup of then monarchist Iraq, its regional rival, by turning to Moscow for arms. Russia quickly took advantage of the opportunity to gain entry into the Arab world and a toehold in the Middle East. (Until then Moscow had been thwarted by the Truman Doctrine, had been forced to remove its troops from Iran, and had been denounced by the Arabs for supporting the partition of Palestine.) Within a few years the USSR was able to exploit regional differences in the Middle East and to sign arms agreements with several Arab states. As a result, in the late 1950s and early 1960s, the Soviets came to be regarded by the radical Arab states as their main support in their struggle with Israel.

EISENHOWER DOCTRINE. In 1956 Britain, France, and Israel jointly invaded the Suez Canal Zone (by Britain and France) and the Sinai Peninsula (by Israel). The invasion followed Egypt's illegal nationalization of the Suez Canal and refusal to allow Israeli ships to use it. Nevertheless the U.S. government condemned the invasion as a violation of U.N. principles, although it had the approval of many Americans. Combined U.S.–Soviet pressure caused Britain, France, and Israel to call off their military action and thereby helped save Egypt from a disastrous military defeat.

As a result of their invasion and withdrawal from the Canal Zone, Britain and France suffered a major diplomatic defeat. Their already-declining prestige in the Middle East almost disappeared completely. The British lost their position of predominance in Jordan and Iraq. Jordan requested the withdrawal of British advisers and military experts. Iraq's pro-Western monarchy was overthrown in 1958, and the country came under control of a radical Arab government. At approximately the same time civil war broke out in Lebanon.

Termination of the Anglo–French role as the major defender of Western interests in the Arab world created a "power vacuum." In an attempt to prevent the Soviet Union from taking advantage of the increasingly unstable situation in the Middle East, the United States issued the *Eisenhower Doctrine*. This doctrine took the form of a joint resolution of both houses of Congress, drafted at the urging of President Eisenhower. It stated that the United States was prepared to aid any Middle East nation requesting assistance against armed aggression by any country inspired or controlled by "international Communism."

The Eisenhower Doctrine was aimed at preventing the Soviet Union from expanding its influence in the region. It was also a response to the activities of radical groups that threatened the pro-Western governments in Jordan and Lebanon.

In 1958 the Eisenhower Doctrine was applied for the first (and only) time.

PRESIDENT EISENHOWER DISCUSSING AMERICAN INTERVENTION
IN LEBANON IN 1958

When Soviet and Nasser-backed Muslims tried to overthrow the Maronite Christian government of Lebanon in 1958, President Camille Chamoun asked the United States to intervene. President Eisenhower responded by dispatching 15,000 U.S. marines to Lebanon. They were withdrawn several months later. This was the only application of the Eisenhower Doctrine (see text). Shown above are President Eisenhower and Rashid Karame, Prime Minister of Lebanon, discussing the situation. Eisenhower Library

In that year pro-Nasser opponents of the pro-Western regime of President Camille Chamoun in Lebanon tried to overthrow the government. The attempt was Soviet-encouraged. At the request of President Chamoun, President Eisenhower ordered 15,000 troops to Lebanon. He declared that Lebanon's independence was vital to the U.S. national interest and to world peace. Eisenhower charged that the United Arab Republic[3] and the Soviet Union were attempting to overthrow the government of Lebanon by force. The United States withdrew its forces three months later, after the rebellion was put down.

CENTO. U.S. attempts to organize an anti-Communist alliance in the Arab world collapsed in 1958 with the downfall of the monarchy in Iraq. In a military coup, the pro-Western regime was replaced by one favorable to the Soviet Union. The new Iraqi regime immediately withdrew from the Baghdad Pact, causing its remaining members to reorganize their alliance as the Central Treaty Organization (CENTO), consisting of Britain, Turkey, Iran, and Pakistan (1959). To reassure the remaining former members of the Baghdad Pact of its continuing support, the United States helped in the organization of CENTO and also made even more specific pledges to come to the defense of Turkey, Iran, and Pakistan (all non-Arab states) in case of Communist aggression or subversion.

Although every American president reemphasized the United States's commitment to protect the Middle East from Communist aggression and to uphold the territorial integrity of Israel and the Arab nations, CENTO remained a largely inactive defense pact until 1979 when it collapsed after Iran and Pakistan withdrew, following the overthrow of the Iranian monarchy.

ARMS SALES TO MIDDLE EAST NATIONS. To counterbalance the influence gained by the USSR through arms sales to Middle East nations favorable to Soviet policies, the United States has supplied missiles, tanks, planes, and other military equipment to the same nations. U.S. arms sales to Iran enabled that country to play the role of "guardian" of the Persian Gulf in the 1970s. The United States has also sold increasing quantities of arms to Israel since the 1960s, in order to maintain the military balance between Israel and its Arab enemies. The Soviets helped rebuild Egypt's military forces after Egypt's disastrous defeat by Israel in 1967. They also have supplied arms to Syria, Iraq, Libya, and South Yemen.

U.S.–SOVIET NAVAL RIVALRY. To help achieve their tactical and strategic short-range and long-range objectives, the United States and the USSR

[3] The United Arab Republic was a short-lived union of Egypt and Syria lasting from 1958 to 1961. (See p. 106.)

INDIAN OCEAN: The U.S. and the Soviet Presence

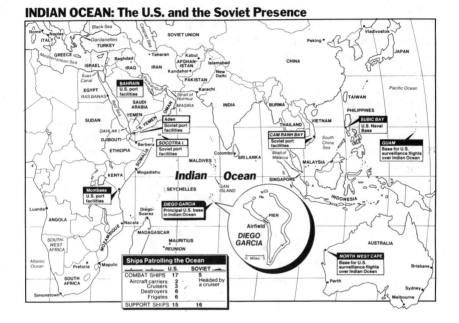

SUPERPOWER RIVALRY IN THE MIDDLE EAST

United States-Soviet superpower rivalry in the Mediterranean has in recent years been extended to the Red Sea, the Persian Gulf and the Indian Ocean, as this New York Times map shows (April 19, 1981). New York Times

have become naval rivals in the Mediterranean Sea and the Indian Ocean.

Since World War II the United States has maintained task forces of the Sixth Fleet in the Mediterranean to sustain its strategic interests. In 1958 this fleet was deployed to Lebanon to help the government quell a rebellion that was supported by Egypt and the USSR. During the Arab–Israeli Six Day War of 1967, the capabilities of U.S. Mediterranean naval forces were instrumental in blocking the threat of Soviet intervention on the Arab side. Sixth Fleet units assigned to NATO have had access to naval facilities in Greece, Turkey, and Cyprus.

In spite of American naval power in the area, since the Six Day War Soviet naval power in the Mediterranean has grown to the point where it now seriously rivals U.S. strength. The Soviets have built a modern and powerful fleet and have taken full advantage of passage rights through the Turkish Straits and naval facilities in Syria.

The United States has become increasingly worried about the overall Soviet buildup. It is concerned that in a future Arab–Israeli crisis, Spain and other European nations might again — as they did in the 1973 war — refuse to grant refueling rights to American supply planes heading for Israel. In addition, the continuing dispute between Turkey and Greece over Cyprus may endanger NATO naval facilities in either or both countries.

Superpower rivalry in the Mediterranean has been matched by growing rivalry in the area of the Red Sea, the Indian Ocean, and the Persian Gulf. In recent years increased Soviet naval activity in the region has been made possible by Soviet installations in Iraq, at the head of the Persian Gulf, in South Yemen and Somalia, and on opposite sides of the Gulf of Aden (between the Red Sea and the Indian Ocean). When in 1978 Somalia closed down a Soviet naval base because of Russian support of Ethiopia in an ongoing war between Somalia and Ethiopia, the USSR sought new bases in Ethiopia on the Red Sea.

To counter the Soviet threat and protect its valuable oil supply route from the Persion Gulf to the West, the United States has obtained docking facilities at Bahrain for a small naval force in the Persian Gulf. This makes possible a U.S. presence in the area and facilitates U.S. naval patrols along the southern coast of the Arabian Peninsula and the east coast of Africa. In 1975 the United States began to develop naval and air-support facilities on Diego Garcia, a British-owned atoll in the Indian Ocean 1,000 miles south of India.

MILITARY PRECAUTIONS. In 1973, during the fourth Arab–Israeli war, the United States acted to prevent a possible Soviet troop movement into the Middle East by placing U.S. military forces on a worldwide alert. Since they have been as anxious as the United States to avoid a direct military confrontation, the Soviets abandoned whatever plans they may have had for such an action. Prior to the war both superpowers had replenished the participants with large quantities of arms to enable them to rebuild the military strength drained by the Six Day War of 1967.

CHANGING U.S. MILITARY POLICY. Since the U.S. embassy in Iran was overrun by Islamic militants and American hostages were taken in November 1979, the United States has been developing a new military strategy for the Middle East, in order to be able to better protect its oil and other interests in the region. President Jimmy Carter announced the new strategy in his State of the Union address in January 1980: "An attempt by any outside force to gain control of the Persian Gulf region will be repelled by any means necessary, including military force." The United States has since taken a number of steps to implement the "Carter Doctrine."

—It has organized and trained a small but growing Rapid Deployment Force that can be moved swiftly into crisis spots in the Middle East and elsewhere. This force has been field tested in maneuvers in Egypt. By the mid-1980s U.S. military planners hoped to be able to transport a force of

100,000 to the Middle East within thirty-five days, including heavy equipment — a task that would have taken up to six months at the beginning of the decade.

—It has equipped this and other U.S. forces in the region with the latest weaponry. During the hostilities between Iraq and Iran, four highly sophisticated radar aircraft warning planes (AWACS) were placed on patrol over Saudi Arabia to detect any threats of air attack on oil fields in the Gulf area.

—It has gained expanded access to military facilities in Oman, Somalia, and Kenya in the Persian Gulf and Indian Ocean regions, and has strengthened its naval base on the island of Diego Garcia in the Indian Ocean. Egyptian President Sadat offered the United States full use of his nation's military facilities in the event of crises in the Gulf.

—Over $5 billion a year has been committed to the purchase of planes and ships needed for transporting troops and supplies to the Middle East.

The U.S. buildup has been hastened by the Soviet invasion of Afghanistan in December 1979 and the war between Iraq and Iran, which began in September 1980.

President Ronald Reagan, on assuming office in January 1981, criticized the Carter administration's Middle East policy as inadequate and pledged to make the defense of the Persian Gulf from Russian domination his main Middle East objective. He later asked Congress to approve a massive $8.5 billion military sales program for Saudi Arabia, including five AWACS, sophisticated surveillance planes. President Reagan also promised continued military support for Egypt and Israel.

Support for Israel

In recent years the United States has become the world's most steadfast supporter of Israel's security and survival. A special relationship has developed between the two countries since the time when the United States gave its support to the U.N. partition plan and recognized Israel as an independent nation. President Ronald Reagan has continually emphasized that Israel, with the most effective army in the Middle East, is vital as a deterrent to possible Soviet aggression and thus essential to America's national interest. The special relationship between the United States and Israel has not, of course, prevented differences of opinion on many occasions.

Although Israel's survival is important if not vital to the United States for strategic as well as emotional reasons, American foreign policy in part reflects the conflict between sympathy for Israel and U.S. economic and political interest in maintaining good relations with the Arab world because of its oil resources.

PRESIDENT TRUMAN AND PRESIDENT WEIZMANN OF ISRAEL
Within minutes after the British left Palestine and the new state of Israel was declared (May 14, 1948), President Truman of the United States recognized Israel. Here Dr. Chaim Weizmann, first President of Israel and lifelong advocate of a Jewish homeland in Palestine, presents a Torah (Scroll of Holy Scriptures) to President Truman during a visit to the White House shortly thereafter expressing the gratitude of the Jewish people. Truman Library

REASONS FOR U.S. SUPPORT OF ISRAEL. President Harry Truman was the first world leader to recognize Israel. Since then every U.S. president and Congress has expressed America's commitment to Israel.[4] This position has had widespread public support.

The United States has supported Israel for a number of important reasons:

1. Israel is the only democracy in the entire area and a reliable anti-Communist bastion. It is the only Middle East nation linked with the West whose future does not depend on the survival or whim of an autocratic ruler or military regime.

2. Israel's existence as a strong pro-West state is in the national strategic interest of the United States. In any major confrontation with the Soviet

[4] Despite these expressed declarations of official support, there has been fairly strong pro-Arab sentiment within each administration.

Union in the Middle East, over oil or for any other reason, Israel could be a key defense point for the United States. It could serve as a supply depot, a refueling base, and a tactical support for American military force. Israel's own military capabilities could be pooled with those of NATO or the United States.

3. Support for Israel is in line with the American moral tradition of sympathy for victims of persecution and for people striving for nationhood.

4. The attachment to Israel of the overwhelming majority of America's six million Jews as well as tens of millions of sympathetic Christians has created a special bond between the two countries.

U.S. AID TO ISRAEL. The United States has given Israel political, economic, and military aid.

Political Aid. The United States has been a firm supporter of Israel's right to exist. After the 1967 Arab–Israeli war, President Johnson stressed the right of each nation in the Middle East to live without attack or fear of extinction. Every American president has since expressed the same principle, which became part of U.N. Security Council Resolution 242, promulgated later the same year (November 12, 1967). The resolution calls for the acknowledgment, respect, and guarantee of "the sovereignty, territorial integrity and political independence of every state in the area and their right to live in peace within secure and recognized boundaries free from threats or acts of force."

The United States has also refused to brand Israel an "aggressor" in Soviet- and Third-World-encouraged U.N. debates on Arab-sponsored resolutions. In 1975 the United States and other Western nations condemned and voted against a resolution adopted by the U.N. General Assembly that labeled Zionism "a form of racism and racial discrimination." Many nations that voted for the resolution did so under pressure from the Arab nations on whom they were dependent for oil or petrodollars.

Economic Aid. In line with America's policy of supporting and strengthening its allies around the world, the United States has given Israel considerable amounts of economic assistance, largely in the form of government loans and grants. Additional aid has been raised for Israel's social and humanitarian needs through private sources. Advocates of continued aid for Israel point out that it is particularly essential because Israel has had to divert the largest portion of its budget to military expenditures in order to assure its own survival.

By giving economic aid to Israel and other Middle East nations in order to improve living standards, the United States has hoped to deter instability and conflict. In 1955 the United States became involved in efforts to promote a plan to permit Jordan and Israel to share the waters of the Jordan

AMERICAN STUDENT VOLUNTEERS IN ISRAEL
Many American student volunters have spent their summer vacations in Israel, touring, learning the language, and — as shown here — working on a kibbutz. Israel Government Tourist Office

River for their mutual benefit. The plan could never be implemented because of Arab–Israel tension.

Over the years the willingness of the United States to supply arms to Israel has depended on its view of what has been most needed to achieve American goals in the Middle East. During the 1950s and early 1960s, U.S. policy was based on the judgment that *economic* development was the best means of helping to stabilize the Middle East and counter Russian influence. The United States joined with Britain and France in 1950 to issue a Tripartite Declaration opposing an arms race and the use of force in the region. Despite Soviet arms shipments to Egypt after 1955, the United States refused to sell arms to Israel on the ground that this would lead to an Arab–Israeli arms race.

Military Aid. In the early 1960s the United States became concerned that the growing sale of Soviet arms to Egypt, Syria, and Iraq was beginning to threaten the military balance in the Middle East, to the advantage of the USSR. As a result the United States began to reconsider its position on supplying weapons to Israel. In 1962 Israel was able for the first time to buy limited quantities of U.S. antiaircraft missiles.[5] In 1965 it received U.S. tanks, and in 1966 Israel began to receive U.S. combat aircraft.

After France decided to stop selling arms to Israel in 1967, the United States stepped up the quantity of its arms sales. In recent years the United States has become Israel's major arms supplier. Since 1967, it has sent arms to Israel when it has felt that Soviet arms aid to Arab nations endangered the military balance. In 1971, expressing "great concern over the deepening involvement of the Soviet Union in the Middle East and the clear and present danger to world peace resulting from such involvement, which cannot be ignored," Congress authorized the transfer of increased quantities of aircraft and supporting equipment to Israel. During the Arab–Israeli war of 1973, massive quantities of U.S. military supplies were airlifted to Israel to prevent it from being defeated by the Soviet-equipped forces of Egypt and Syria.

Since 1973 the United States has continued to sell military equipment to Israel as well as to other Middle East nations. Although President Carter declared that Israel was entitled to arms because of its "special relationship" with the United States, the decision of the Carter administration in early 1978 to also sell jet aircraft to Egypt and Saudi Arabia became a matter of great controversy, particularly in Congress, and caused temporary strains in U.S.–Israeli relations.

Critics have argued that recent U.S. arms policy has contributed to an arms race in the Middle East and that selling arms to all sides can have harmful consequences. Supporters of the policy, including Presidents Ford, Carter, and Reagan, have argued that U.S. arms sales strengthen our allies, preserve regional balances of power, and help us maintain influence in countries that receive the arms. Although President Carter called for a reduction in U.S. worldwide arms sales, during his administration these sales reached all-time highs with the Middle East the biggest customer.

After Israel destroyed the Iraqi nuclear reactor, President Reagan suspended delivery of fighter planes which the U.S. had sold to Israel, pending a determination as to whether American planes had been used in the raid. The embargo was continued when Israel bombed the PLO's Beirut headquarters, but was later lifted. When Prime Minister Begin visited the White House in September 1981, President Reagan declared that the security of Israel was a principal objective of his administration and that

---

[5] Whereas Israel has received its arms aid through loans and *purchases*, Soviet aid to Arab nations has largely taken the form of *gifts* (grants), without the expectation of repayment.

U.S. ARMS TO ISRAEL
The United States has given considerable economic and military assistance to both Israel and the Arab states. These are military weapons and equipment sold to Israel. Israel Consulate

"we regard Israel as an ally in our search for regional stability." The two leaders discussed steps for strengthening strategic ties, including joint planning to counter the Soviet Union, joint naval maneuvers, increased sharing of intelligence information, use of Israeli facilities to repair American military craft, and stockpiling of medical equipment in Israel for use in emergency U.S. military action in the Middle East.

Maintaining Good Relations with the Arab World

At the same time that the United States supports Israel, it has attempted to maintain friendly and supportive relations with as many Arab and other states in the Middle East as possible, and particularly those with a pro-Western orientation. This "evenhanded policy" has been in evidence on many occasions and has been a consistent thread in U.S. Middle East diplomacy since World War II.

AID TO PALESTINIAN REFUGEES. The United Nations has supported Palestinian refugees since the first Arab–Israeli war of 1948. The United States, as part of its U.N. responsibilities, has been the major source of financial aid to the Palestinians through the U.N. Relief and Works Agency (UNRWA). The Arab states and the Soviet Union have given little or no support. The United States has also supported the principle of Palestinian participation in the determination of their future.

ECONOMIC AND MILITARY ASSISTANCE. Billions of dollars in U.S. economic and military loans, grants, and sales have gone to many Arab and other Middle East nations to win their support or counter Russian aid. Egypt, Israel, Iran, Jordan, and Turkey have received the largest portions of U.S. economic assistance. Iran, Saudi Arabia, Turkey, Israel, Jordan, and Kuwait have received the most military aid. The United States did not oppose British shipments of arms to Iraq, Jordan, and Egypt in the late 1950s, while at the same time it refused Israeli requests for such supplies (until the 1960s).

MILITARY RESTRAINTS ON ISRAEL. Although the United States has been concerned about Israel's survival as an independent state, it has not allowed Israel to determine the character of the peace on the basis of Israeli military victories.

In each of the wars between Israel and the Arabs, the United States has joined with the Soviet Union to demand a halt to Israeli military advances against the Arabs. After the Suez War of 1956, a U.S. threat to impose economic sanctions forced Israel to remove all its forces from the Sinai. After the 1967 war, the United States and other members of the Security Council unanimously approved Security Council Resolution 242, calling for withdrawal of Israeli forces from territories occupied during the war — but only, of course, on the basis of Arab willingness to negotiate a genuine peace.

The United States supplied military equipment to Israel during the Arab–Israeli war of 1973 to correct the military imbalance caused by the Soviet Union's military aid to Egypt and Syria. Nevertheless it joined with the USSR in calling for a cease-fire when the Israelis succeeded in breaking through Arab lines on the two fronts, crossing the west bank of the Suez Canal in the west and advancing in the east to within twenty miles of Syria's capital, Damascus.

Washington officials and especially Secretary of State Henry Kissinger felt that a total Israeli victory would hamper U.S. efforts in a number of directions—improving relations with Arab states, assuring a steady supply of Persian Gulf oil to the West and Japan, and bringing about peace negotiations between Israel and the Arab states. Moreover, there was the possibility that Russia would intervene militarily rather than lose face with the Arab world.

In addition, though firmly committed to Israel's security, the United

States has indicated disapproval of certain of Israel's policies on a number of occasions since 1973, particularly with regard to establishment of additional settlements in the West Bank during the peace negotiations that dealt with autonomy for the West Bank. The Regan administration, however, broke with the position of the Carter administration by stating that new Israeli settlements on the West Bank were not illegal (as Carter had stressed) though they might be unwise.

CORDIAL RELATIONS WITH KEY NATIONS. To protect the oil flow to the West and to promote regional stability, the United States has given military and economic assistance to Arab and non-Arab states. It has as a result maintained cordial relations with a number of key countries in the region, including Turkey, Saudi Arabia, Jordan, and Iran (until its 1978–1979 revolution). In the post-1973 period Egypt has reversed its relations with the Soviet Union and "tilted" toward the United States. Consequently, the United States today is the only superpower with major influence on both of what until recently were the two main protagonists in the Arab–Israeli conflict.

Turkey. Turkey has been linked to the United States through its membership in NATO. It supplies ground forces to the Western military alliance. To strengthen and maintain ties with Turkey, the United States has given it generous amounts of economic and military aid. In return for its assistance the United States has been permitted to establish a number of electronic bases or "listening posts" in Turkey to monitor Soviet nuclear and missile development.

Turkey has for the most part been pro-West in its foreign policy. Nevertheless, U.S.–Turkish relations deteriorated for several years after Turkey's invasion of Cyprus in 1974. Its use of American arms in the venture resulted in a U.S. embargo on arms to Turkey. This in turn caused Turkey to close down the U.S. surveillance bases within its boundaries. With the lifting of the arms embargo by Congress in 1978, the use of these monitoring stations was restored to the United States.

Although Turkey is still an important member of NATO, it has been careful in recent years not to antagonize its powerful northern neighbor by allying itself too closely with the United States. In 1978 it signed a nonaggression pact with the Soviets and has since improved its economic relations with them.

Iran. Before the overthrow of the Shah in 1979 American relations with Iran were friendly. Until violent and growing opposition to the Shah and his policies manifested itself in the late 1970s, Iran seemed to the U.S. government to be one of the more stable Middle East regimes. Massive sales of U.S. arms to Iran under the Shah strengthened its ties to the United States as well as its determination to become the dominant power in the Persian Gulf region. The United States depended on Iran for a large share of its imported oil and considered its ties with the Shah's regime an important offset to Soviet ambitions.

The overturn of the Shah in 1979 and the establishment of an Islamic republic headed by Ayatollah Khomeini has had serious political and economic consequences for the United States and the rest of the world. The taking of American hostages and the violent denunciation of the United States by the Ayatollah have led to a breaking of ties between the two countries. The United States has expelled Iranian diplomats and imposed an embargo on American exports to Iran. Iran has ceased selling oil to the United States. (See Chapter 3 for a discussion of the recent Iranian crisis.)

Saudia Arabia. The United States has maintained close relations with Saudi Arabia since World War II. For many years its influence in the oil-rich Arab state has been greater than that of any other foreign power. Aside from disagreements over American support for Israel, relations between the Saudis and the United States have for the most part been cordial.

In the past few years Saudi Arabia has become the most influential and richest Arab state in the Middle East. Its annual oil income has exceeded $90 billion, and it has the fastest-growing military arsenal of any Arab state. At

THE UNITED STATES AND SAUDI ARABIA

The United States has had close relationships with Saudi Arabia for most of the period since World War II. Here top level Saudi diplomats meet in Washington, D.C., with Vice President Mondale, Foreign Affairs Advisor Brzezinski and Secretary of State Cyrus Vance during the Carter Administration. Aramco Photo

various times the Saudis have been the chief financial backers of Egypt, Jordan, Syria, and the PLO. But the Saudis were leaders in putting teeth into the Arab oil embargo of 1973 and have been influential in determining the rises in oil prices fixed by the Organization of Petroleum Exporting Countries (OPEC).

The Saudis do not maintain diplomatic relations with any Communist state and have strongly opposed the spread of Communist influence in the Muslim world. They are suspicious of the radical socialist regimes established in Syria, Libya, Iraq, and South Yemen, and of the support given these regimes by the USSR. In the past they saw themselves as counterbalancing Iran's growing economic and military strength in the Persian Gulf, in order to be sure that Arab interests in the area were protected.

The formerly close relationship between Saudi Arabia and the United States has cooled somewhat in recent years because of American sponsorship of peace negotiations between Egypt and Israel. The Saudis were further disillusioned by the failure of the Carter administration to take more effective steps to obtain the release of American hostages taken by the Khomeini regime in Iran, and also by the failure of the United States to act effectively against the USSR for its invasion of Afghanistan.

Since the United States began to take a firmer military posture during the last year of the Carter administration and especially since the inauguration of President Reagan, the Saudis have once again become somewhat more favorably disposed toward the United States. In response to their request for help in warding off a possible Iranian attempt to block the Strait of Hormuz at the mouth of the Gulf or to take action against Gulf states aiding the Iraqi war effort, including Saudi Arabia itself, President Carter sent four AWACS (Airborne Warning and Control System) aircraft to Saudi Arabia to patrol the Gulf, together with ground radar units and 600 technicians. The U.S. move was seen as a turning point in reversing the Saudi feeling that the United States had turned its back on its Middle East Arab allies.

In the fall of 1981, President Reagan informed Congress that he proposed to sell Saudi Arabia an $8.5 billion military package, consisting of five radar surveillance planes (AWACS) plus range-extending fuel tanks, air-to-air missiles, and tanker aircraft that the Saudis had requested to enhance the sixty-two F-15 fighter planes scheduled for delivery in 1982 or 1983. The Israelis feared that Saudi Arabia would be able to cripple Israel's defenses with the increased range and destructive power of the F-15s and the sophisticated monitoring capability of the AWACS.

Many U.S. Senators and Representatives objected to the sale. They pointed out that the AWACS would constitute a serious threat to Israel's security. In addition, the Saudis had not supported American peace efforts in the Middle East, and there was a danger that American secret technology would fall into the wrong hands (including the U.S.S.R.) if the Saudi government were overthrown, as the Shah of Iran had been. The Reagan administration defended the sale on the grounds that it would enhance the defense of the Persian Gulf.

Jordan. American relations with Jordan have also for the most part been friendly for many years. Since 1946, the United States has sold Jordan well over half a billion dollars worth of missiles and other military equipment and has granted it loans to make such purchases possible. Jordan has received over a billion dollars in U.S. economic aid. In 1970 and 1971 the United States, along with Israel, was supportive of King Hussein's efforts to put down a major attempt by Palestinian guerrillas (supported by Syrian tanks) to overthrow his regime. Although he has consistently supported the Arab cause, Hussein has—relatively speaking—taken a less extremist attitude toward Israel than the PLO and the "rejectionist" Arab states (Syria, Iraq, Libya, and South Yemen). As in the case of Saudi Arabia, U.S.–Jordanian relations cooled after the peace agreement between Israel and Egypt and have remained somewhat strained since.

U.S. AID TO JORDAN

In its effort to maintain good relationships with Arab states in the Middle East, the United States has given much economic assistance and advice. Above Dr. Lyle Hayden, former Executive Director of the Near East Foundation, discusses olive tree growth with Jordanian officials. Near East Foundation

Egypt. Following a period of cordial relations after the July 1952 revolution in Egypt (which overturned the monarchy), relations between the two countries deteriorated. President Nasser was angered when the United States withdrew a promise to help finance the Aswan Dam. He opposed the Baghdad Pact and the Eisenhower Doctrine as attempts to block Arab unity under Egyptian leadership.

After the invasion of the Suez Canal Zone in 1956 by Britain and France in coordination with Israeli military actions in the Gaza Strip and the Sinai, Nasser turned to the Soviet Union for economic and military assistance. After the war of 1967, the USSR rebuilt the Egyptian military arsenal and provided military advisers. During this period Egypt broke off diplomatic relations with the United States.

In 1972 Nasser's successor, President Anwar Sadat, expelled the Russians. Relations with the United States were resumed after the 1973 war with Israel. Since then Egypt has increasingly looked to the United States for support.

Since 1974 President Sadat increasingly relied on the United States to bring about a general Middle East settlement, and relations between the two nations have improved considerably. Sadat believed that the United States, because of Israel's dependence on it, was the only country that can persuade Israel to make concessions to the Arabs. In 1978, in an effort to further cement relationships, the United States agreed to sell military aircraft to Egypt. American assurances to Egypt (as well as to Israel) helped pave the way for a peace treaty between Israel and Egypt in 1979. Today, America's commitment to Egypt, the major power in the Arab world with half of all Arabs in the Middle East, is greater than that to any other Arab state and President Sadat was eager to cooperate with the United States to counter what he and American officials fear may be a growing Soviet threat in the Persian Gulf region.

Attempts to Preserve Peace and Stability in the Middle East

To achieve its primary goal of preserving strategic access to the Middle East and its oil resources, the United States has, to the extent possible, tried to bring peace and stability to the Middle East. At times U.S. involvement has been very direct; at other times it has been less active. But since 1973, as we shall see in the next chapter, the U.S. role has become more active than ever before.

Mastery Activities

1. Briefly explain or identify each of the following names or terms as used in this chapter:

Cold War
U.N. Partition Plan for Palestine
U.S. Sixth Fleet
Superpower rivalry
Holocaust
Truman Doctrine
NATO
CENTO

Tripartite Declaration of 1950 ✓
Suez Crisis (1956)
Diego Garcia
United Nations Relief and Works
    Agency (UNRWA)
Security Council Resolution 242
Eisenhower Doctrine ✓

2. Write the names of the two large bodies of water linked by each of the following strategic water passages:

(a) Suez Canal: connects the ___ *Med, Oc.* ___ with
    the ___ *Red Sea* ___

(b) Straits of Gibraltar: connect the ___ *Atlantic* ___ with
    the ___ *Med. Oc.* ___

(c) Straits of Bab el Mandeb: connect the ___ *Red Sea* ___ with
    the ___ *Indian Ocean* ___

(d) Turkish Straits: connect the ___ *Med Oc* ___ with
    the ___ *Black Sea* ___

(e) Strait of Hormuz: connects the ___ *Persian* ___ with
    the ___ *Indian Oc.* ___

3. Following is a graph showing the extent of the sale of military arms and equipment by the United States to Saudi Arabia during the 1970s.

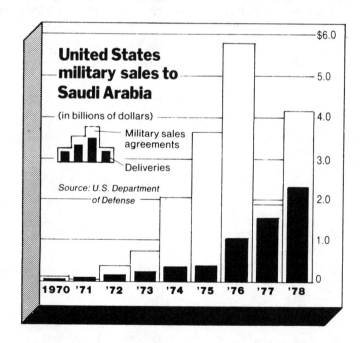

United States military sales to Saudi Arabia

(in billions of dollars)

Military sales agreements

Deliveries

Source: U.S. Department of Defense

$6.0
5.0
4.0
3.0
2.0
1.0
0

1970 '71 '72 '73 '74 '75 '76 '77 '78

Show your understanding of this graph by printing in the space to the left of each statement a T, F, or NS to indicate whether, on the basis of the information given, it is true, false, or there is not enough information to make such a judgment.

___ (1) The information in the graph is based on official sources.

___ (2) Military deliveries but *not* military sales rose steadily from 1970 to 1978.

___ (3) For the period shown, U.S. military sales exceeded $20 billion.

___ (4) Saudi Arabia has been the largest single recipient of U.S. arms in the Middle East.

___ (5) Total U.S. military sales to Saudi Arabia from 1970 to 1978 were greatest in 1978.

Questions for Homework and Discussion

1. Why did the United States become directly involved with the Middle East after World War II?

2. Explain how the need for oil has shaped U.S. policy in the Middle East.

3. What has the United States done to check the growth of Soviet influence in the Middle East? How successful has it been?

4. Explain why and how the United States has supported Israel politically, militarily, and economically since World War II.

5. In addition to supporting Israel since World War II, the United States has tried to maintain good relations with Arab and other key countries in the Middle East.
   (a) Discuss three steps taken by the United States to stay on good terms with Muslim states in the Middle East.
   (b) Explain one problem faced by the United States in maintaining cordial relations with each of the following: Egypt, Iran, Jordan, Saudi Arabia, Turkey.

7

The United States and Attempts to Preserve Peace and Stability in the Middle East

Tension and instability in the Middle East stem at least as much from inter-Arab and regional disputes as from the Arab–Israeli conflict. For this reason the United States has been concerned with many developments in the area for over three decades.

American concerns climaxed during the Carter administration in late 1979 and 1980 because of crises resulting from the taking of American hostages by the new Islamic regime of Ayatollah Khomeini following the overthrow of the Iranian monarchy, the Soviet invasion of Afghanistan, and the Iran–Iraq war. An additional, pressing challenge was created by the growing mobilization of anti-imperialist Muslim sentiments into a specifically anti-American movement — including the prolonged holding of the hostages in Iran and attacks on U.S. embassies and consulates in other parts of the Muslim world.

The Truman Administration (1947–1953)

The United States has tried to deal with the Arab–Israeli conflict since shortly after Israel's independence. During the first Arab–Israeli war (1948–1949) the United States adopted a policy of neutrality and support for U.N. actions. The Truman administration hoped that the war and the armistice agreements negotiated by U.N. mediator Ralph Bunche (an American) would be followed by permanent peace and economic and social progress in the Middle East. The premise was that instability and conflict would be avoided if living conditions improved.

195

NOBEL PEACE PRIZE WINNER RALPH BUNCHE U.N. mediator Ralph Bunche, an American, negotiated the armistice agreements bringing the Arab-Israel War of 1948-49 to an end. In 1950 he received the Nobel Peace Prize for this achievement. He is seen examining the certificate awarded to him in Oslo shortly after the awards ceremony. Wide World

The Eisenhower Administration (1953–1961)

The administration of President Dwight D. Eisenhower tried to strengthen the position of the United States in the Arab world in order to counteract growing Soviet influence. John Foster Dulles, secretary of state in the Eisenhower administration, became the first U.S. secretary of state to visit the Middle East. When he returned he urged a policy of "impartial friendship."

To contain Communism, the Eisenhower administration sponsored the Baghdad Pact and issued the Eisenhower Doctrine. In an attempt to show "impartial friendship" it played down its support for Israel and criticized Israel's retaliatory actions against Arab terrorist raids from the Gaza Strip and the demilitarized zone between Syria and Israel.

Strains between Israel and the United States developed when the latter refrained from providing Israel with arms to counteract the growing Middle East military imbalance in the 1950s. Relations worsened considerably after the Suez invasion of 1956, when America threatened sanctions against Israel to compel it to withdraw its troops from the Gaza Strip and Sinai Peninsula.

U.S. attempts to build a Middle East anti-Communist alliance backfired when the new revolutionary regime in Iraq withdrew from the Baghdad Pact and Egypt under President Nasser turned to the Soviet Union for arms and economic aid. Although U.S. relations with Jordan and Lebanon improved as a result of U.S. intervention in Lebanon in 1958, the U.S. position in the region as a whole was weakened because of criticism by other Arab states of this action.

The Kennedy Administration (1961–1963)

The Kennedy administration tried to regain some of the influence in the Arab world lost to the USSR in the preceding years. It gave large-scale economic aid to Egypt and assured Egyptian President Nasser and other

PRESIDENT JOHN F. KENNEDY AND ISRAELI PRIME MINISTER DAVID BEN-GURION
President Kennedy of the United States believed that it was essential to maintain a balance of power in the Middle East. During his Administration the U.S. began to sell arms to Israel. He is shown meeting with Israeli Prime Minister David Ben-Gurion, one of the founders of the Jewish state. Zionist Archives

Arab leaders of its understanding of the region's problems, including the need to do something about the problem of Arab refugees. It also gave up U.S. attempts to build a Middle East military alliance, recognizing that they had failed.

President Kennedy also became convinced that it was necessary to correct the growing arms imbalance against Israel. He indicated that a "balance of power" would be a guiding principle of American Middle East policy. In 1962, for the first time, the United States began to sell arms to Israel (antiaircraft missiles).

The Johnson Administration (1963–1969)

In the early 1960s the United States became increasingly concerned with President Nasser's attempts to encourage pro-Nasser coups in Syria and other Arab states as part of his campaign for pan-Arab unity under Egypt's leadership. The Johnson administration became particularly concerned about Nasser's intervention on the side of the rebels in the civil war in Yemen, with Russian support.

In the belief that Nasser's expansionist foreign policies were a threat to the more cooperative regimes of Saudi Arabia and the Persian Gulf principalities, Johnson decided to adopt a hard nosed policy of phasing out economic assistance to Nasserite Egypt. He also decided to continue to supply arms to Israel to restore the military balance. Offensive weapons, including tanks and advanced fighter-bombers, were sold by the United States to Israel for the first time.

The Arab–Israeli war of 1967 marked a significant turning point in U.S.–Israeli relations. Although the United States had been "neutral" during the war, it saw in Israel's remarkable victory a means of achieving its own goal of Middle East stability. For the first time since Israel's birth, American policy makers recognized that a *strong* as well as a secure Israel might be in the best interest of the United States.

The Johnson policy emerged after the war. In June 1967 President Johnson set forth four general principles he believed essential to any overall peace settlement in the Middle East, namely: (1) Every Middle East nation has the right to exist and live without attack; (2) the Arab refugee problem must be settled by all concerned nations, with justice; (3) all Middle East nations must respect the international waterways in the region; and (4) the political independence and territorial boundaries of each nation must be recognized.

Although it continued to pursue the goal of maintaining good relations with friendly Arab nations, the Johnson administration took a number of steps to implement its new policy decisions with regard to Israel. Unlike in

1956 (during the Suez War), the United States did not join the Soviets and Arabs in calling for withdrawal by Israel from territories captured in the 1967 war. Moreover, it helped Israel resist diplomatic and military pressure for such a pullback.

Although it voted for Security Council Resolution 242—the U.N. statement of guiding principles for an overall Middle East peace settlement—the United States interpreted the principle of return of occupied territories in the same spirit as did the Israelis, namely, as part of an overall peace settlement of Arab–Israeli differences. In the U.N. debates following the 1967 war, the United States refused to condemn Israel as an aggressor.

When it became evident, after the war of 1967, that the Soviets had rebuilt the Egyptian and Syrian arms stockpiles to a point where Egypt and Syria might consider going to war to recover Israeli-occupied territory, Johnson decided to discourage such a possibility. In a move that nearly doubled the capacity of the Israeli air force, he agreed to sell Israel fifty powerful fighter-bombers.

The Nixon and Ford Administrations (1969–1977)

On assuming office in January 1969, President Richard Nixon stated that the Middle East was becoming an explosive "powder keg" that needed to be defused "because the next explosion, I think, could involve very well a confrontation between nuclear powers, which we want to avoid." From 1969 to the beginning of the fourth Arab–Israeli war in 1973, the Nixon administration undertook a number of peace initiatives that for the first time involved the United States actively in efforts to negotiate a settlement.

From 1968 to 1970, in a departure from previous policy, the United States carried out a series of bilateral talks with the Soviet Union, as well as four-power talks with the Soviet Union, Britain, and France. In the course of these talks, Secretary of State William P. Rogers outlined a new U.S. position that called on Israel to withdraw from Arab territories occupied in the June 1967 war in return for Arab assurances of a binding commitment to a Middle East peace settlement. The U.S. proposals were rejected by both Israel and the Arabs.

The United States also continued to support the efforts of Gunnar Jarring, the U.N. envoy, to mediate an Arab–Israeli settlement. At the same time it recognized that little was being achieved by the U.N. talks or by its own discussions with the Soviet Union, Britain, and France. As a result, in 1970 Nixon affirmed U.S. support for Israel's call for direct peace negotiations with the Arabs.

In 1970, a U.S.-proposed and Soviet-supported cease-fire agreement between Egypt and Israel was accepted by both parties. The agreement temporarily ended the Nasser-inspired "War of Attrition" that had been going on since the 1967 war along the Suez Canal as well as along the Israel–Syrian and Israel–Jordanian borders. (See Chapter 4.)

The cease-fire agreement was soon violated when—with Soviet support— Egypt placed antiaircraft missile installations in what was supposed to be a neutral buffer zone. This development caused the United States openly to restate its support for Israel's security and its pledge to "rectify" the military imbalance.

In 1971 and 1972, the United States made additional proposals. These called for U.S.-mediated discussions by Israel and Egypt of a number of U.S. suggestions for an interim peace settlement, including a troop pull-back, the reopening of the Suez Canal, and a return to pre-1967 borders. Negotiations on these "Rogers proposals" made little headway, since Israel in particular was unwilling to discuss a return to its 1967 borders without concrete measures to ensure its security.

Like Israel, the United States was caught by surprise when Egyptian and Syrian armies launched the fourth Arab–Israeli war in October 1973 by attacking Israeli forces on Yom Kippur, the holiest day in the Jewish calendar. Eight days later the United States began to airlift large quantities of sorely needed military supplies to Israel in order to redress the imbalance caused by continuing massive Soviet arms shipments to Egypt and Syria. (By this time the Israelis had already checked both offensives and Israeli forces had crossed the Suez Canal into Egypt.)

After initial Arab advances during the first days of the war, the tide of battle turned in favor of the Israelis. At this point, two weeks after the hostilities began, the United States and the USSR sponsored Resolution 338 in the Security Council. It called for a cease-fire and implementation of Security Council Resolution 242 of 1967 as a basis for peace negotiations. Egypt and Israel accepted the cease-fire.

The two superpowers acted when they did to prevent a clear-cut Israeli victory. Both felt that another Arab defeat would increase hostile feelings in the Arab world and thereby increase the threat of a direct U.S.–Soviet confrontation, which neither wanted. The United States, in addition, feared that the Arabs would be so humiliated by such a defeat that they would resist joining in any postwar search for a peace settlement.

In December 1973 a multination conference was convened at Geneva. Representatives of the United States, the Soviet Union, Israel, Egypt, Jordan, and the United Nations agreed on the need for peace negotiations. In January 1974, following one formal session of the Geneva conference, Egypt and Israel agreed on the "disengagement" of their forces along the Suez Canal.

The cease-fire ending the Arab–Israeli war of 1973 and two disengagement agreements with Egypt and one with Syria (1974 and 1975) were

MIDDLE EAST PEACE TALKS 1973

Following the cease-fire ending hostilities in the Arab-Israeli War of 1973, the need for immediate peace negotiations was agreed upon at a multi-nation conference in Geneva. Seen as they deliberated are representatives of Jordan, the United States, the U.N., Israel and the U.S.S.R., in the order listed (clockwise, beginning with Jordan, lower left). U.S. representative Henry Kissinger, seated at the U.S. table, was instrumental in working out the final disengagement agreements in 1974 and 1975. Laurent/Gamma-Liaison

worked out largely through the diplomatic efforts of U.S. Secretary of State Henry Kissinger, who had succeeded Rogers as secretary of state.[1] In what was referred to as "shuttle diplomacy" Kissinger traveled back and forth among the capitals of Egypt, Israel, and Syria to piece together the various pacts through step-by-step consultations and negotiations. By offering economic aid to Egypt and additional military aid to Israel, he was able to effect Israeli withdrawals from Egyptian territory in the Sinai and from former Syrian territory in the Golan Heights on the Israeli–Syrian border.

The disengagement agreements strengthened the position of the United States in the Arab world. Syria and other Arab states reestablished diplomatic relations broken off during the war of 1973. The Arabs also terminated their oil boycott of the United States. President Richard Nixon visited Egypt, Syria, Jordan, and Israel, met with regional leaders, and pledged closer cooperation with the Arab states. After the American withdrawal from Southeast Asia following the Vietnam War, the United States

[1] See p. 129 for terms of the Sinai I (1974) and Sinai II (1975) disengagement pacts.

PRESIDENT NIXON AND KING HUSSEIN

President Nixon met with Middle East leaders here and abroad and pledged closer cooperation with Arab states. At the same time he assured Israel of continuing concern for her interests. Nixon and King Hussein are seen above, when the Jordanian ruler visited to explore approaches to peace in the Middle East. International Communication Agency

decided to rely on regional powers rather than U.S. military intervention in order to preserve peace and stability (a policy called the "Nixon Doctrine"). Accordingly, in the Middle East President Nixon stepped up military aid to the Shah of Iran to help make his country the "guardian" of the Persian Gulf and protector of the vital oil supply route to the West.

Nixon and later Gerald Ford (who became president when Nixon resigned in 1974 as a result of the Watergate scandal) tried to reassure Israel of their continuing concern. Nevertheless, it was clear after the war of 1973 that Israel had become more dependent than ever on U.S. economic and military aid and political support. As Israel's dependence on the United States grew, Washington during the Ford administration increased pressure on Israel to yield territory in order to get the Arabs to the peace table. Thus, in 1975, when Israel under the Rabin government resisted Secretary of State Kissinger's pressure to make concessions necessary to secure the Sinai II agreements, the Ford administration declared a "reassessment" of its entire Middle East policy and temporarily restricted the flow of economic and military supplies to Israel. After strong objections by more than three-fourths of the U.S. Senate, President Ford and Secretary of State Kissinger withdrew their objections.

The Carter Administration (1977–1981)

Although his goal for the Middle East were basically the same as those of his predecessors, President Jimmy Carter took an even more active role as a key conciliator, mediator, and negotiator, particularly in the search for an Arab–Israeli peace accord.

Early in his presidency Carter reaffirmed the U.S. commitment to Israel's security and survival. At the same time, he gave Arab leaders assurance of his awareness of their needs and concerns. Despite much criticism in the United States and Israel, Carter agreed to sell fighter planes to Egypt and Saudi Arabia as well as to Israel.

In 1978 President Carter received great credit at home and abroad for helping to get President Sadat and Prime Minister Begin to sign agreements designed to pave the way for an Egyptian–Israeli peace treaty and autonomy for Palestinians living on the West Bank and the Gaza Strip. The accords were worked out at a conference at Camp David, Maryland in September 1978. Following the Camp David conference, the United States took an active part in working out the details of a peace treaty between Egypt and Israel based on the principles agreed on at Camp David. The American president's key role as a "full partner" in the Camp David discussions and in the negotiations that followed was considered an outstanding diplomatic triumph.

The Carter administration also helped persuade the other members of the Security Council to send a U.N. peacekeeping force to southern Lebanon in 1978, following a large-scale Israeli incursion into Lebanon to destroy Palestinian terrorist bases being used as staging areas for terrorist raids on Israeli territory.

In late 1978 and early 1979, during riots and turmoil that overturned the Shah, the United States helped evacuate Americans from Iran. Very much concerned with the outcome of the Iranian crisis, the seizure of American hostages by Iran in November 1979, the dispatch of Soviet troops to Afghanistan in December 1979, and the Iraq–Iran war of 1980–1981, the Carter administration announced it would strengthen its military presence in the Middle East and elsewhere to protect its interests and forestall moves by the Soviet Union to take advantage of the situation.

In his January 1980 State of the Union address, President Carter warned the Soviet Union to stay out of the Persian Gulf. In what is now referred to as the "Carter Doctrine," he indicated that an attempt by any outside force

PRESIDENT CARTER AT THE SIGNING OF THE
ISRAELI-EGYPTIAN PEACE TREATY
One of President Jimmy Carter's most notable achievements was his influential
role in the negotiations that paved the way for peace between Egypt and Israel. He
is shown with President Sadat of Egypt and Prime Minister Begin at the signing of
the Israeli-Egyptian Peace Treaty at the White House, March 26, 1979. Israel
Consulate

to gain control of the Persian Gulf region would be regarded as an attack on
the vital interests of the United States; and that such an assault would be
repelled by any means necessary, including military action. Critics were
quick to assert that the nation's armed forces had been so weakened during
the first three years of the Carter administration that the Soviet government
would look on the Carter Doctrine as an empty threat with little substance
to back it up. Some Republicans even likened it to "talking big and carrying
a small stick." It was also charged that one of the centerpieces of the Carter
Doctrine, the Rapid Deployment Force, would take some time to properly
develop and make ready for any eventuality.

The Reagan Administration (1981–   )

As it came into office in 1981, the Reagan administration proposed a
major increase in military spending as a way to meet the Soviet threat to
the Persian Gulf. Unlike the Carter administration, President Reagan sees

the major problem in the Middle East, as in other areas, as part of an East–West confrontation in which the Soviet government attempts to destabilize sensitive regions of the world.

For the Reagan administration, the Russian invasion of Afghanistan, as well as the Iran–Iraq war and its potential for interference by the Soviet Union, have overshadowed the Arab–Israeli dispute, which had remained a major focus of U.S. diplomacy in the Middle East during the Ford and Carter administrations. The concerns of previous administrations with this continuing source of tension had been based on the belief that of all Middle East crises prior to the Iranian and Afghanistan crises of 1979 to 1980, the Arab–Israeli conflict had the greatest potential for sooner or later bringing the United States into a direct confrontation with the Soviet Union — a situation that could explode into a third world war. President Reagan and Secretary of State Alexander Haig have differed with this previous approach, believing that Soviet probing in sensitive areas of the world is the principal cause of East–West tension. Secretary of State Haig and Richard Allen, national security advisor to President Reagan, have even accused the USSR of training and supplying terrorist groups such as the PLO as a means of undermining the Western democracies.

United States Involvement in Recent Middle East Peace Negotiations

Since the signing of the Sinai pacts leading to an official cease-fire between Egypt and Israel following the war of 1973, the United States has continued its attempts to help work for an overall peace settlement.

At first, the Carter administration tried to get Egypt and Israel to resume peace negotiations at another Geneva conference at which the United States, the USSR, Arab states, and Israel would again be represented. Israel was reluctant to attend such a conference. It opposed a settlement of Arab–Israeli differences by parties not directly involved in the dispute (particularly the Soviet Union). It also opposed PLO representation at any conference convened to work out a settlement so long as the PLO continued to seek Israel's destruction. Interestingly enough, Egypt was also opposed to such a conference, which it feared would bring the Soviet Union into the Middle East with an agenda for trouble rather than resolve conflict.

At the same time relations between Israel and the United States became somewhat strained, particularly as a result of President Carter's criticism of the Israelis for continuing to establish new settlements in occupied territories. Israel was also angered by a joint U.S.–USSR statement calling for the recognition of the "legitimate rights" of Palestinians to a homeland as one of the necessary prerequisites for a Middle East peace agreement.

EGYPTIAN PRESIDENT SADAT VISITS ISRAEL
Egyptian President Anwar Sadat's historic visit to Jerusalem at the end of 1977 opened the way for the establishment of friendly relationships and to peace between Egypt and Israel. He is welcomed by Israeli citizens on the occasion of his visit (above). Gamma-Liaison

Sadat–Begin Peace Talks

A significant breakthrough occurred at the end of 1977, when Israeli Prime Minister Menachem Begin invited President Anwar Sadat of Egypt to address the Israeli parliament. Sadat accepted, and his visit to Jerusalem to talk to Begin and other Israeli leaders was the first by an Arab leader since Israel was founded in 1948.[2] In a historic address to the Israeli Knesset, Sadat said he accepted the existence of Israel and stated his willingness to work for a lasting peace. However, he emphasized that such a peace would depend on Israel's withdrawal from occupied Arab lands and recognition of the rights of the Palestinians.

[2] It has become clear that Egypt, like Israel, did not want another Geneva conference. Sadat felt such a meeting would give the USSR and the "rejectionist" Arab states the opportunity to nullify Egypt's growing determination to work for peace with Israel. As a result of this joint desire to bypass a second Geneva conference that seemed to be in the planning, a secret meeting took place in Morocco between Egyptian and Israeli representatives shortly before Sadat's trip, to feel each other out on the possibility of such a visit to Israel if Sadat were invited to come. This paved the way for what followed.

Although the "Sadat initiative" received great praise in the United States, Western nations, and in Egypt, most Arab leaders condemned it as a surrender and betrayal of Arab interests. Efforts by Syria, Iraq, Libya, Algeria, and Southern Yemen to prevent continued Egyptian–Israeli negotiations led to a split with Egypt.

Peace talks begun hopefully at the end of 1977 soon bogged down. Discussions gave way to bickering and name-calling and were suspended by Egypt early in 1978, with each side making proposals for the most part unacceptable to the other. Attempts by the United States to get both sides back to the peace table proved difficult until President Carter's personal diplomacy with a whirlwind visit to Egypt and Israel in March 1979 brought agreement between Egypt and Israel.

Issues in the Arab–Israeli Dispute

Differences over several major issues were primarily responsible for the initial difficulties of the Sadat–Begin talks.

WITHDRAWAL FROM OCCUPIED TERRITORIES. Egypt insisted that Israel withdraw from all lands occupied since the 1967 war.[3] Israel insisted it needed "defensible borders." It was willing to remove its settlements and return all of the Sinai to Egypt (including major airfields and billions of dollars in oil wealth) as part of an overall accord; but it was unwilling to yield certain parts of the Golan Heights or Judea and Samaria (the West Bank), which it considered vital to its security.

ESTABLISHMENT OF A PALESTINIAN HOMELAND. Egypt called for self-determination (self-government) for the Palestinians living in the West Bank and the Gaza Strip. Israel was willing to grant the Palestinians limited self-rule but insisted on a continued Israeli military presence for the time being to safeguard Israeli settlers and public order.

ISRAELI SETTLEMENTS IN OCCUPIED TERRITORIES. Egypt demanded the removal of all Israeli settlements in Arab territories captured in the 1967 war. Israel insisted on the right of its citizens to live in these areas along with Arabs. It claimed that Jews have a right to settle in these areas since they were originally part of the Palestine mandate as given to Britain after World War I. In addition, Israel made the point that Jews have lived there since biblical times.

---

[3] Although Egypt, unlike most other Arab states, now recognizes the existence of Israel and has been willing to negotiate for peace, its views on this and other issues are for the most part identical with those of other Arab states.

EAST JERUSALEM. Egypt insisted that Israel withdraw from East Jerusalem (the Old City). It favored placing holy places under international supervision. Israel refused to accept any proposal that would again divide Jerusalem—its capital city. It insisted on continued Israeli control of all of Jerusalem with access to holy shrines guaranteed to members of all faiths.

The Camp David Conference

Early in September 1978, President Sadat, Prime Minister Begin, and President Carter met at Camp David, Maryland to break the deadlock and resume the momentum of negotiations. President Carter played a leading and forceful role in two weeks of intense and difficult discussions and hard bargaining that were climaxed by the signing of historic agreements. Noteworthy in the process of these negotiations was the personal courage of both Begin and Sadat in compromising their own initial positions in order to find an accommodation that would result in meaningful steps toward peace.

The Camp David Accords

Two major agreements were reached by Prime Minister Begin and President Sadat at Camp David. The "Framework for Peace in the Middle East" set forth general principles for the establishment of self-government for the Arabs on the West Bank of the Jordan River and the Gaza Strip over a five-year period. The "Framework for the Conclusion of a Peace Treaty between Egypt and Israel" established guiding principles for the signing of a peace treaty between the two countries, for Israeli withdrawal from the Sinai, and return of that area to Egypt.

Significance of the Camp David Agreements

The Camp David agreements were considered an extraordinary diplomatic achievement. Although a peace treaty still had to be drafted and accepted by both sides, with a number of key issues left unresolved and with months of difficult negotiations ahead, the agreements brought new hope for an end to thirty years of a state of war between Israel and Egypt.

President Sadat and Prime Minister Begin felt that President Carter deserved the most credit for bringing about the agreements and complimented him highly for his successful endeavors. Begin and Sadat were jointly awarded the Nobel Peace Prize for 1978 for their efforts.

The Egyptian cabinet approved the agreements unanimously. The Israeli cabinet and parliament voted to support the agreements by a wide margin after Begin convinced them that given the alternatives of peace or continued war, there was little option but to accept them.

Most of the other Arab states and the Soviet Union denounced the agreements as a complete surrender to Israel and as going against basic Arab rights. The leaders of Syria, Algeria, South Yemen, and Libya severed relations with Egypt and pledged to work for the "fall" of Sadat's peace policies.

Signing of a Peace Treaty by Egypt and Israel in 1979

On March 26, 1979, sixteen months after the peace negotiations began with Sadat's visit to Jerusalem and six months after the Camp David conference, President Sadat and Prime Minister Begin signed a peace treaty between Egypt and Israel in Washington, D.C. The treaty ended the thirty-one years of a state of war between Egypt and Israel. It provided for the return to Egypt of the entire Sinai Peninsula in stages culminating in 1982 and the initiation of negotiations for self-rule for Palestinians on the West Bank and the Gaza Strip. The treaty was based on the Camp David Accords. It was considered a "political miracle."

To prevent a deadlock that might endanger the signing of the treaty, President Carter again personally intervened during a week-long trip to the Middle East shortly before the signing. As a result of his meetings with

ISRAELI REACTION TO THE PEACE TREATY WITH EGYPT
On March 26, 1979, in joyful celebration, thousands of Israelis gathered in front of giant screens that transmitted the signing of the Israeli-Egyptian peace treaty live from the White House. Katz/Gamma-Liaison

Sadat and Begin and follow-up discussions between the representatives of both nations, final agreements were hammered out, some almost at the last minute.[4]

Provisions of the Peace Treaty

The following are the main provisions of the peace treaty between Egypt and Israel.

1. The state of war will end and peace will officially begin when the treaty is signed and ratified.[5]

2. Israel will evacuate its military and civilian forces from the Sinai Peninsula in stages over a three-year period (phased withdrawal). Within nine months, two-thirds of the peninsula will be turned over to Egypt. (Implementation took place ahead of schedule.)

3. Much of the Sinai will be demilitarized.

4. To monitor the agreement, United Nations forces will be stationed in a demilitarized border zone twelve to fifteen miles wide — in the Sinai along the Israeli border and extending down to the Gulf of Aqaba and Sharm el-Sheikh. If the Security Council declines to station such forces, other multinational forces will police a buffer zone between the Egyptians and the Israelis. In addition, early-warning stations manned by the United States may exist to ensure compliance with the accord.

5. After the initial nine-month period of withdrawal from the Sinai, normal and friendly relations will be established. These will include cultural exchanges, free movement of nationals across the borders, and the end of Egypt's economic boycott and discriminatory economic practices against Israel. Ambassadors will be exchanged ten months after ratification.

6. Israeli ships and cargoes will be given the same rights of free passage

---

[4] Included in these last-minute agreements was an agreement that Sinai oil fields would be returned to Egypt seven months after the treaty was ratified, instead of the nine months Israel had preferred and the six months Egypt had earlier asked for. In addition, Mr. Begin agreed to turn over the El Arish area of the Sinai within two months instead of the three months originally proposed by Israel. An arrangement was also made assuring Israel of the right to buy oil at the prevailing world price from the fields it was returning to Egypt. It is estimated that Israel lost approximately $2 billion a year (at 1980 oil prices) plus oil self-sufficiency by returning these fields.

[5] In international relations treaties do not become official until they are "ratified." Ratification takes place when the lawmaking bodies or councils of the countries involved give their approval. When this is done, "instruments of ratification" are exchanged and the treaty goes into effect. The Israel Knesset (parliament) and cabinet ratified the treaty within a week after its signing. Ratification by the Egyptian government came soon after and was overwhelmingly approved in a national referendum with more than ninety-five percent of the Egyptian people voting in favor. Accordingly, it officially went into effect on April 25, 1979.

through the Suez Canal and its approaches (the Gulf of Suez, the Straits of Tiran, and the Gulf of Aqaba) as are given to vessels of other nations.

7. Israel will be permitted to purchase oil from the Sinai oil fields being returned to Egypt.

8. Within a month after ratification of the treaty, Egypt and Israel will begin negotiations for putting into effect the Camp David agreement on self-rule for Palestinians on the West Bank and the Gaza Strip. (According to a letter signed by President Sadat and Prime Minister Begin that accompanied the treaty, these negotiations were supposed to end in about a year, and elections for local self-rule councils were to take place shortly thereafter. The councils are to operate during a five-year transition period. However, failure to meet this timetable will not be considered a cause to cancel other provisions of the treaty.) After the establishment of such administrative councils, the Israeli military government will be dismantled and Israeli troops withdrawn into special "security locations."

9. Other Arab parties to the dispute are invited to join in the peace process with Israel, guided by the principles and procedures in the Camp David Accords and the peace treaty between Egypt and Israel.

THE SPIRIT OF CAMP DAVID
The hopeful spirit resulting from the Camp David Accords is shown as Prime Minister Begin and President Sadat embrace at the signing ceremony at the Maryland conference site on September 17, 1978. The Camp David Accords led to the drafting of a treaty of peace between Egypt and Israel six months later. Wide World

REOPENING OF THE SUEZ CANAL TO ISRAELI SHIPPING
The peace treaty between Israel and Egypt in 1979 reopened the Suez Canal to Israeli shipping. The Ashdod was the first Israeli vessel to pass through the Canal (May 1979). El Koussy/Gamma-Liaison

Role of the United States

It was clear that without the participation and intervention of President Carter in the negotiations no treaty would have been signed. He was praised by both Prime Minister Begin and President Sadat for his role and personal assistance in resolving difficult issues. In addition to his diplomatic efforts and the growing indications he gave that the United States was determined to significantly increase its military presence in the Middle East, President Carter gave important assurances of military and economic assistance to both nations. These helped greatly to pave the way for the signing of the accords.

The following were among the specific economic and military promises made by the United States to Egypt and Israel.

1. Loans and grants amounting to at least $5 billion in military and economic aid will be given by the United States to Egypt and Israel over the next three years—in addition to $2.5 billion already earmarked for these two countries for 1979. (Included in the grant to Israel is American help in financing Israel's plan to build two new air bases in the Negev region to replace air bases in the Sinai that will be given up.)

2. The United States guarantees to supply oil to Israel for fifteen years if

it is unable to buy what it needs from Egypt or elsewhere. (Included to give Israel insurance against any future Egyptian boycott of Israel.)

3. The United States promises active American participation in the negotiations for Palestinian self-rule. (Included to enable President Sadat to answer Arab charges that by conducting a separate peace he is betraying the Palestinian cause.)

4. If the Egyptian–Israeli peace treaty is violated, the United States will take appropriate diplomatic, economic, and military measures to deal with the situation.

5. If Israel's security is threatened, the United States will urgently consider "the strengthening of its presence in the area." It will also provide emergency supplies to Israel and exercise its maritime rights to end any naval blockade.

6. The United States will take steps to prevent the unauthorized transfer of U.S.-supplied weapons for use in an armed attack on Israel.

7. To promote full treaty observance, Washington will make surveillance flights over the Sinai.

Why Egypt and Israel Signed

Behind the signing of the peace treaty were certain basic realizations for both Israel and Egypt that overcame all other considerations. For Egypt, signing meant accusations of betraying the Arab cause plus stepped-up sanctions. For Israel, signing meant overcoming mistrust of the Arabs, dismantling air bases, giving up direct access to oil supplies adequate for self-sufficiency, removing thousands of settlers from new and cherished homes, yielding strategic and in-depth defenses on which they had depended for eleven years, and preparing to replace the Israeli administration in the West Bank and Gaza. Why then did they sign?

Egypt's economic situation had been going from bad to worse. The nation was becoming increasingly unable to provide public and other services to its rapidly growing population. It had survived only because of aid from the richer Arab nations and the United States. However, it needed much more assistance than it had been getting. Sadat understood that the growing discontent with the situation could be politically dangerous.

In addition, Sadat feared growing Soviet influence in the region and was alarmed by the collapse of Iran. He knew he could not count on large-scale U.S. economic aid or major arms deliveries until there was peace with Israel, plus an agreement not to use such arms against it.

The Egyptian leader also recognized that if there was no agreement he might have to turn to Russia for arms once more and would be faced with the continued financial burden of preparing for an inevitable war with Israel. When that war came, Egypt, as in previous conflicts, would have to do most of the fighting, in spite of the knowledge that it would probably be defeated again by Israel, the most technologically advanced and militarily strongest nation in the area.

Israel was faced with equally compelling reasons for wanting peace, even at a great price and in the knowledge that a miscalculation might lead to another tragic war with the loss of many lives.

Like Egypt, Israel was also facing severe economic problems. It owed large sums of money to other nations and was suffering from crippling inflation. It desperately needed to reduce military spending and to apply its resources to solving pressing economic and social problems.

Although Israelis at times resented U.S. pressure for concessions to Egypt and the Palestinians, they realized that the United States was their only protector and in the last analysis their greatest source of outside support.

In addition, Israelis recognized that no overall peace with the Arabs was possible unless a beginning was made somewhere — and preferably with Israel's most powerful antagonist, Egypt, with one-half the population of all the Arab nations combined, thus eliminating the danger of war from that entire front.

Begin knew that he would be accused of giving away too much — both by his supporters and by leaders of conservative, nationalist, and other groups who felt that returning the entire Sinai to Egypt as well as any change in the status of the West Bank was a sellout. Nevertheless, he believed that peace with security guarantees might end further wars and prevent new losses of lives that Israel could ill afford. Begin was also aware that there were strong forces in Israel, particularly among the younger generation, that were calling for an accommodation with Egypt on almost any reasonable terms.

Significance of the Peace Treaty

The treaty between Israel and Egypt was significant for several important reasons.

1. It brought to an end over thirty years of war that cost the lives of more than 50,000 Egyptians and Israelis in four bitter wars.

2. It made it clear that the United States was determined to be more active than ever before in attempting to underpin the security of the entire region where required. This included greater willingness to consider taking direct military action and to spend additional billions to achieve cooperation between former enemies by becoming their economic and military provider.

3. Although only a first step, the peace pact started a process that could ultimately lead to the comprehensive settlement that is essential for the stability and prosperity of the entire area.

ISRAELI AMBASSADOR IN CAIRO
This picture of Eliahu Ben Elissar, the first Israeli Ambassador to Egypt, on the balcony of his temporary headquarters in the Sheraton Hotel in Cairo, symbolizes the new era of peace and friendship between Israel and Egypt that stemmed from the establishment of peaceful relations in the late 1970s. Neumann/Gamma-Liaison

4. The accord also confirmed the continuing U.S. policy of trying to counter and limit growing Soviet influence in the Middle East.

5. It further emphasized that the United States was the only world power that could influence the two strongest and most stable nations in the area.

Reaction to the Peace Treaty

Reaction to the peace treaty was quick and as expected.

Most Arab leaders denounced the treaty as a sellout and a betrayal of the Arab cause. At an Arab League conference in Baghdad (despite some initial differences over how severe the "punishment" of Egypt should be) resolutions were passed by the foreign ministers of eighteen Arab countries and the PLO declaring a total economic boycott of Egypt. This was to include an end to all Arab financial and economic aid, trade, and oil supplies, as well as a boycott of any Egyptian business concerns that had dealings with Israel. In addition, the ministers announced immediate withdrawal of their ambassadors from Cairo, recommended complete severance of diplomatic relations within a month, and suspended Egypt's membership in the Arab League. The Sudan (one of the most populous Arab nations aside from

Egypt) and Oman, two of the only three Arab League members to support Egypt's action, did not send representatives to the meeting.[6]

In a predictable response, Egypt recalled its ambassadors from eight Arab countries (Bahrain, Jordan, Kuwait, Morocco, Qatar, Saudi Arabia, Tunisia, and the United Arab Emirates).[7] However, diplomats below the rank of ambassador were not recalled.

Most Egyptians received the news of the treaty with joy mixed with restraint. They seemed confident that President Sadat would pull them through the difficult days ahead as he had in the past. There was also general belief that Egypt could count on full American economic and military support in the future. Egyptians expected President Carter to solve the difficult problem of self-rule for the Palestinian Arabs when negotiations took place in the near future. They hoped that the United States would pressure Israel to make major concessions in this direction. Above all was their feeling of relief at being able to look forward to an end of thirty-one years of warfare that had taken many Egyptian lives. Many Egyptians resented the fact that Egypt was constantly called on by Arab nations to fight other people's battles without proper support or appreciation.

Although at the same time there were some "dissident voices," primarily among Egyptian university students and intellectuals on the left and Islamic groups on the right, who warned that Egypt's separate peace with Israel was dangerous, the overwhelming majority supported President Sadat's initiative. The matter was resolved in a plebiscite when more than ninety-five percent of the Egyptian population voted their approval of their president and his action in developing the Camp David accords.

Israeli gratification with the treaty, as a means of officially recognizing their existence, normalizing relations, and avoiding another war, was mixed with serious doubts and worries. There was fear that if President Sadat were swept away by a coup or another development, Egypt's commitment to peace might disappear. There was also recognition that whereas withdrawal from the Sinai was technically difficult but possible, pulling back from the West Bank and granting autonomy to the Palestinians was an entirely different and more difficult matter. No one was prepared to see the newly unified city of Jerusalem again divided. Also, initially, there was a fear of the buildup of a Syria-Iraq-Jordan front on Israel's eastern border. Therefore Israeli military forces were kept in a state of alert and no immediate reductions in the military budget were planned.

[6] Somalia maintained relations with Egypt but later criticized the peace treaty.

[7] Six months earlier (after the Camp David pacts) Mr. Sadat had broken relations with five more militant Arab nations — Algeria, Iraq, Libya, Southern Yemen and Syria, in retaliation for their formation of a "steadfastness front" to fight his peace policy.

The peace pact was generally well received in the United States as a hopeful first step in the direction of a possible comprehensive settlement. President Carter, like President Sadat, hoped that although the immediate response of most of the Arab world was hostile to the treaty and Egypt, in time most Arab states would join in the process of making peace with Israel and solving other mutual problems. Carter administration officials anticipated Saudi Arabian and Jordanian acceptance and were surprised at their reluctance to support the Camp David accords. Americans also recognized that the U.S. role in the Middle East — as chief mediator, peacemaker, guardian, banker, and arms supplier — would be bigger, riskier, and costlier than ever before.

Few diplomats on either side, as well as in the United States, expected further peace talks to be anything but extremely difficult and complex. None would or could predict success because of the wide gap between the positions of Israel and the Arabs on a number of unresolved issues. With regard to Palestinian self-rule in the nearby Gaza Strip and on the West Bank of the Jordan River, the Egyptians insist that the autonomy plan must be a step toward the creation of an independent Palestinian state.[8] The Israelis maintain that they will never permit the establishment of such a state, which they perceive will be a Soviet "client state"[9] with expansionist ambitions and in all likelihood dominated by the PLO. (The PLO National Covenant calls for the destruction of Israel and accepts no compromise.) They hope to negotiate a more limited plan for Palestinian home rule. Opposite views on the future status of Jerusalem — an issue not mentioned in the peace treaty — present another knotty problem. Egypt and the other Arab states call for Israel's withdrawal from East Jerusalem (the Old City). Israel insists that it will not accept any proposal that results in the division of Jerusalem, its capital city, and will continue with its policy of open access and protection of the holy places of all religions.

An equally difficult and as yet unresolved problem is Syria's insistence on the return of the Israeli-occupied Golan Heights (formerly used by the Syrians to shell Israeli settlements in the valley below) and Israel's resolve not to give up the Heights even if there is peace with Syria.

Putting the Peace Treaty into Effect

It was clear to all sides that implementing and keeping the peace would be even more difficult than negotiating the treaty itself.

As a result of continuing cooperative negotiations between Egyptian and

[8] In addition, the Palestinians and Jordan have indicated that because they are opposed to the treaty they will not participate in negotiations on the subject.
[9] The term "client state" or "client nation" is used to describe a country that is very dependent on another country for essential support.

POLICING THE SINAI

Prior to the peace treaty between Egypt and Israel the U.N. Emergency Force in the Middle East provided a military buffer between Israeli and Egyptian armies in the Sinai Desert. In the photo above the head of the Italian forces confers with his Israeli counterpart, framed by the UNEF soldiers. After the treaty the U.N. force was to be initially replaced by a joint Egyptian-Israeli police force and then by contingents from anti-communist nations, including an American "early warning" force. Religious News Service

Israeli leaders in the months following the signing, Israel had withdrawn its forces from nearly two-thirds of the Sinai by early 1980, ahead of schedule, and was scheduled to pull out of the remaining third by the spring of 1982. Another sign of good faith was Egypt's agreement to let Israeli soldiers stay in the Sinai to patrol jointly with Egyptian troops supervising Israeli withdrawal. The joint patrols were a temporary solution following the Soviet Union's rejection of a resolution that would have permitted U.N. troops to remain in the Sinai and Israel's objection to the substitution of U.N. "observers" as inadequate. President Sadat also agreed to sell Israel two million tons of Egypt's annual oil production in the Sinai.

Negotiations on autonomy for the West Bank and Gaza were stalled in 1980 despite President Carter's efforts to develop a new momentum. Hopes for agreement on the complex autonomy arrangements were revived in the fall of 1981 when President Sadat and Prime Minister Begin were to resume the negotiations.

Even though President Reagan devoted most of his energies during the first few months of his presidency to restoring an ailing economy, the rough contours of a Reagan foreign policy had begun to emerge. A major change from the Carter administration and from the policy of some of our West European allies was that the Reagan foreign policy team did not consider the Palestinian issue its first concern in the area. Instead, the major priority of the United States was the protection of the Middle East in general and the Persian Gulf area in particular from any Soviet adventure. The administration's major concern is East–West rivalry rather than Arab–Israeli, Iran–Iraq, Syria–Jordan, Libya–Egypt, or Morocco–Algeria conflict. The United States has therefore decided to concentrate on the Soviet challenge in the Middle East instead of focusing on the Palestinian issue.

Indeed, Secretary of State Alexander Haig spoke out against the PLO as an example of a terrorist group that is supplied and trained by the Soviet Union as a means of undermining the stability of Western democracies. Richard Allen, President Reagan's national security advisor, also said that Israeli raids into southern Lebanon constituted hot pursuit of a sort and were therefore "justified."

In a departure from the policy of the Carter administration, President Reagan expressed the view that although Israel's continued build-up of new settlements in the West Bank might be unwise during a period of negotiations, it could not be considered illegal.

Israel's final withdrawal from the Sinai Peninsula was conditional on the establishment of a force to police compliance with the treaty. The Reagan administration moved ahead with Egypt and Israel, under the terms of the treaty, to form a multinational force and observer unit, with American troops making up half of the force. Columbia, Uruguay, and Fiji agreed to participate along with the United States.

Continuing Crises in the Middle East

The Crisis in Lebanon

Syria stepped up its attacks on Christian enclaves in Lebanon in the spring of 1981. The fighting around the Syrian-besieged Christian town of Zahle and the Christian enclaves in Beirut was the worst violence in Lebanon since 1978 and threatened to spread to other parts of the country and even beyond.[10] Israel's foreign minister declared that Israel would not stand by and let Syrian troops "massacre" Lebanese Christians. In response to Israel's aid to the embattled Christians, Syria installed Soviet SAM-6 and SAM-9 missiles inside Lebanon.

[10] In the spring of 1981 there were fears that renewed fighting in Lebanon would lead to the dismemberment of the country, with the Muslim areas absorbed by Syria and the Christian enclaves becoming a separate state under Israeli protection.

Mounting violence, during which the PLO bombarded Israel's northern settlements with Soviet Katyusha missiles, was climaxed by an Israeli raid on the PLO headquarters in Beirut. To defuse the continuing crisis in Lebanon, President Reagan's special envoy, Philip Habib, engaged in a round of "shuttle diplomacy" to Lebanon, Syria, Israel, and Saudi Arabia. The Reagan administration continued to adhere to the policy of not dealing with the PLO until it recognizes Israel's right to exist. Saudi Arabia, a major backer of the PLO, was credited with convincing the PLO to agree to a cessation of hostilities. By summer's end, although the siege of Zahle had been lifted, Syria had still not removed the missiles from Lebanon, and it remained to be seen how long Israel would refrain from taking action against the missiles.

The Hostage Crisis in Iran

Toward the end of 1979 a dangerous crisis in American-Iranian affairs caused the United States to reexamine its role in maintaining peace and stability in the Middle East.

CAUSES AND NATURE. The crisis developed when sixty-six American hostages were seized by militant followers of the Ayatollah Khomeini who occupied the United States embassy on November 4, 1979. The price for the release of the hostages was the return of the deposed Shah of Iran, then under treatment in a New York hospital for cancer, to face trial and almost certain death. After releasing fourteen of the hostages, the Iranians continued to hold fifty-two hostages until January 20, 1981.

Even after the Shah had left the United States several weeks later for asylum in Panama, the Islamic authorities continued to threaten that hostages suspected of being spies would be tried in Islamic courts unless the Shah was returned.[11] The militant "students" guarding the American hostages threatened to kill them and blow up the embassy if there were attempts at rescue. Indeed, mines were placed around the embassy compound by the PLO, which also voiced solidarity with the terrorist takeover of the embassy and the holding of the hostages. In addition, the defense agreement with the United States was scrapped and oil shipments to the United States were suspended (after President Carter announced that the United States would no longer import oil from Iran).

REACTION BY THE UNITED STATES AND THE WORLD. President Carter condemned the seizure as an act of terrorism as well as a violation of inter-

---

[11] The Shah later died of cancer in 1980 while in exile in Egypt, the one Muslim nation that offered him long-term asylum and protection.

AMERICAN HOSTAGES IN IRAN

For over a year world attention was focused on the American hostages seized and held by militant followers of the Ayatollah Khomeini in Iran. Fifty-two of the hostages were held for 444 days, from November 4, 1979, to January 20, 1981. Above a blindfolded American hostage is questioned by his captors. Mingam/Gamma-Liaison

national law and the rules of world diplomacy. Although he insisted that the United States would not yield to "blackmail," he stated that military force would not be used except as a last resort—a policy of restraint that was initially praised throughout the world and was adopted so as not to jeopardize the lives of the hostages.

Repeated efforts throughout 1980 by the United Nations Security Council, U.N. Secretary General Waldheim, and the World Court failed to obtain release of the hostages. A Soviet veto prevented the Security Council from applying economic sanctions against Iran.

President Carter's efforts to free the hostages were frustrated throughout 1980, his final year in office. Sudden switches in Iranian policies foiled repeated U.S. attempts to reach a settlement. In April a dramatic rescue attempt had to be discontinued when, because of flawed equipment, several U.S. helicopters malfunctioned after landing in the Iranian desert, causing the death of eight American servicemen. Negotiations for the release of the hostages were finally concluded in January 1981, with Algerian diplomats serving as mediators. Iran, near bankruptcy from its debilitating war with Iraq, gave up the hostages in exchange for the release of $2.9 billion, part of its assets that had been frozen by the U.S. government when the hostages were seized.[12] In what appeared to be a deliberate act by the Iranians to deprive President Carter of the credit for the liberation of the hostages while he was still in office, the fifty-two Americans were not allowed to take off from Teheran airport until minutes after President Reagan was inaugurated to succeed President Carter.

REASONS FOR IRAN'S ACTIONS. The reasons for the uncompromising demands and furious outburst of anti-Americanism whipped up by Khomeini were rooted in Iranian history and in the rigid moral absolutism of the Ayatollah and his religious supporters.

Several important factors may be identified: (1) There has been bitter feeling against the United States in Iran dating back to 1953, when, with United States CIA help, the Shah was reinstalled and the nationalist government of Mohammed Mossadegh was overthrown. (2) Before the Shah was deposed in 1979 there was increasing opposition to his dictatorial powers, particularly to the use of the dreaded secret police (the SAVAK) and its methods of stamping out opposition through torture, murder, and other denials of human rights. Religious leaders opposed the Shah's programs of industrialization and modernization, feeling that they corrupted or eroded basic Islamic values. (3) Iranian leaders felt that by admitting the Shah for medical treatment, the United States was deliberately insulting the Iranian revolution and the Iranian people. They believed it was the religious duty of America to send the Shah back for trial. (4) It is also thought that the Ayatollah provoked the crisis when he did because it was necessary to reunite Iranians and divert their attention from the growing dissatisfaction with his authoritarian rule and the deteriorating economic condition of the nation.

GROWING ISLAMIC MILITANCY. Equally destabilizing regionally and internationally and given new impetus by the U.S.–Iranian crisis was the violent wave of Islamic militancy that swept across the Muslim world in late 1979. Stirred by Khomeini's verbal offensive, with its denunciation of the United States and call for an Islamic religious crusade, Muslim extremists in Pakistan, Bangladesh, India, and Turkey attacked American diplomatic headquarters and other installations, causing the United States to evacuate diplomatic personnel.

[12] The United States froze about $12 billion of Iranian assets. When the hostages were released, the United States transferred $8 billion to the Bank of England, including the $2.9 billion immediately released to Iran and $5.1 billion that was set aside to pay off Iranian debts to American and European banks. Much of the remaining $4 billion was tied up by lawsuits brought by companies with claims against Iran.

ANTI-U.S. SENTIMENT IN IRAN

During the revolution in Iran which brought the Ayatollah Khomeini regime to power, anti-American feeling was whipped up to a fury. Above is a mural painted on the wall of the American Embassy in Teheran that reflects the Iranian mood at the time. de Wildenberg/Gamma-Liaison

The causes of mounting religious fervor and the anti-Americanism that has been sweeping the lands of Islam in the wake of the Iranian revolution are varied and complex. Several basic factors can be identified: (1) Muslims for many years have been anxious to redress decades of humiliation at the hands of Western colonialists. There has been a growing mood of rejection of Western standards and values among peoples conscious of a past glory and a belief in their own religious and cultural superiority. (2) Memories of old Islamic grandeur and Arab empires have sharpened the belief that the West in general and the United States in particular, as its dominant power, have through their industrializing and modernizing influences found a new way to perpetuate the subjection once achieved by force. (3) This sense of shared frustration has been intensified by the fact that decolonization and independence for nations once under colonial imperialist domination have not improved the peoples' lot. (4) The Iranian revolution and its perceived success in defying the power of the Western world, plus the feeling among oil-exporting nations that they have a new source of power, have given tremendous impetus to this mood of rejection of the West. (5) The United States, as the world's strongest nation, is seen as the symbol of continuing

Western imperialism and aggression against Islam, and the Ayatollah Khomeini's initial defiance of American power has given some in the Muslim world a new sense of pride.[13]

IMPACT OF THE IRANIAN CRISIS ON U.S. EFFORTS TO MAINTAIN PEACE AND STABILITY. The continuing crisis in Iran caused the Carter administration to initiate a radical shift in its defense posture. The change in policy was primarily caused by two developments: (1) growing evidence of an expansionist Soviet drive that posed a threat to Middle East oil states from recently or newly developed military footholds in Afghanistan, Ethiopia, and South Yemen, and (2) the Iranian crisis, including the upsurge of Muslim militancy triggered by Iran's Islamic revolution, which was viewed as especially dangerous because of repercussions in Saudi Arabia, America's number one source of imported oil.

After its withdrawal from direct involvement in the war in Vietnam during the 1960s and early 1970s, the United States adopted a policy that was followed until the Iranian crisis. Under the so-called "Nixon Doctrine" the United States withdrew from direct military involvement in areas of its concern outside its borders and instead called on local countries to act as regional "policemen" in order to keep peace and stability. Under this policy the United States helped Iran militarily and encouraged it to act as guardian of the Persian Gulf.

During this period critics of U.S. policy in the Middle East argued that the lack of direct American military involvement and of a show of military strength during regional crises was causing America to lose face among Arab and other nations and making it possible for the Soviet Union to gain influence at the expense of the United States.

The aim of the new policy that seemed to be emerging as the 1980s began—and that became more pronounced when President Reagan assumed office—was to build a significant American military presence in the troubled Indian Ocean–Persian Gulf region (the principal oil source for the Western world) strong enough to deter the Soviet Union and help friendly nations through other crises that may be ahead. The Carter administration undertook to develop a Rapid Deployment Force to deal with emergencies in remote areas. It also negotiated for new naval and air base facilities in Egypt (at Mersa Matruh), Kenya (Mombassa), Oman (Masira Island off the Omani coast), and Somalia (Berbera). In addition to the present tiny base in Bahrain in the Persian Gulf, which can only accommodate two destroyers and a small command ship, the nearest U.S.

---

[13] Other Muslim rulers are either fearful that Khomeini's militant Shiite Muslim ideology might bring revolution to their borders or are embarrassed by the image that Khomeini has given Muslims in the eyes of the Western world.

AMERICAN POPULAR REACTION TO IRANIAN OIL CUT-OFF

In the billboard editorial above, Americans are urged to consume less gasoline by observing the 55 mile-per-hour speed limit, in order to fight back against the cutting off of oil shipments to the United States by Iran, following the Revolution in 1979. Pozarik/Gamma-Liaison

naval facility of any size (but still considered relatively small) was on the small British-owned island of Diego Garcia in the Indian Ocean, about 2,500 miles southeast of the Persian Gulf.

When President Reagan came into office in 1981, he criticized Carter's increase in military spending as inadequate to maintain a balance of power with the Soviet Union (not to mention superiority). President Reagan recommended substantial military increases, including funds to reinvigorate the U.S. navy into a powerful three-ocean fleet that, it was hoped, could make the Middle East secure and prevent Soviet expansion into the Persian Gulf.

President Sadat was reluctant to permit the United States to establish "bases" in Egypt, but did agree to provide temporary "facilities" which would remain under Egyptian control.

For the first time, the United States was prepared to station ground combat troops in the Middle East. American troops would thus gain experience in the area and American equipment would be tested on-site in the hope of preventing the kind of technical problems and mishaps that plagued the aborted hostage rescue mission in Iran. The U.S. presence might also help condition the American public to the idea of GIs being based elsewhere in the region, for instance in the vicinity of the Persian Gulf which the Reagan administration believed is of major importance in preventing incursion into this oil-rich area by the Soviet Union or its surrogates like Libya, Syria, or the People's Democratic Republic of Yemen.

The Crisis in Afghanistan

The grave threat of Soviet ambitions and growing involvement in the Middle East has been underscored by events in Afghanistan since 1979.

In 1978, pro-Soviet leftists seized power in Afghanistan in a bloody military coup and signed a twenty-year economic and military pact with the USSR. At the end of December 1979, dissatisfied with continued disorder and opposition to the new regime, as well as with what it considered less than satisfactory cooperation, the Soviet government supported the ouster of the president in a coup carried out with the assistance of tens of thousands of Russian troops. The Soviets installed a new leader believed to be more willing to cooperate with the USSR and to take effective action against anti-government terrorism and insurgency. However, in the spring of 1981, approximately 100,000 Russian troops were mired in Afghanistan, unable to subdue the armed opposition of rebel groups that refused to recognize the pro-Soviet government of Afghanistan.

SOVIET INVASION OF AFGHANISTAN

The invasion and taking over control of Afghanistan, beginning in late December 1979, to support a weak pro-Soviet regime, brought heavy criticism from Islamic as well as Western nations. It also created a new balance of force in the Middle East, posing a challenge to American foreign policy. Soviet troops moving into Afghanistan in January 1980 are shown above. Philippot/Sygma

In 1980, his last year in office, President Carter denounced the use of Soviet forces outside Russia's borders as a grave threat to peace. He warned the USSR to withdraw its forces from Afghanistan or face "serious consequences" in its relations with the United States. President Reagan and Secretary of State Haig were even more blunt, accusing the Soviet government of lying and cheating and using its own forces or the armies of its Communist client states to achieve its goals, and of funding and supporting international terrorist groups such as the PLO to undermine pro-American governments. Iran and Pakistan in particular felt directly menaced and also denounced the Soviet action. In January 1980, the United States called for U.N. action on the Soviet invasion of Afghanistan. After the USSR vetoed a Security Council resolution condemning Russian aggression, it suffered a major diplomatic and psychological defeat when the General Assembly, by a vote of 104 to 18, strongly deplored the armed intervention and called for the immediate, unconditional, and total withdrawal of foreign troops from Afghanistan.

Mastery Activities

1. Briefly identify or explain each of the following terms and names as used in this chapter.

Names

Ralph Bunche	Anwar Sadat
John Foster Dulles	Menachem Begin
Henry Kissinger	Mohammed Reza Pahlevi
Cyrus Vance	Ayatollah Khomeini
Gunnar Jarring	Alexander Haig

Terms

War of Attrition	Palestinian self-rule
Yom Kippur War	Rejectionist front
Resolution 242	Sinai Peninsula
Geneva Conference	Straits of Tiran
Shuttle diplomacy	Gulf of Aqaba
Old City of Jerusalem	Gaza Strip
Balance of power in the Middle East	Golan Heights

2. Answer each of the following questions with regard to U.N. Security Council Resolutions 242 and 338 (below), by selecting the letter of the choice that most correctly completes the statement.

A. Resolution 242 calls for all of the following *except*
   (a) withdrawal of Israeli armed forces from all territories occupied as a result of the Arab–Israeli war of 1967

(b) lasting peace in the Middle East
(c) recognition of the right of each nation in the Middle East to live in peace within secure boundaries
(d) free navigation through the Suez Canal and the Straits of Tiran

B. Resolution 338 calls for
(a) settling the refugee problem
(b) sending a U.N. representative to the Middle East
(c) a general cease-fire
(d) implementation of certain provisions of U.N. Security Council Resolution 242

C. Both resolutions aim to help solve differences between
(a) Muslims and Christians
(b) Arabs and Jews
(c) the United States and the Soviet Union
(d) Turkey and Greece

D. Both resolutions were drafted
(a) after the Six Day War
(b) after the Camp David conference
(c) before the Holocaust
(c) after Egypt and Israel signed a peace treaty

E. Resolution 338 does *not* refer to
(a) Egypt
(b) Syria
(c) Iran
(d) Israel

U.N. Security Council Resolution 242, Nov. 22, 1967

The Security Council
Expressing its continuing concern with the grave situation in the Middle East,

Emphasizing the inadmissibility of the acquisition of territory by war and the need to work for a just and lasting peace in which every State in the area can live in security,

Emphasizing further that all Member States in their acceptance of the Charter of the United Nations have undertaken a commitment to act in accordance with Article 2 of the Charter,

1. *Affirms* that the fulfillment of Charter principles requires the establishment of a just and lasting peace in the Middle East which should include the application of both the following principles:
(i) Withdrawal of Israeli armed forces from territories occupied in the recent conflict;
(ii) Termination of all claims or states of belligerency and respect for and acknowledgement of the sovereignty, territorial integrity and political independence of every State in the area and their right to live in peace within secure and recognized boundaries free from threats or acts of force;

2. *Affirms further the necessity*
(a) For guaranteeing freedom of navigation through international waterways in the area;
(b) For achieving a just settlement of the refugee problem;

(c) For guaranteeing the territorial inviolability and political independence of every State in the area, through measures including the establishment of demilitarized zones;

3. *Requests* the Secretary-General to designate a Special Representative to proceed to the Middle East to establish and maintain contacts with the States concerned in order to promote agreement and assist efforts to achieve a peaceful and accepted settlement in accordance with the provisions and principles in this resolution;

4. *Requests* the Secretary-General to report to the Security Council on the progress of the efforts of the Special Representative as soon as possible.

U.N. Security Council Resolution 338, Oct. 22, 1973

The Security Council

1. *Calls* upon all parties to the present fighting to cease all firing and terminate all military activity immediately, no later than 12 hours after the moment of the adoption of this decision, in the positions they now occupy;

2. *Calls* upon the parties concerned to start immediately after the cease-fire the implementation of Security Council Resolution 242 (1967) in all of its parts;

3. *Decides* that, immediately and concurrently with the cease-fire, negotiations start between the parties concerned under appropriate auspices aimed at establishing a just and durable peace in the Middle East.

Questions for Homework and Discussion

1. Explain one step taken by the administrations of each of the following American presidents to achieve peace and stability in the Middle East.
   (a) Harry Truman
   (b) Dwight Eisenhower
   (c) John Kennedy
   (d) Lyndon Johnson
   (e) Richard Nixon
   (f) Gerald Ford
   (g) Jimmy Carter
   (h) Ronald Reagan

2. As U.N. representative for Egypt before the 1979 peace treaty, how would you have argued in regard to each of the following issues in the Arab–Israeli dispute?
   (a) Israeli withdrawal from occupied territories
   (b) establishment of a Palestinian homeland
   (c) Israeli settlements in occupied territories
   (d) Israeli control of all of Jerusalem

3. As Israel's U.N. representative, how would you have replied to the Egyptian arguments given in answer to the previous question?

4. Explain with regard to the Camp David agreements:
   (a) why they were considered so significant when they were drawn up in 1978
   (b) how they influenced the peace treaty signed by Egypt and Israel six months later

5. The peace treaty between Israel and Egypt was signed on March 26, 1979. Write a 200-to-500 word editorial that might have appeared the next day in a newspaper you read that comments on the significance and future prospects of this historic development. Give your editorial an appropriate title.

6. It has been said that the crisis in Iran, following the overthrow of the Shah and the establishment of an Islamic republic, clearly shows that the Arab–Israeli conflict is not the main cause of Middle East instability.
   (a) What is meant by this statement?
   (b) Explain why you agree or disagree with it.

8

Dilemmas of United States Foreign Policy in the Middle East

Middle East problems will continue to be among the most difficult challenges to U.S. foreign policy for some time to come. Critical questions facing the United States in the Middle East include how to avoid or contain war, how to protect its oil and strategic interests, how to explain to some of the Arab and Muslim nations its image as a world power that supports Israel, and how to thwart Soviet ambitions in the Middle East in general and the Persian Gulf in particular. Many complicating factors in the Middle East are often beyond the ability of the United States or any other nation to contend with. The chief factors contributing to the dilemmas the United States faces in developing its future policy in the region need to be reviewed and understood.

United States Goals and International Politics

U.S. security interests in the Middle East are linked to international politics. The United States looks on the Middle East–Mediterranean area as a region in which its power must be effectively employed. Since the area is also considered strategic by the Soviet Union, there has been a continuing possibility of U.S.–USSR confrontation. This possibility has been most evident six times: in 1956, 1967, and 1973 during the last three Arab–Israeli wars, since 1979 in the ongoing Iranian revolution, in 1980–1981 during the Iran–Iraq war, and since 1979 when the Soviet Union invaded and occupied Afghanistan. It could arise again. It is essential that the United States contain those conflicts that might provide opportunities for the USSR or any other hostile power to move into the region, directly by way of troop and naval bases or emplacements, or indirectly as arms suppliers. American awareness of this need has caused the United States to be vitally concerned with the Arab–Israeli and the Greek–Turkish disputes, the Russian invasion of Afghanistan, the serious danger posed by the Iran–Iraq war, the ongoing problem of oil flow from the Middle East, as well as with the impact of political change and the upsurge of religious militancy in Iran and elsewhere.

The Arab–Israel Dispute

Until the crises following the overthrow of the Shah in Iran and the subsequent Iran–Iraq war, the most explosive issue seemed to be the Arab–Israel dispute. Still at issue in this conflict, and not settled by the Camp David accords and peace treaty between Egypt and Israel in 1979, are problems of Israel's security, the future status of the Palestinians, and the disposition of territories occupied by Israel since the war of 1967.

Territory

Each of the warring "confrontation" groups with territorial involvements has its demands and points of view. The Israelis demand a secure existence and believe that giving up territory will endanger that security. The Palestinians demand an independent Palestinian state. They view any solution short of this as destroying the Palestinian cause. The Egyptians, Jordanians, and Syrians view Israeli occupation of territory formerly held by them as illegal.

Emotional Factors

The emotions that accompany the territorial claims of each side in the Arab–Israel dispute are shared by millions beyond their borders. Jews in the United States and Europe look on Israel as a long-sought homeland for an oppressed people. They view any threat to Israel's survival as a threat to all Jews. Muslims generally have sided with the Arabs, as members of the Islamic brotherhood and as victims of Western imperialism, of which they consider Israel a symbol. Many non-Islamic nations share this feeling.

The conflict with Israel has caused Arab leaders to patch over their differences and animosities from time to time, although the bitter hatred that exists between these nations has at times boiled over in bloody combat such as the protracted Iran–Iraq conflict. It has also drawn the attention of the poverty-stricken masses away from their suffering and their needs. The smoldering Arab–Israeli conflict has also resulted in the growth of Saudi political influence and prestige in the Arab world, since some of the Arab confrontation states and the PLO depend on Saudi funds to continue their struggle against Israel.

OPPOSITION TO MIDDLE EAST ARMS SALES
Many Americans are opposed to arms sales to Middle East nations and particularly to those who support PLO terrorism. This demonstration in Washington, D.C., protested such sales to Saudi Arabia because the oil-rich and very influential monarchy has become the PLO's chief financial backer. Moore/Gamma-Liaison

The passions aroused by the Arab–Israel dispute are so strong that they often override what the participants believe might be in their best national interests. The intensity of such feelings was best seen when the leaders of Egypt and Israel, the two major parties in the dispute, agreed to end the state of war and negotiated a peace treaty. President Sadat's peace mission to Israel, his willingness to undertake direct negotiations and to sign a peace treaty with the Israelis brought angry denunciation by other Arab leaders as well as initial economic and political sanctions against Egypt. Prime Minister Begin's agreement to turn over Israeli-occupied Arab territories in the Sinai Peninsula (an action he had vigorously opposed previously) in return for a peace pact brought severe criticism of him by some factions in Israel.

Religious Aspects

The religious aspects of the dispute make the situation even more complex. Both Jews and Muslims claim the "Old City" of Jerusalem (East Jerusalem) as theirs because it contains important religious shrines considered holy to each faith. It is the holiest city for the world's Jews and ranks after Mecca and Medina as the third holiest site for Muslims. The government of Israel, remembering that Jews were banned from visiting their holy sites when Jordan held the Old City from 1948 to 1967, have gone out of their way to protect the holy sites and to make them available without discrimination to the world's Christians, Muslims, and Jews. Arabs and other Muslims demand the return of Jerusalem for religious reasons. Jews maintain that Jerusalem must remain the united capital of Israel. In the name of religious solidarity, as well as for other reasons, many Muslim states in Asia and Africa support the Arab position aganist Israel.

Impact of the War of 1973

The Arab–Israel war of 1973 had a significant impact on the role and foreign policies of both the United States and the Soviet Union in the Middle East. It also had important policy and psychological impacts on Israel and the Arab states.

The Arab oil embargo and the development of closer relations between Egypt and Saudi Arabia during and after that war (until the diplomatic break following the peace treaty between Egypt and Israel) caused the Ford and Carter administrations to give up their previous assumption that the oil and Arab–Israeli issues could be handled separately. The Reagan administration has returned to some extent to the earlier assumption. The war also challenged the assumption that the Israelis were militarily strong enough to handle any confrontation with the Arabs without additional military equipment from the United States.

In addition to bringing about military reassessments, the war had important psychological effects on both the Israelis and Arabs. For the Israelis, the shocking initial success of the Arab attack showed that the military gap between Israeli and Arab forces was narrowing and that the Arabs were becoming increasingly united against Israel. Their belief, particularly after the Six Day War of 1967, that time was on their side and that militarily they had nothing to fear from the Arabs was brought into serious question. For the Arabs, the war reversed their negative self-image and encouraged a belief that their honor had been restored. As was to be seen several years later in the role President Sadat of Egypt played in the peace negotiations between Egypt and Israel, the war made the Arab world feel that time was now on its side and that the Arab states could now negotiate from a position of strength rather than weakness.

The Peace Treaty between Egypt and Israel (1979)

The risks of failure to achieve a peace pact between Egypt and Israel were high, not only for each nation but also for the United States.

For Egypt, failure would have imposed new military burdens on the nation's already strained economy — and might have led to explosive unrest among the country's masses who were hoping for a peace that might relieve them from their extreme poverty. In addition, if his peace efforts had failed, Sadat would have been further criticized severely by his radical enemies, who had already called for his overthrow. President Sadat's political future was clearly at stake.

For Israel, failure to reach a peace agreement increased the chances of additional strains with its Arab neighbors, including increased terrorism by the PLO and tensions that could erupt into a fifth Arab–Israel war. Failure would also have given additional political ammunition to those Israelis who opposed Begin's ultimate decision to trade some occupied territories for peace.

For the United States and other Western nations, failure to achieve a Middle East peace could jeopardize important strategic and economic interests. Danger of renewed Arab–Israel war could further destabilize the already unstable Middle East by strengthening Soviet-backed radicals and weakening traditional U.S. ties to more moderate and conservative Arab countries such as Jordan and Saudi Arabia. These increased tensions would come at a time when Iran was in turmoil and transition and Soviet influence was growing in Afghanistan, Southern Yemen, and Ethiopia. Such developments constituted a growing potential threat to the oil deposits and supplies in the Persian Gulf on which the U.S., Western Europe, and Japan depend heavily.

The Greek–Turkish Dispute over Cyprus

The United States has been anxious to resolve the dispute between Greece and Turkey over Cyprus through U.N. or NATO channels.

The dispute has worsened relationships of both countries with both NATO and the United States. After the Turkish invasion of Cyprus, Greece blamed the United States for not acting strongly enough to prevent Turkey's armed intervention. As a consequence, it restricted the use of Greek military facilities by U.S. forces and reduced its participation in NATO activities.

Turkey was angered by the U.S. arms embargo levied against it for using U.S. arms in the invasion of Cyprus. In retaliation Turkey also closed down a number of missile and nuclear monitoring bases previously available to the United States. Despite the repeal of the embargo in 1978 and the regranting of permission to the United States to use its electronic listening-posts, there were fears that Turkey might turn to the Kremlin (the USSR) for arms, a turn of events that could "unhinge" the southern flank of

GREEK CYPRIOTS STORM AMERICAN EMBASSY IN NICOSIA

After the Turkish invasion of Cyprus in 1974, Greece blamed the United States for not acting strongly enough to prevent Turkey's invasion. In retaliation Greece restricted American use of its military facilities and reduced its participation in NATO activities. Here angry Greek Cypriot demonstrators rip the American flag from the U.S. Embassy in Nicosia during a demonstration against American policy. The American Ambassador, Roger P. Davies, was killed by gunfire in the incident. Wide World

NATO. Although Turkey has remained pro-West, its signing of a nonaggression pact with the Soviet Union and the increase in trade relations since then have caused continued concern on the part of both NATO and the United States.

Oil Diplomacy

The United States and other industrial nations have become increasingly dependent on oil as a source of energy. To ensure continued oil flow, to keep prices from again rising as sharply as they did after the Arab–Israeli war of 1973, and to forestall another oil embargo, the United States has had to give the Arab oil-producing states concrete assurances of its sympathetic interest in their concerns. It has sold arms and provided technological assistance to Saudi Arabia and Kuwait as well as to Iran under the Shah. Moreover, U.S. diplomacy has been actively geared to keeping the support of Saudi Arabia and Kuwait, who have increasingly become key Middle East states in matters of OPEC oil pricing and production policies.

The Danger of Nuclear Proliferation

In the spring of 1981 there was much concern in both the State Department and the Senate that militant and unstable countries in the Middle East might, with outside resources and aid, be able to manufacture nuclear bombs that could further destabilize the entire region. It has been believed for some time that the most erratic and unstable ruler in the region, Colonel Qaddafi of Libya, is funding a Pakistani attempt to create an "Islamic atomic bomb." More recently various U.S. senators have accused Iraq of blackmailing oil-dependent West European nations to acquire nuclear fuel and start a crash program to become a nuclear power. Other officials have asserted that some West European nations, led by France, have in their assistance to Iraq and Pakistan's nuclear efforts inadvertently developed a clear and present danger to U.S. security interests in the Middle East. Some American officials saw both Iraq and Pakistan becoming nuclear powers by the end of 1982; others put the date slightly later.

At the start of their war, Iran had unsuccessfully attempted to bomb and destroy Iraq's nuclear facilities. It is also known that Libya's strongman, President Qadaffi, who preaches revolution in the Middle East, has been trying to buy nuclear weapons and technology in the open market. Early in 1981 some members of Congress asked the administration to consider ending nuclear-supply relationships with West European countries such as France that have been aiding in the dangerous nuclear proliferation in the Middle East. Iraq's capability to produce nuclear weapons was crippled in June 1981 when Israeli jets bombed the reactor under construction near Baghdad.

Some say that Israel already has nuclear capability. Israeli leaders have repeatedly declared that Israel would never be the first to introduce nuclear warfare into the Middle East.

In the spring of 1981, following Egypt's ratification of the international treaty banning the spread of nuclear weapons, the United States and Egypt completed a nuclear-power accord that will enable Egypt to purchase nuclear reactors and fuel for a power-generating program.

Political Dynamics in the Middle East

Shifting political balances, internal unrest, and inter-Arab differences have made it difficult to make predictable policy assumptions or to apply any single rational solution to Middle East problems. The Arab world has been and continues to be divided and unstable.

Continuing Instability

In recent years there have been many examples of the instability that characterizes the Middle East—and particularly the Arab world: Libya and

Egypt have massed troops on one another's borders as have Syria and Jordan; Iraq and Iran were involved in a debilitating war through 1980 and 1981; North and South Yemen have engaged in long-standing conflicts; Iraq has tried to seize territory in Kuwait; South Yemen has supported guerrilla warfare in Oman; Arab Christians have fought Muslims, Syrians, and PLO terrorists in Lebanon—while Israel has given support to the Christians; Jordan has used its armed forces to violently expel the PLO; and feuding Syrian and Iraqi PLO terrorists have assassinated one another's leaders. In addition, the attempted modernization of Saudi Arabia and of Iran (under the Shah) has encountered the growing opposition and resistance of conservative Muslims and Muslim leaders, for whom entry into the modern world implies breaking with a society based on Islamic law and customs. The Iranian revolution and the rising tide of Islamic unrest (for example, the attack on the Grand Mosque in Mecca, Saudi Arabia) added new complexities to an already complicated and turbulent situation.

An additional complicating factor to differences among regimes in political outlooks, traditions, religious sectarianism, history, and geography has been the bewildering shifts in alliances in recent years. There have been alliances between Syria and Egypt against Jordan; between Syria and Iraq against Egypt; betwen Syria and Jordan against Iraq and Egypt; between Jordan and Iraq against Syria; and between Syria and Iran against Iraq. Libya, the most militant of the Arab nations, has joined in or made plans for temporary unity with almost all Arab nations and then has disengaged.

American Relations with Key Middle East Nations

Although often accused of taking sides in these and other disputes, the United States has tried where possible to maintain a low profile in order to hold on to its leverage with Middle East nations, particularly with the Arab world. At the same time the United States has made extra efforts to strengthen its relationships with several key Middle East states, notably Egypt, Saudi Arabia, Jordan, and, until the overthrow of the Shah's regime by the Ayatollah Khomeini, Iran.

EGYPT. Egypt is considered "pivotal" because President Sadat committed himself to the principles of peace negotiations and recognition of the existence of Israel. Moreover, Egypt is committed to noninvolvement with the Soviets; Sadat actually expelled thousands of Soviet advisers and technicians. Egypt is also the most populous and most militarily powerful Arab state and, until its peace treaty with Israel, had much influence with the oil-producing Arab states which President Sadat predicted will be renewed after other Arab states realize both the necessity for peace with Israel and the danger of Soviet intrusion in the area. In turn, the Egyptians need the United States as an alternative to the Soviet Union for vital military and economic aid.

AWACS IN FLIGHT

American Aircraft Warning and Control System Planes (AWACS) are the world's most advanced surveillance planes. A promise by the Reagan Administration to sell Saudi Arabia five AWACS produced strong reaction in Congress and the nation. Department of Defense

SAUDI ARABIA. An equally important policy "dynamic" has been U.S. awareness of the influence of Saudi Arabia in the Arab world. Saudi Arabia has replaced Egypt as the Arab nation most looked to for pan-Arab leadership and, to some, has also become the most important power to be reckoned with in the Middle East. The Saudis have a vast oil income and huge monetary reserves. As the world's top oil exporter and a leading member of OPEC, Saudi Arabia has great influence on the oil cartel's decision on how much oil goes to the United States and Western Europe and for what price.

The Saudis have used their wealth to develop the fastest-growing military arsenal in the Arab world. In 1978 the Carter administration, after heated debate in the U.S. Senate, authorized the purchase of sixty-two F-15 planes by Saudi Arabia. President Carter made a commitment to the Senate that further offensive capabilities for the planes would not be authorized. In the fall of 1980, during the heated Carter–Reagan presidential campaign, Saudi Arabia requested that the F-15s now be equipped with air-to-air missiles, extra fuel tanks, bomb racks, and KC-135 tankers. The Defense Department recommended, during the closing days of the campaign, that Saudi Arabia's request be approved even though this would violate the commitment made to the Senate and enable the planes to reach and attack Israel.

President Carter decided to postpone the decision until after the election. President Reagan decided to sell the Saudis five AWACS (Airborne Warning and Control Systems), electronic surveillance planes, as well as advanced air-to-air missiles, seven KC-135 aerial tankers, and attachable fuel tanks for the F-15 fighter planes already on order. But he put off the Saudi request for bomb racks for the F-15s. President Reagan notified Congress of the proposed sale in September 1981. Unless a majority of both houses of Congress voted to block the sale, it would be automatically approved. In October 1981, the House voted against, but the Senate (by a narrow 52 to 48 vote) approved the sale.

The Saudis have become the chief financial backers of Syria, Jordan, and even the PLO (some say to prevent the PLO from meddling in Saudi domestic affairs). Saudi Arabia also gave substantial aid to Egypt, but this was cut off when Egypt signed the peace treaty with Israel in 1979.

Saudi Arabia is strongly anti-Communist and very conservative. It seeks to prevent the "radicalization" of Arab states. Saudi leaders were badly shaken by the overthrow of the Shah of Iran, by the fact that Iran's new masters preached violent change, even beyond Iran's borders, and by the attack on the Grand Mosque in Mecca allegedly inspired by outsiders in late 1979. The Saudis were also concerned with Ayatollah Khomeini's continuing contacts and relationship with the PLO, the Muslim Brotherhood, and other Middle East radicals.

Saudi Arabia is strongly anti-Israel and like other Arab states seeks recovery of territories lost in 1967 and Muslim holy places in Old Jerusalem. Despite its opposition to Israel and to Egypt's signing a separate peace with it, the Saudi attitude toward peace negotiations has at times been less hostile than that of the more radical regimes in Syria, Iraq, Libya, other rejectionist states, and the PLO. At other times, it has called for *jihad* (holy war) against Israel.

American influence with the Saudis had been strengthened by the Saudis' need for U.S. political support against radical elements on the Arabian Peninsula, particularly in Syria, Libya, South Yemen, and more recently Iran; as well as by the Saudis' need for continuing American military and technological assistance. In addition, U.S. support is seen as a counterforce to Soviet influence in the region. The Saudis hope, too, that if there were to be a showdown with Iran, their chief rival for supremacy in the Persian Gulf area, U.S. support would "tilt" toward them.

After the revolution in Iran and the Israeli–Egyptian peace treaty, Saudi leaders were reluctant to fall in step with U.S. policies. They felt that the United States should have intervened actively to help the Shah of Iran in time to save the country from revolutionary chaos. They opposed the continuing efforts of Israel and Egypt to move toward a more comprehensive peace settlement with U.S. support. Despite the announced decision by the Carter administration in late 1979 and in 1980 to develop a military task force to deal with emergencies in the Middle East and elsewhere, Saudi leaders were still not fully assured that the United States had the will and ability to stop growing Russian encroachment in Persian Gulf and Red Sea areas. After President Reagan's election, definite signals were given in early 1981 that the United States would take a stronger military posture in the area than had the Carter administration. Indeed, the Reagan administration hoped eventually to develop greater strategic coordination in the Middle East between Egypt and Israel as well as Jordan and Saudi Arabia. It remained to be seen whether the Reagan administration could develop such coordination among countries that do not recognize each other (Jordan and Saudi Arabia do not recognize the existence of the State of Israel) or have recently broken off ties (Saudi Arabia and Jordan have broken off diplomatic and economic ties with Egypt because Egypt made peace with Israel).

IRAN. For over a decade prior to the overthrow of the Shah the United States attempted to cultivate friendly relations with Iran. Iran was a member of CENTO, the Middle East anti-Communist military alliance, until the leaders of the Islamic regime that replaced the Shah in 1979 took it out of the defense pact. Iran was also a leading source of American oil imports and, like Saudi Arabia, had been generally pro-West in its political leanings. At one time Iran's leading ally and arms supplier, the United States provided the Shah's government with substantial technological advice and assistance and sold it large quantities of equipment, including combat aircraft.

The turmoil in Iran that began in 1978 toppled the Shah from his throne in January 1979 and has posed serious threats to American interests and policy in the Middle East. Riots and demonstrations in Iran were often violently anti-American, clearly indicating the deep resentment of Washington's support for the Shah until shortly before his forced departure. The taking of American hostages by Iran, following the admission of the Shah to the United States in 1979 for medical treatment, heightened the tension between the two countries and created a crisis with major consequences for the United States and the world. The release of the hostages in January 1981 defused some of the immediate tension but did not resolve the basic differences between the United States and Iran.

In addition to the damage to American prestige in the region and the economic squeeze caused by the cutback in Iranian oil production, the United States was seriously concerned with the anti-U.S. and anti-West posture of the new Islamic regime. This called for a reassessment by the United States of its Persian Gulf and other Middle East strategies, including the possibilities of an increase in the USSR's influence in the Persian Gulf and adjacent regions and of Iran's being drawn into the Soviet orbit.

During its last year the Carter administration's recognition that the increasingly turbulent situation in the Persian Gulf might require some kind of military action resulted in a "watershed change" in American foreign policy and the decision to establish a Rapid Deployment Force to meet emergencies. In late 1979 the United States initiated a search for new bases in the region to support such a force.

The decision to establish new bases was not without problems and dilemmas. The governments of the Gulf region want an American presence to balance the potential Russian threat to their security but do not want American forces on their soil. Some Americans feel that the establishment of bases may provoke further Soviet military aggression (as in Afghanistan). Some critics of the plan feel that the bases will sooner or later involve the United States in the tangled politics of the region, with the likelihood of American involvement in support of right-wing feudal governments with which it has little in common. Others argue that there is no real need for additional bases and that frequent visits to the region by powerful naval-air forces would be sufficient to protect American interests in any crisis.

Although criticism of the base program is likely to continue, the feeling of the President and top military and strategic planners in the Pentagon is that additional bases are necessary for the protection of American interests, particularly the security of the oil fields and oil-shipping routes.

Client-State Relationships

Closely tied in with American relationships with key Middle East nations is the issue of client-state policy. The overthrow of the monarchy in Iran caused the United States toward the end of the Carter administration to reexamine its diplomacy in this matter. It thought it would have to make some determination as to whether or not to give up the policy of recent administrations, begun when John Foster Dulles, secretary of state under President Eisenhower, tried to shape an interlocking set of regional pacts designed to halt the spread of Communism. Under the so-called "Nixon Doctrine" in the early 1970s, client states in critical areas — for example, Iran and Saudi Arabia in the Persian Gulf — were armed by the United States and played an important role in U.S. strategic planning.

Recent events in Iran have called client-state diplomacy into question by making clearer than ever what had already become apparent, namely, that client states can be unreliable, burdensome, and embarrassing. Thus, the United States, because of its strong support for the Shah, became the target of abuse by anti-Shah Iranian groups that helped overthrow his regime. In addition, the decision of the new Iranian government to cancel over $7 billion in new orders for American military hardware was a severe economic blow to defense and defense-related industries.

The U.S. has also found that friendly relations with Saudi Arabia and Iran (under the Shah) did not prevent these countries from supporting major increases in oil prices and from cooling off their relationships with the United States after the Shah's overthrow. Moreover, the Carter administration's emphasis on human rights appeared to be in conflict with American support for autocratic or repressive regimes in the Shah's Iran, Saudi Arabia, and other Middle East states.

On the one hand it is clear that the cost of client-state support is high and has become an increasing economic burden for the United States. On the other hand it is recognized that insufficient economic and military aid and political involvement can cause a client to alter its allegiances — as the Soviets learned when Russian advisers were ousted from Egypt in the early 1970s.

The United States faces a client-state dilemma. It knows that in an era of growing Soviet military power, and of a reluctance on the part of the United States to commit its own forces to regional conflicts (the result of its Vietnam experience), the importance of alliances has grown. At the same time there are serious drawbacks to such linkages. It has been suggested that the solution might be *not* to end existing security ties but rather to reinforce them by helping clients develop greater economic and political self-reliance, as for example in the case of Egypt and Israel since the peace treaty.

Since the election of President Reagan, the United States has decided to go further than previous administrations and attempt to stimulate greater strategic coordination among the major pro-Western nations in the area — Egypt, Israel, Jordan, and Saudi Arabia.

Policy Considerations and Options

Although there are continuing tensions and crises in the Middle East, the desire for peace and stability continues to be the prime consideration for the United States. Because it has felt until recently that the Arab–Israel dispute was potentially the most dangerous of all Middle East crises, the United States has been actively involved in attempting to work out a Middle East settlement, as demonstrated by its participation in peace negotiations between Egypt and Israel.

The Policy of Evenhandedness

For many years the United States has adopted an official policy sometimes referred to as "evenhandedness" or "balanced diplomacy." It has tried to ensure Israel's basic security while respecting basic Arab claims. It has at the same time attempted to protect its economic interest in the delivery of Middle East oil and its political and strategic interest in keeping the region as free as possible of Soviet domination.

The United States has endorsed U.N. Security Council Resolutions 242 of November 22, 1967 and 338 of October 22, 1973, each based on a balancing of Arab and Israeli interests. Resolution 242 calls for "withdrawal of Israeli armed forces from territories occupied in the Six Day War of 1967" and for "acknowledgement of the sovereignty, territorial integrity and political independence of every state in the area and their right to live in peace within secure and recognized boundaries." It also calls for "a just settlement of the refugee problem." Resolution 338 calls for negotiations based on the principles set forth in Resolution 242, "under appropriate auspices aimed at establishing a just and durable peace."

Increased Presence in the Middle East

More recently the United States has also been vitally concerned with the upheavals in Iran that have resulted in the dissolution of the monarchy and its replacement by a militant Islamic republic, the Iran–Iraq war, the in-

ARAFAT AND GROMYKO

The United States has become increasingly concerned with Russia's attempts to keep the Middle East destabilized. The Palestine Liberation Organization has received Soviet support for its terrorist activities. Here, its leader Yasser Arafat, confers with Soviet Foreign Minister Gromyko in Moscow. United Press International

vasion of Afghanistan by Russian troops, and the potential for further Soviet intrusion in the area. Toward the end of the Carter administration, there was growing evidence that the United States intended to increase its military presence and role in the region.

The new Reagan administration indicated its intention to increase the quantity and quality of America's commitment beyond what President Carter had considered. Its major concern was possible Soviet intrusion in the area and shoring up our major allies (Israel, Egypt, Saudi Arabia, Jordan) to prevent this from happening. The administration was convinced that if the U.S. helps strengthen Saudi Arabia against Soviet influence in Ethiopia and South Yemen, as well as internal subversion from Islamic radicals, then the Saudis will be more likely to join Arab-Israeli peace efforts. During separate visits to Washington by President Sadat and Prime Minister Begin, President Reagan assured the two leaders of continued American support for their countries and his intention to involve both Egypt and Israel in forging a strategic alliance to curb Soviet penetration.

Besides more military aid for the area, the Reagan administration hoped to establish a U.S. military presence, including the Rapid Deployment Force and a U.S. contingent in the proposed multinational Sinai peace force. It also planned to gain access for U.S. forces at additional military facilities in the Middle East.

United States policies in the Middle East have been both defended and criticized.

Defense of United States Middle East Policies

Supporters of recent U.S. policy in the Middle East, particularly of evenhandedness, have made the following arguments.

1. *America has important economic and political interests in the Arab Middle East.* These should be given as much consideration as the U.S. commitment to Israel. Because the United States in the 1950s and early 1960s did not give sufficient consideration to developing positive relations with the Arab world, the Soviet Union was able to turn much of this world against the United States and the West and to greatly extend its influence in the region. By giving increased attention to Arab concerns since the late 1960s, the United States has developed a counterbalance to attempted Soviet domination of the region.

2. *U.S. efforts to gain more influence among the Arab states have worked.* Today the United States is the only key country with substantial influence on both sides of the Arab–Israeli dispute. During the late 1960s (before Sadat), when President Nasser ruled Egypt and Russian influence in Egypt and Syria was at its height, the United States had few friends in the Arab Middle East other than Israel and a decreasing number of Arab kingdoms.

3. *U.S. policy makers have been overly influenced by the pro-Israel lobby in Congress and elsewhere.*[1] It is time to review some aspects of America's Middle East position.

4. *The evenhanded policy of the United States made it possible for Egypt eagerly to accept President Carter's leadership role in working out the Camp David agreements between Egypt and Israel and the peace treaty that followed* — one of the most hopeful developments in the Middle East in many years.

5. *Recent Carter and Reagan administration policies have shored up U.S. strength in the Middle East and will cause the Soviets to think twice before embarking on further adventurism in the region.*

Criticism of United States Middle East Policies

Critics of past American policy in the Middle East have made the following arguments.

1. *American policy in the Middle East has been a failure. It has not achieved its objectives.*

Despite U.S. attempts to block or limit Soviet penetration, the Soviets have established many footholds in the Middle East. Efforts to develop a strong anti-Soviet alliance and check expansion of Soviet influence have been ineffective.

---

[1] For a number of years pro-Israeli and pro-Arab groups have been represented by officially registered lobbies in Washington, D.C.

Pro-Israel groups in the United States have been ably represented by the American Israel Public Affairs Committee (AIPAC). It has the support of most of the American Jewish community and considerable non-Jewish support, especially among members of Congress. The continued willingness of the United States to reaffirm the nation's commitment to Israeli security and continued economic and military aid has been in significant measure a result of the persuasiveness and influence of the AIPAC.

In recent years and especially since the war of 1973, more and more of the AIPAC's attention has been devoted to countering the lobbying of the increasingly active pro-Arab lobby. It has also vigorously opposed and exposed U.S. business firms boycotting Israel despite the illegality of such a boycott. It is felt that the pro-Israel lobby has been a crucial factor in balancing the "evenhanded" approach of "Arabists" in the State Department who have long favored less support for Israel. The Arab cause in the United States is represented by the National Association of Arab-Americans (NAAA). The NAAA works closely with the Arab Information Centers established by the Arab League. It has the support of virtually all cultural, religious, and charitable Arab organizations in the United States.

The Arab lobby has the additional financial backing of oil interests in the United States. As a result of greatly expanding its Capitol Hill operation, its influence has been growing steadily since the early 1970s, when it was officially established. With the support of members of Congress of Arab-American descent, the NAAA has focused its efforts on acting as a counterforce to the pro-Israel lobby as well as on making the administration and Congress aware of Arab concerns. At the same time it has tried to get the government to reassess its foreign policies in the Middle East and abandon what the NAAA considers a pro-Israel policy.

The Arab oil embargo and the sharp price rises approved by OPEC since the Arab–Israeli war of 1973 have demonstrated that the United States and the West have, as a result of poor energy policies, become too dependent on Middle East oil and in addition can no longer be sure of an uninterrupted Middle East oil flow at reasonably stable price levels. Moreover, in the event of future confrontation with the United States or the West, the USSR could, through its growing military and naval presence in and around the Persian Gulf, choke off the oil flow from the region.

Efforts to get Arab states to "tilt" toward the West have not borne real fruit. Aside from the more conservative Arab regimes, which are as fearful and suspicious of the more radical regimes as they are of Israel, most Arab states remain nonaligned, eager to accept aid from both sides and to manipulate U.S.–Soviet rivalry to their own advantage.

In spite of its hopes and its policies, the United States has been unable to do much to prevent continuing Middle East instability. In addition, military rule rather than democracy has become the prevailing form of government in the Middle East.

LEBANESE PROTEST SYRIAN AND PLO INTERVENTION
Syria and the PLO have intervened actively in the civil war in Lebanon. Here several thousand American Lebanese stage a protest march in New York City against the Syrian and PLO intervention. Some also protested against the regime of Col. Qaddafi of Libya for also attempting to stir up trouble in Lebanon.
Gubb/Gamma-Liaison

2. *Past U.S. Middle East policy has been self-defeating.* It shows poor judgment and indecision.

Recent escalating U.S. arms sales to Arab and other Middle East nations have made future military confrontations possible. This could be counterproductive to the American desire for peace and stabilty.

During the decades in which the USSR has been establishing its presence in the Middle East, the United States did little to effectively counteract this development.

The United States has also seriously misread the political situation in the Middle East. It has, until the Reagan administration, mistakenly proceeded on the assumption that the Arab–Israeli conflict is the central issue in the politics of the Middle East. It has insufficiently recognized that the region would be unstable even without this conflict, as recent crises reveal. The belief that a settlement of the Arab–Israeli dispute will automatically lead to a decline in Soviet influence and an improvement in relations between the United States and the Arab states is at best questionable.

American leaders have over-relied on the Saudis to help "broker" or support an Arab–Israel peace settlement. The existing situation of "no war, no peace" works to the Saudis' advantage. Peace in the region would focus the attention of the impoverished and overpopulated Arab states on Saudi Arabia's oil wealth. The Saudis have given only very limited support to efforts for a comprehensive peace settlement in the Middle East. Their rejection of the peace agreement between Israel and Egypt has complicated the situation. Furthermore, some analysts fear that the absolute monarchy of the Saudi regime will not last into the next decade. Moreover, say the critics, the United States should abandon the illusion that Saudi Arabia is a "moderate" Arab state. In their opposition to Israel and their backing of the PLO, the Saudis are almost as determined as Libya, Syria, and revolutionary Iran. Sadat and Begin rejected a Saudi Mideast plan in September 1981.

3. *One of the greatest weaknesses of past American policy in the Middle East has been its failure to place more emphasis on what could be Israel's strategic value to U.S. security.*

Israel's military value to the United States comes from its location and from the strength and sophistication of its armed forces. It has shown its superiority over the combined forces of Arab enemies in four wars and is, in the judgment of most analysts, still the strongest military power in the region.

By its victory in the Six Day War in 1967, Israel prevented Nasser from making a deal with Russia (then his ally) that might have opened opportunities for Soviet access to Middle East oil. In 1970, an Israeli threat to intervene to aid Jordan (then fighting to prevent a PLO takeover) prevented Syria from attempting to invade Jordan to rescue the PLO and made it unnecessary for the United States to go through with its plan to send supplies to Israel to help it ensure Jordan's victory. In addition, Israel's support for the Christians in the civil war in Lebanon has prevented Syria from completely taking over that country.

Toward the Future: United States Policy in the Middle East

The advent of the Reagan administration in 1981 moved American policy in the Middle East toward recognition of Israel as a strategic asset and a major ally of the United States. As the 1980s began, the United States continued to be confronted with the many currents of crisis, tension, and change that have characterized the Middle East for over a quarter of a century. The following glimpses of the state of the region in 1981 illustrate the simmering cauldron that is the Middle East today.

• *Iran* was slipping into a state of chaos. The ongoing war with Iraq had destroyed most of Iran's oil refineries, moving the nation closer to bankruptcy. Mismanagement of the economy by the Khomeini regime had resulted in decreased production, increased unemployment, and greater inflation. Opposition to the government was growing among leftists, nationalists, secularists, those opposed to religious rule, and other groups that had initially helped overthrow the Shah. Additional and more violent opposition to the government was growing among the Kurds, Turkomans, Baluchis, Azerbaijanis, Arabs, and other ethnic minorities desiring self-rule. Civil war had been threatened in 1980 by the moderate and prestigious

MIDDLE EAST PERSPECTIVES

This cartoon appeared in December 1980, shortly after Ronald Reagan was elected President of the United States. What is the main idea of the cartoon? Who is speaking to Reagan? What events is he referring to? How might the cartoon be updated if the artist re-drew it today? Arab Perspectives, December 1980

Ayatollah Kazem Shariat Madari of Azerbaijan who opposed Khomeini's dictatorial power.

The Iranian–American crisis had been intensified by the seizure of the American hostages by Iranian militants in November 1979 and their retention for fourteen months. The crisis continued to boil through 1980 with growing regional and worldwide repercussions. The hostages were finally released in January 1981 but tensions continued when some of the former hostages revealed the humiliating and brutal treatment they received at the hands of their captors.

The summer of 1981 was a time of tragedy and upheaval for Iran. In quick succession, President Abolhassan Bani-Sadr was ousted; a bomb blast blew up the headquarters of the ruling Islamic Republican Party, killing 74 prominent political leaders; the newly-elected president and his prime minister were assassinated in another bomb explosion; the chief of police and many other politicians were assassinated; the clergy-led government retaliated by arresting thousands of leftists and secularists and executing hundreds of "counterrevolutionaries."

Encouraged by the revolution in Iran, Muslim fundamentalists tried to gain greater influence in other countries of the Middle East and anti-American militancy spread across the Muslim world. These destabilizing factors presented further opportunities for Soviet expansionism.

● *Saudi Arabia* continued to be rocked by the brief seizure of the Grand Mosque in Mecca, Islam's holiest shrine, by a group of several hundred armed extremists in late 1979. Following the retaking of the mosque by Saudi forces, the surviving rebels were summarily tried and over sixty were beheaded. The Saudis were also shaken by the outbreak of violence in the kingdom's oil-producing Eastern Province. Outside influences allegedly from Libya, the USSR, and Southern Yemen, seemed to be involved in a plot against the regime. Saudi leaders and leaders of other conservative kingdoms in the United Arab Emirates were increasingly worried that the revolutionary spirit in Islam touched off by recent events in Iran might affect the stability of their governments.

● Although peaceful relations had been established between *Israel* and *Egypt*, with Israel returning the major portion of the Sinai Peninsula to Egypt (including valuable oil fields and airfields) ahead of schedule in an agreed-upon phased withdrawal, the issue of self-rule for the Palestinians was deadlocked. The new Reagan administration, unlike the Carter administration, considered the issue of Palestinian self-rule secondary to stopping Russian intrusion in the area.

● In *Turkey*, a junta led by General Kevan Evren took control in 1980 in the wake of general dissatisfaction over high unemployment and soaring inflation, near civil war among extremists, rightists, and leftists, and bloody

MILITARY GOVERNMENT IN CONTROL IN TURKEY

In September 1980 Turkish military forces seized power for the third time in twenty years, to prevent Turkey from sliding into political, religious, and economic chaos. In less than a year the new ruling junta (the National Security Council) was able – with popular support, to sharply reduce terrorism, slow down inflation, and ease unemployment. Restoration to the United States of several military bases once again gave NATO an important air-force capability in the region, together with electronic listening posts for surveillance of the Soviet Union. Here General Evren and members of the National Security Council are leaving the Prime Ministry. Guler/Gamma-Liaison

riots between majority Sunni Muslims and minority Shiites in major cities. Three thousand people had been killed in two years of civil strife. The leaders of the military coup, in the tradition of Kemal Ataturk, were regarded as modernist, secular, and nationalist. During 1981, the junta clamped down on dissidents and took stern measures to restore stability. Elections were planned to return Turkey to civilian rule.

• A recently installed military regime held power in anti-Communist *Pakistan* under President Zia. Martial law had been imposed in order to keep anti-government demonstrations from escalating into rebellion.

• *Afghanistan*, on Iran's eastern border, had become a virtual Russian satellite since its takeover by a Marxist government in 1978. Rebel Afghan groups, unwilling to accept Soviet domination or to recognize the Soviet-supported regime, continued to pose a serious problem for 100,000 Russian troops.

● Reports continued to circulate that the USSR was trying to get the Marxist government of *Southern Yemen* to stir up a rebellion in Dhofar, a strategically located province in Oman at the southern entrance to the Persian Gulf. (In 1975 Iranian troops had helped the Sultanate crush a previous insurrection of Soviet-assisted rebels.)

● In 1979 *Iraqi* authorities accused the Khomeini regime of fomenting revolt among Iraq's Shiite Muslims and abrogated a 1975 agreement in which Iraq had yielded disputed border territory in return for Iran's ending its support for Kurdish rebels in Iraq. Iranian authorities once again became fearful of an Iraqi attack that could spark a full-scale uprising in the province of Khurzestan. Claims were also being made that the Iraqi regime, armed by the USSR, was continuing to initiate efforts to overthrow the pro-Western governments of Saudi Arabia and Kuwait.

In September 1980, Iraq attacked Iran in a war that continued into 1981, with Iraq gaining the upper hand and destroying most of Iran's oil facilities but without the immediate and dramatic victory it had anticipated. Iran's

WAR BETWEEN IRAQ AND IRAN

The outbreak of war between Iraq and Iran in September 1980 dramatically highlighted the instability and rivalry that has made the Middle East one of the world's most troubled and explosive regions. The hostilities, which began when Iraq sent military forces into Iran, climaxed growing tension between the Baathist socialist government of Iraq and the Islamic Khomeini regime. This photo shows an Iraqi soldier near blazing Iranian oilfields. Golestan/Gamma-Liaison

war effort was handicapped by its concerns over the possible spread of insurgency by its ethnic minorities. These included the four million Kurds who had been fighting a guerrilla war since long before Iraq's invasion, as well as the one million Baluchis, the million or more Turkomans, and eight million Azerbaijanis.

Western observers felt that even though the Kurds, in their desire for an independent or autonomous Kurdistan, had been a problem to central governments in Iran for over a century, unrest among other minorities might be equally if not more dangerous, since the Azerbaijani, Baluchi, and Turkoman peoples might turn to the USSR for military and economic assistance.

● U.S. jets flying over the Gulf of Sidra downed two Soviet-made *Libyan* planes in the summer of 1981. Libyan dictator Qadafi claimed that the American planes, then on naval maneuvers in the Mediterranean, violated his country's territorial waters. The U.S. rejected this claim and insisted that the Libyans had attacked first without provocation. The incident seemed to show that the Reagan administration would no longer tolerate military adventurism from Libya or elsewhere.

U.S. Policy Reassessment

In the face of religious and racial warfare, political violence, social conflict, and military instability that was gripping nations from southern Africa through the Middle East and into Afghanistan and Pakistan in Asia, the United States was being forced to seriously reconsider its policies in the Middle East. According to critics, this reassessment was long overdue.

In the Middle East the "arc of instability" that had developed included: the rift in the Arab world caused by the negotiations preceding and the situation following the signing of a peace agreement between Egypt and Israel; the Iraq–Iran war; the growing wave of militancy throughout the Islamic world; the unsettling political developments in Iran and Turkey; the termination by Iran of the Shah-adopted (and U.S.-supported) role of "guardian" of the Persian Gulf region, its adoption of pro-Palestinian and pro-Arab policies, and its termination of the sale of oil to Israel; and the growing influence of the Soviet Union in the eastern Mediterranean, the Red Sea, the Horn of Africa, and Afghanistan. The Libyan invasion and takeover of Chad in December 1980 further heightened tensions in this area and frightened most of black Africa as well as Egypt, Sudan, Somalia, and the North African Muslim nations.

Particularly compelling was the fear that "ripple effects" of the situation could shift the global balance of power against the United States and its allies. Should a pro-Soviet government emerge in Iran, as it already has in

Afghanistan, the Russians could gain a long-sought land link to the Persian Gulf, plus the capability of disrupting oil exports from Iran, Saudi Arabia, Iraq, Kuwait, and the United Arab Emirates.

Among the courses of action being recommended for consideration by U.S. government leaders in the 1980s were:

(1) Swift follow-through on the Carter administration's late decision to expand the American military presence in the Middle East with combat forces that would be available in an emergency to help prevent the fall of other pro-Western governments and safeguard the oil routes to and from the Persian Gulf region.[2] The Reagan administration was moving very quickly to increase military support for America's friends in the Middle East at a much more rapid and extensive pace than had previously been anticipated.

(2) Recognizing Israel's value as an ally that can defend itself and reinforcing its military strength or using it as a base as an alternative to sending American forces to the area.[3]

(3) Making greater efforts than ever before to reduce U.S. dependence on Middle East oil in order to end its being "hostage" to events in the region that endanger this vital source of energy.

(4) Supporting opposition forces or arming insurgent forces in nations where anti-Western regimes directly jeopardize American interests (for example, Iran, Afghanistan).[4] Leading officials in the Reagan administration have recommended to the President and the Secretary of State that our government follow this pattern.

United States policies directed toward preventing possible Soviet domination of the area, assuring continued access to Middle East oil, and resolving the Arab–Israel dispute are likely to shape the course of Middle East and global affairs for many years to come.

[2] Many foreign officials friendly to the United States as well as many Americans have urged a show of force as the best way to avoid engaging in its actual use. Some have gone further and argued for a takeover of Middle East oil fields (without saying how to hold them or keep them working).

[3] An open letter to President Carter in January 1979, signed by more than 170 retired generals and admirals, pointed out that "in a non-nuclear conflict between the Soviet Union and the United States in the Middle East, Israel alone might deter Soviet combat forces intervention." Despite this strong statement the Carter administration did not adopt such a policy for fear of antagonizing the Arab world, further reducing the chances of reaching an overall Arab–Israeli peace settlement, and endangering U.S. oil supplies. Leading officials in the Reagan administration are closer to the position of the retired military officers.

[4] It has been pointed out that a major difficulty in such a course of action is that there are no grounds for knowing how such forces would act when in power.

Mastery Activities

1. Identify or briefly explain each of the following terms as used in this chapter:

Arab–Israeli dispute   Nixon Doctrine
Greek–Turkish dispute   The Arab lobby
The oil flow problem   The Israel lobby
Old City of Jerusalem   Détente
The Arab oil embargo   Arc of instability
Petrodollar pressures   Iraq–Iran war
Soviet invasion of Afghanistan   Lebanese civil war
Evenhandedness

2. Bring to class and be prepared to discuss a newspaper or magazine article written within the past two weeks that:
(a) deals with one or more current important crises or events in the Middle East, and
(b) presents important problems or challenges for the United States in the Middle East.

Questions for Homework and Discussion

1. One dictionary definition of the word "dilemma" is: "a situation that requires one to choose between two equally balanced alternatives." Another definition is: "a situation that seemingly defies a satisfactory solution." Using either of the above definitions with regard to *three* of the following situations, events, or issues, explain:
(a) why it has been an American dilemma,
(b) what steps or policies the United States has taken to solve the problem or problems presented by the dilemma, and
(c) the extent to which you agree or disagree with U.S. policy in respect to each of the Middle East dilemmas you discuss.
1. The Arab–Israeli dispute
2. The Greek–Turkish dispute over Cyprus
3. American relations with client states in the Middle East
4. Peace negotiations between Israel and Egypt since the Camp David agreements
5. Maintaining a continued oil flow from the Middle East
6. Growing Russian influence in the Middle East
7. Arms sales in the Middle East
8. The revolution in Iran (1979–1980)
9. The American hostage crisis in Iran (1979–1980)
10. The Iraq–Iran war (1980–1981)

2. In 1979, 1980, and 1981 the United States decided to significantly increase its military presence in the Middle East.

(a) Explain why and how it intends to do this.

(b) Discuss your reasons for agreeing or disagreeing with the new policy.

President Anwar El-Sadat of Egypt was assassinated on October 6, 1981, by Muslim extremists. Vice President Hosni Mubarak immediately took his place as president, declaring martial law and arresting hundreds of militants and Muslim extremists. President Mubarak asserted that the would fulfill President Sadat's obligations and continue to work with the United States for peace in the Middle East in accordance with the Camp David Accords.

It was too early when this book went to press to try to assess the impact and ramifications of this tragic development. However, at the very least, the assassination of Anwar El-Sadat plunged the already volatile Middle East into a new period of uncertainty.

Bibliography

Akhavi, Shahrough. *Religion and Politics in Contemporary Iran: Clergy-State Relations in the Pahlavi Period.* Albany: State University of New York Press, 1980.

American University. Foreign Area Studies. *Iran: A Country Study.* Washington, D.C.: U.S. Government Printing Office, 1978.

———. *Israel: A Country Study.* Washington, D.C.: U.S. Government Printing Office, 1978.

———. *Syria: A Country Study.* Washington, D.C.: U.S. Government Printing Office, 1978.

Antonius, George. *The Arab Awakening.* Staten Island: Gordon Press, 1976.

Arberry, Arthur J. *Religion in the Middle East.* 2 vols. London: Cambridge University Press, 1969.

Badeau, John S. *The American Approach to the Arab World.* New York: Harper & Row, 1968.

Begin, Menachem. *The Revolt.* Plainview: Nash Publishing Corp., 1977. (Reprint)

Blair, John M. *The Control of Oil.* New York: Pantheon, 1977.

Cohen, Michael J. *Palestine, Retreat From the Mandate: The Making of British Policy, 1936-1945.* New York: Holmes and Meier, 1978.

Coon, Carleton S. *Caravan: The Story of the Middle East.* Huntington: Krieger, 1976 (rev. ed.).

Curtis, Michael et al., eds. *The Palestinians: People, History, Politics.* New Brunswick: Transaction Books, 1975.

Eban, Abba. *My People: A History of the Jews.* New York: Random House, 1968.

Fisher, W.B. *The Middle East: A Physical, Social and Regional Geography.* 7th ed., London: Methuen Inc., 1977.

Gibb, Hamilton A. *Mohammedanism: An Historical Survey.* London: Oxford University Press, 1973.

259

Gilbert, Martin. *Atlas of the Arab-Israeli Conflict*. New York: Macmillan, 1975.

Haim, Sylvia G., ed. *Arab Nationalism: An Anthology*. Berkeley: University of California Press, 1974.

Halpern, Manfred. *Politics of Social Change in the Middle East and North Africa*. Princeton: Princeton University Press, 1970.

Harkabi, Yehoshafat. *Arab Attitudes to Israel*. New Brunswick: Transaction Books, 1974.

Hertzberg, Arthur. *Zionist Idea: A Historical Analysis and Reader*. New York: Atheneum, 1969.

Hourani, Albert H. *Arabic Thought in the Liberal Age, 1798-1939*. London: Oxford University Press, 1970.

——. *Minorities in the Arab World*. New York: AMS Press, 1977 (reprint of 1947 ed.).

Issawi, Charles. *The Economic History of the Middle East: 1800-1914; a Book of Readings*. Chicago: University of Chicago Press, 1976.

Keddie, Nikki R., Ed. *Scholars, Saints and Sufis: Muslim Religious Institutions Since 1500*. Berkeley: University of California Press, 1972.

Kerr, Malcolm H., ed. *Elusive Peace in the Middle East*. Albany: State University of New York Press, 1975.

Laqueur, Walter. *A History of Zionism*. New York: Holt, Rinehart and Winston, 1972.

——. *The Israel-Arab Reader, A Documentary History of the Middle East Conflict*. New York: Bantam, 1976.

Lenczowski, George C. *The Middle East In World Affairs*. 4th edition. Ithaca: Cornell University Press, 1980.

Lerner, Daniel. *The Passing of Traditional Society: Modernizing the Middle East*. Glencoe: Free Press, 1964.

Lewis, Bernard. *Arabs in History*. New York: Harper Torchbooks, 1960.

——. *Emergence of Modern Turkey*. 2nd ed. London: Oxford University Press, 1968.

——. *The Middle East and the West*. New York: Harper Torchbooks, 1968.

Meir, Golda. *My Life*. New York: Putnam, 1975.

Migdal, Joel S. *Palestinian Society and Politics*. Princeton: Princeton University Press, 1980.

Nasser, Gamal Abdel. *The Philosophy of the Revolution*. Buffalo: Smith, Keynes and Marshall, 1959.

Pickthall, Mohammed M. *Meaning of the Glorious Koran*. New York: New American Library, 1974.

Polk, William R. *The United States and the Arab World*. 3rd ed. Cambridge: Harvard University Press, 1975.

Pullapilly, Cyriac K., Ed. *Islam in the Contemporary World*. Atlanta: Cross Roads, 1980.

Quandt, William B. *Decade of Decisions: American Policy Toward the Arab-Israeli Conflict, 1967-1976*. Berkeley: University of California Press, 1977.

Reich, Bernard. *The Quest for Peace: United States-Israel Relations and the Arab-Israeli Conflict*. New Brunswick: Transaction Books, 1977.

Rubin, Barry. *Paved with Good Intentions: The American Experience and Iran*. London: Oxford University Press, 1980.

Sacher, Howard M. *A History of Israel: From the Rise of Zionism to Our Time*. New York: Knopf, 1979.

Sadat, Anwar El. *In Search of Identity. An Autobiography*. New York: Harper & Row, 1978.

Safran, Nadav. *Israel: The Embattled Ally*. Cambridge: Harvard University Press, 1978.

Salibi, Kemal S. *Crossroads to Civil War: Lebanon, 1958-1976*. Delmar: Caravan Books, 1976.

Sampson, Anthony. *The Seven Sisters*. New York: Bantam, 1976.

Shwadran, Benjamin. *Middle East Oil: Issues and Problems*. Cambridge: Schenkman, 1977.

Sweet, Louise E. *Peoples and Cultures of the Middle East*. 2 vols. New York: The Natural History Press, 1970.

Tibawi, A.L. *American Interests in Syria, 1800-1901*. Oxford: Clarendon Press, 1966.

———. *A Modern History of Syria*. New York: St. Martin's Press, 1970.

Index

4-20-86 Abu Nidal (Sabry al-Banna)
Palestinian Terrorist c̄ Libyan backing